Mirror Worlds

Mirror Worlds

or the Day Software Puts the Universe in a Shoebox ...
How It Will Happen and What It Will Mean

DAVID GELERNTER

Department of Computer Science
Yale University

New York   Oxford   Oxford University Press   *1991*

Oxford University Press

Oxford   New York   Toronto
Delhi   Bombay   Calcutta   Madras   Karachi
Petaling Jaya   Singapore   Hong Kong   Tokyo
Nairobi   Dar es Salaam   Cape Town
Melbourne   Auckland

and associated companies in
Berlin   Ibadan

Library of Congress Cataloging-in-Publication Data
Gelernter, David Hillel.
Mirror worlds on the day software puts the universe in a shoebox :
how it will happen and what it will mean / David Gelernter.
p. cm.   Includes bibliographical references (p.) and index.
ISBN 0-19-506812-2
1. Computer software. 2. Software engineering.   I. Title.
QA76.754.G45   1991   005—dc20   91-19178

9 8 7 6 5 4 3 2 1

Printed in the United States of America
on acid-free paper

These *DBT*'s are for
my grandmother Dorothy Rothchild Lewis,
my mother,
and my Jane

Contents

Contents

List of Figures

Mirror Worlds

No changing of place
at a hundred miles an hour,

      You can't imagine how strange it seemed
      to be journeying on thus, without
      any visible cause of progress
      other than the magical machine,

nor making of stuffs a thousand
yards a minute,

      with its flying white breath and
      rhythmical, unvarying pace,
      between these rocky walls, which are
      already clothed with moss and
      ferns and grass;

will make us
one whit stronger, happier
or wiser.

      and when I reflected that

There was always more
in the world
than men could see,
walked they ever so slowly;

      these great masses of stone had been cut
      asunder to allow our passage thus far
      below the surface of the earth, I felt that

they will see it no better
for going fast.
JOHN RUSKIN[1] (1856)

      no fairy tale
      was every half so wonderful
      as what I saw.
      FANNY KEMBLE[2] (1830)

Prologue

This book describes an event that will happen someday soon: You will look into a computer screen and see reality. Some part of your world—the town you live in, the company you work for, your school system, the city hospital—will hang there in a sharp color image, abstract but recognizable, moving subtly in a thousand places. This Mirror World you are looking at is fed by a steady rush of new data pouring in through cables. It is infiltrated by your own software creatures, doing your business.

People are drawn to these software gadgets: When you switch one on, you turn the world (like an old sweater) inside out. You stuff the huge multi-institutional ratwork that encompasses you into a genie bottle on your desk. You can see over, under and through it. You can see deeply into it. A bottled institution *cannot* intimidate, confound or ignore its members; *they* dominate *it*. And your computer's screen is transformed, into a clear surface with brilliant multi-colored life unfolding just beyond. People will stop looking at their computer screens and start gazing into them.

Mirror worlds will transform the meaning of "computer." Our dominant metaphor since 1950 or thereabouts, "the electronic brain," will go by the boards. Instead people will talk about crystal balls, telescopes, stained glass windows—wine, poetry or whatever—things that make you see *vividly*.

Don't like computers? Unamused by technology? For most people, technology is the ocean on a bright cool Spring day. Sparkling in the far distance; breathtakingly cold; exhilarating once you've

1

plunged in. At any rate, not to be over-delicate: This cold and beautiful Ocean is coming to meet you. Mirror Worlds mean another overwhelming rise in sea level. If you don't choose to jump in, what exactly *do* you choose?

Why not give it a try? Hold your breath. Let's plunge.

Chapter 1

Mirror Worlds?

What *are* they?

They are software models of some chunk of reality, some piece of the *real world* going on outside your window. Oceans of information pour endlessly into the model (through a vast maze of software pipes and hoses): so much information that *the model* can mimic *the reality's* every move, moment-by-moment.

A Mirror World is some huge institution's moving, true-to-life mirror image trapped inside a computer—where you can see and grasp it whole. The thick, dense, busy sub-world that encompasses you is *also*, now, an object in your hands. A brand new equilibrium is born.

Suppose you are sitting in a room somewhere in a city, and you catch yourself wondering—*what's going on out there?* What's happening?

At this very instant, traffic on every street is moving or blocked, your local government is making brilliant decisions, public money is flowing out at a certain rate, the police are deployed in some pattern, there's a fire here and there, the schools are staffed and attended in some way or other, oil and cauliflower are selling for whatever in local markets... This list could fill the rest of the book. Suppose you'd like to *have* some of this information. Why? Who are *you* to be so nosy? Let's say you're a commuter or an investment house or a school principle or a CEO or journalist or politician or policeman or even a *mere*, humble, tax-paying citizen. Let's say you're just curious. You want to browse, take in the big picture (it's your city, isn't it?)—form some impression of how well the whole thing is working.

So you build a model. You lay out a detailed map on your living room floor. You add little model buildings and bridges and cars and policemen and so on, and lots of blackboards. On the blackboards you will record information that doesn't correspond to any physical object—the state of the budget, the weather; thousands or maybe millions of other tidbits. The blackboards are scattered all over. Given the blackboards, you don't really *need* the map, the buildings and so on—the city-in-miniature. But you've realized that you'll need some way to *organize* all the data you intend to collect; and a recognizable image is a powerful organizing device. If you dump lots of little cars onto currently slow-go streets, use unfinished buildings to indicate construction projects and so on—you can grasp at least *certain* kinds of data quickly. And you can deploy the blackboards in "reasonable" locations—the stock-prices blackboard in front of the little stock exchange building; which gives you at least some hope of finding them.

You buy some long tables and set them up around your model. You have a few dozen phone lines installed. You hire a bunch of people. Most of them will staff the phones; the rest will maintain the model, moving things around and updating the blackboards to reflect the latest information.

Now you hire several thousand more people (let's say) and send them out into the city. Some are posted permanently at interesting points: you'd like to know traffic conditions *everywhere*. Some are assigned to particular institutions: What are the city council, the board of education, the police department, the mayor's office doing at the moment? How's water quality and the value of city bonds holding up? Your researchers are in constant phone-contact with the staffers back in your living room, passing in the latest data for instant transfer to the model.

Good work. (Glad you didn't just sit there brooding...)

Now, whenever that *"what's going on?"* mood is upon you, you need merely rise from your sofa, glance (languidly) at your model and *you know*.

Yes, *but*—it was difficult and a tad expensive to set up; and how good is it, really? Certainly it's a lot better than nothing. But it's interesting that... If you do the smart thing, chuck the whole set-up and build the model *out of software* instead—

You don't merely get something that's *plausible*—that's achievable, where the hardware version is obviously ridiculous, for most people in any case. More important: the software model is staggeringly more powerful than the best hardware model could possibly be.

The *software* model of your city, once it's set up, will be available (like a public park) to however many people are interested, hundreds or thousands or millions at the same time. It will show each visitor exactly what he wants to see—it will sustain a million different views, a million different focuses on the same city simultaneously. Each visitor will zoom in and pan around and roam through the model as he chooses, at whatever pace and level of detail he likes. On departing, he will leave a bevy of software alter-egos behind, to keep tabs on whatever interests him. Perhaps most important, the software model can remember its own history in perfect detail; and can reminisce pointedly whenever it is asked. And everything is up to date, to the millisecond.

Such models, such *Mirror Worlds*, promise to be powerful, fascinating, and gigantic in their implications. They are scientific viewing tools—microscopes, telescopes—focused not on the hugely large or small, but on the *human-scale* social world of organizations, institutions and machines; promising that same vast *microscopic, telescopic* increase in depth, sharpness and clarity of vision. Such Mirror Worlds don't exist, yet. But most of the necessary components have been designed, built and separately test-fired, and we are now entering the assembly stages that will produce complete (albeit small-scale) prototypes. The intellectual content, the *social* implications of these software gizmos make them far too important to be left in the hands of the computer sciencearchy. The rest of this book explains why.

Sounds Like Fun, but So What?

Software today offers assistance to the specialist (in everybody) — not to the citizen. The mere citizen deals with the increasingly perilous complexity of his government, business, transportation, health, school, university and legal systems unaided. Mirror Worlds represent one attempt to change this state of affairs.

You set up a software mirror wherever you like, then allow some complex real-world system to unfold before it. The software faithfully reflects whatever is going on out front. But this is a three-dimensional kind of reflection: The program reaches out and engulfs some chunk of reality. Like a child-sized play village modeled precisely on a real town and tracking reality's every move, the Mirror World supplies a software object to match and track every real one.

A hospital Mirror World has a software version of every patient, doctor, bed, room—and every abstract entity that's important: cash in the bank, drugs on order and so on. Through permanent sensors and ordinary terminal-based record-keeping, the Mirror World reflects the real one. When a patient is scheduled for surgery, the date is noted in the software *Doppelgänger*. When the patient is transferred to the X unit, the software version is too. The organization's current status is presented in the form of an intricate and constantly-changing *picture* that you explore from your computer screen, skimming the surface or diving deeper as you like.

What's the point? These Mirror Worlds are like regular old-fashioned databases, to some extent. If you need to find Shmoe's salary or Schwartz's social security number, you can look it up. But they go far beyond this. The Mirror World is directly accessible, twenty-four hours a day, to the population that it tracks. You can parachute in your own software agents. They look out for your interests, or gather data that you need, or let you know when something significant seems to be going on. You consult the Mirror World like an encyclopaedia when you need information; you read it like a dashboard when you need a fast take on current status. Fundamentally these programs are intended to help you *comprehend* the powerful, super-techno-glossy, dangerously complicated and basically indifferent man-made environments that enmesh you, and that control you to the extent that you don't control them.

So Mirror Worlds function *in part* as fire walls opposing the onslaught of chaos. But they aren't *mere* fire breaks. They are beer halls and grand piazzas, natural gathering places for information hunters and insight searchers. Most important, they are *microcosms*—intricate worlds come alive in small packages. Whether in the shape of a Victorian winter garden, an electric train layout, a Joseph Cornell shadow-box or a mere three-inch plastic dome with snowflakes softly settling inside, microcosms are intriguing. They show you patterns and help you make discoveries that you'd never have come across otherwise. At their best, they are thought-tools of great power and evocativeness.

But Mirror Worlds aren't happening in a vacuum. Today's world technology scene is no placid pond, exactly. And the technological context isn't incidental to this story: it will figure in every paragraph. So we need to step back a moment before we begin.

1791

People were pretty sure, in 1791, that the industrial revolution had *happened*. It was history.

The world had been transformed. The spinning jenny and the power loom, the coke-fired blast furnace and above all Watt's all-powerful steam engine were ready and waiting. In 1791, William Hutton frothed over in describing the growth of Birmingham, that industrial super-city. "These additions are so amazing, that even an author of veracity will barely meet belief."[1] Fifteen years *earlier*, Adam Smith had enthused over the "universal opulence"[2] that England's state-of-the-art, machine-driven economy had produced. "Let any person consider the progress of everything in Britain during the last twenty years..."[3] wrote Arthur Young in 1774.

In retrospect, little had changed. There were no railroads. Cotton was a minor industry in Britain. Manchester was a smallish town. Who were these people kidding, patting themselves on the back and congratulating themselves up and down on the advanced state of their technology? On the world-transforming wonders it had wrought? In 1791, the industrial revolution was merely building up a head of steam. The Big Bang came later.

Glancing backwards from a vantage-point two centuries hence, 1991 will look a lot like 1791. The technological world of today has that same pastoral sparsely-settled leafiness. Everything is neat and well-ordered and tentative: a garden in earliest Spring. Nothing basic has changed. Yes, software has accomplished great things. But as Al Jolson so presciently announced in Hollywood's first Talkie, you ain't heard nothing yet. The real software revolution won't have much to do with fancy robots, computers in education, canned "multimedia" hype or the other hot topics that dominate this month's hit parade. It will center instead on software that steps over the crucial boundary between private and public. It will have to do with "public software works," with civil software-engineering, with Mirror Worlds. The software revolution hasn't begun yet; but it will soon.

Public policy will be forced to come to grips with the implications. So will every thinking person: A software revolution will change the way society's business is conducted, and it will change the intellectual landscape. This book is a brief introduction to software and the computers that power it, a guide to the coming revolution, and a toast to that memorable moment not far off when the Design of Software Structures sweeps down the grand staircase to its smashing debut—as a deep and beautiful intellectual effort in its own right.

§ Venice (Quick Visit)

It is widely claimed, of course, that the software revolution has already happened, that we live in an "information age". To grasp why and how this is not so, the *Piazza San Marco* in Venice is a good place to start. The great church is before you. It is in essence a combination of two materials, stone and mosaic: the stone for shape and structure, the mosaic for pizzazz. Both components are part of the church's beauty, but the stones are fundamental, the mosaic in every sense superficial. Today, software as a building material resembles mosaic tile. Modern organizations and intellectual pursuits are extensively plastered with this stuff, and the results are spectacular; but nothing basic has changed. In the future, software will metamorphose into a something more like stone or steel or concrete. The metamorphosis has in fact (just) begun.

New software Saint Marks' will rise. They will monopolize the energy and attention of thousands in the building, will broadcast an aesthetic and a world-view to millions, will mold behavior and epitomize the age...

§ The Building Material

Most people are oblivious to the possibilities; this has a lot to do with a widespread difficulty in understanding software as a building material. Most people conceive of programs (to the extent they bother to conceive of them at all) as "lists of instructions that tell a computer what to do." Examine the business side of a compact disk: You're looking at millions of microscopic bits of information. How would you describe what the disk contains? You might say "a list of instructions that tell the compact disk player what to do," and you'd be right. But your answer would be a little lacking in poetry and insight. "Encoded music" might be a better answer. It puts the emphasis where it belongs. The fact that you will use a compact disk player to perform the decoding is technically crucial but leaves a huge conceptual gap.

The information on the disk is a formula for constructing an event in time. Software is the same. In both cases we are dealing with a kind of instant soup mix that can be reconstituted automatically, the CD into music, the program into a certain kind of machine. A software machine (a reconstituted program) is a real machine, and independent of the electronic box that decodes it, in the same sense that the music coming out of a CD player is an independent reality.

§ Information Refineries

A software machine is an "information machine". Hardware guides and transforms forces, electronic machinery does the same with electrical signals; software machines transform information. It's perfectly legitimate to picture a running program as a kind of factory with information trundled in by software forklifts, dumped into conveyers, fed into and out of sub-assemblies and so on.

This point is crucial to the intellectual moon-mission that software is about to undertake. It's unhelpful to think of programs as mere static lists of instructions. A program is a working structure, a (potentially) huge information refinery buzzing and blazing with activity as masses of information move around inside — a Grand Central Station of information, with crowds sweeping through on many levels. It's still often the case that you run a program, feed it some numbers, get some numbers back and then turn it off. But many programs today run continuously, in future most programs will, and this will become our basic way of *thinking* about programs: as factories, information refineries, operating day and night.

The topic in this book is *information machinery*. Mirror Worlds will likely be the most complex information machines ever built. They might possibly be the most complex machines of *any* kind every built.

But in discussing these prodigies of power and complexity, I'll need to deal, too, with the simplest of information machines.

§ The Paleolithic, Revisited

In the hyper-compressed world of software technology, it's the twenty-first century and the old stone age simultaneously.

At the same time we develop vast complex software worlds, the *simple machines* of information structure are *also* just being invented. The wheel, the ramp, the wedge, the screw, the lever. Much of today's software-structures research amounts precisely to this search for universal, simple information-machines that can support vast complex structures. It makes no sense to reinvent the bolt and the geartrain every time you design a mechanical device. Builders of information machinery too would prefer to start with the universal, basic stuff in hand. But what *are* the simple information machines? It took some time (presumably millenia) to come up with the initial basic five. We'd like five more by this afternoon. If it's not too much trouble.

But you can't merely will them into existence. In some respects, you're faced with a design problem (what engineers do); in others, more a problem of *discovery*. The wheel and the lever are man-made tools. But they're so pervasively important that they look almost like natural phenomena. Not mere engineering doodles; almost *intrinsic* in the logical woodwork of mechanical problem-solving, just waiting to be found out. Chances are, there is a set of basic *information* machines waiting to be found out as well. And Mirror Worlds are *so* complicated that it's especially important that we build them out of simple, universal elements; otherwise, we drown in complexity.

This re-creation of technology on a new footing, in a new way, is an intellectual event of real importance. It's also the sort of event that, by its very nature, is easy to miss. These are *simple* machines we're talking about, after all. Nothing fancy; nothing showy. When the first test-pryings using a prototype lever came off successfully at some Paleolithic research institute (whose funding no doubt had just been slashed)—most likely, no-one held a press conference. A

pivoting stick: big deal. Many thousands of years later, early research trials of the potter's wheel in Ancient Sumeria[4] are unlikely
to have dominated dinnertable conversation at mid-town watering
holes. The Sumerians knew how to write, but this new "wheel" technology hardly ranked up there with cattle inventories as a favorite
topic. We are more technology-conscious today. When a rocket goes
up, we are moderately interested. Far from the camera crews, technologists are doing experiments that are laughably less spectacular.
But, maybe, more important: They are inventing *new* simple machines; recreating the technological universe.

Of course, technology has gone through many phases since the
last bout of simple-machine development culminated, with the wheel,
in rather a big way. New engineering vocabularies arose for making
metal, building structures, harnessing water and wind power, keeping
time, building many kinds of engines: a series of techno-revolutions
of earthshaking importance. And yet, all these machines were made
of *stuff* and, in *one* important sense anyway, an *information machine*
is not. The rise of information machinery may or may not prove
more important, in the end, than the rise of clocks or watermills or
electric power. But it should be clear that *something* is going on
here that is new, different and worth understanding. We're starting
a new chapter in technological history. Chapter one—machines built
out of something; chapter two, machines built out of nothing. Merely
enacted, temporarily *embodied* by an irrelevant hunk of metal, plastic
and silicon called a computer.

And so,

This Book

has three layers. Mirror Worlds don't make sense if they are served in
isolation. They are much happier as the insides of a conceptual Deli
Sandwich. The bottom layer deals with the basic nature of software
and the simple machines we are now in the process of inventing. The
upper layer deals with the ultimate motivation in building Mirror
Worlds—the search for what I will call "topsight." Each chapter
serves up another slice of Mirror World between these wrappers.
The goal is not the usual (for this kind of book) quick stroll down
Wondertech Boulevard, admiring the window displays and then back

on the bus; you should emerge from the last chapter with a detailed, concrete feel for how you would actually build these systems.

The progression of chapters is dictated directly by the character of the problem. Chapter 2 explains what a Mirror World is. The chapters following discuss in step-by-step fashion how we intend to build them.

Mirror Worlds are built out of software. First, then: what is software? (Chapter 3.) The usual warmed-over tripe about those "lists of instructions that tell the machine what to do" won't serve. We need to explore the intellectual shape of this problem, not the trivial details. But it's impossible to grasp software's nature concretely without coming to grips with some fairly subtle points. This chapter is the "hardest" and most detailed in the book. (For all that, it's not terribly hard, and no more detailed than absolutely necessary.) This chapter is also different in character from the others: It deals with the basics, the fundamental facts about software that are well-known to everyone in the field. All subsequent chapters discuss research, and the state-of-the-art. In fact, they grow researchier and researchier until the story culminates with a bang at the doorstep of the large-scale Mirror World itself. Right up to this point, though, I will be discussing *real software* that runs today, not mere hypotheses.

Mirror Worlds aren't ordinary programs. They are software *ensembles*, glued-together out of many separate programs all chattering at once. Chapter 4 explains how you build ensemble programs using the basic elements described in Chapter 3. Once you understand ensembles, you've grasped *the* basic Mirror World technology. You've also seen the software future in general. Ensembles are the natural and inevitable end-point of the three major forces at work in software evolution, the urge to make programs *fast, clear* and *powerful.* Ensembles already loom large on the software scene; before long, they will be ubiquitous.

Then, we start building Mirror Worlds. We look first (in Chapter 5) at the Mirror World "basement," which is full of realtime knowledge plants. A knowledge plant is one type of ensemble program—the Mirror World as a whole is an ensemble of ensembles. These "knowledge plants" are designed for installation in the teeth of onrushing data floods. Their goal is to figure out what's going on—to piece together the big picture out of an endless outpouring of low level detail. Then (Chapter 6) we look at the attic, where bushels of fact are fed into the History Presses ("expert datapools") for transformation into something like "the wisdom of experience." The expert datapools we describe are simple programs with a propensity to behave in complicated ways—to "speculate," to "get distracted," occasionally to "free associate." What would you want with a program that occasionally stops paying attention to you? Good question. I'll get to it...

And finally the Mirror World itself: In Chapter 7 we describe how the whole thing is put together, out of the components and using the technologies we've already explored in some detail.

Discussing Mirror Worlds means discussing the future. But we aren't talking about hazy science fiction. We have arrived at the musing, prototype-building and detailed planning reflected in this book by the fact that the tools and materials for Mirror World building are in hand, and the job is underway.

Chapter 2

The Orb

To use a Mirror World program, you sit down at your computer, which has a large color screen and a connection to the local fiber-optic utility cable. (The screen and the cable are garden-variety technology today.) Or—if you're willing to put up with a smaller picture *and* it's a nice day—you pick up your laptop, tune in Data Radio and head for the hammock. In either case, you flip channels until you find the Mirror World of your choice, and then you see a *picture*. Capturing the structure and present status of an entire company, university, hospital, city or whatever in a single (obviously elliptical, high-level) sketch is a hard but solvable research problem. The picture changes subtly as you watch, mirroring changes in the world outside. But for most purposes, you don't merely sit and stare. You zoom in and poke around, like an explorer in a miniature sub. At every level the display is live: it changes as you watch. You move a viewing-frame around the picture with a mouse or equivalent, probably equipped with knobs for zooming. You meet your software agents and other Mirror World visitors along the way. When your agents have developments to report, or when you choose to ask questions or plant new agents, you pop into a sub-screen that displays ordinary text.

You can enter a Mirror World through any household computer, but a few extra controls come in handy. Your basic Mirror World computer is equipped with a perspective shifter, a diving mouse, a "history" key (with a time-travel velocity knob right next to it), the all-important "experience" key, and finally an "agent" key. There is the ordinary keyboard besides.

(I'm describing hardware gadgets that are similar to what you can buy today at the corner computer store. If you plan to do lots of Mirror Worlding, you'll invest in the Mirror World Value Pack, or whatever; the extra gadgets are tacked onto the computer in the same way your mouse is attached. The "viewpoint shifter" probably looks like a joystick; the diving mouse is the same as any other mouse, but equipped with an altitude-control knob. The time-travel velocity knob is a knob attached to a box. Your three extra keys look like any other keyboard keys. You don't really *need* any of this extra stuff. You can always make do with a regular keyboard and a plain ordinary mouse. But for an extra ten bucks, why not do it right?)

Into the Mirror World

You can look at the typical Mirror World in several different ways. When you shift viewpoints, the contents of the Mirror World don't change, but the presentation does, radically: everything gets re-arranged. The Mirror World is a leading member of a smug but invaluable new class of software, programs that know too much. If we don't sort things out meticulously and arrange them intelligently, you won't know where to start, or which way to turn. The *way things are presented* is a tremendously important aspect of a Mirror World program.

The "geography" perspective is a natural starting point, some-times. The picture you see on your display represents a real physical layout. In a City Mirror World, you see a city map of some kind. Lots of information is superimposed on the map, using words, num-bers, colors, dials—the resulting display is dense with data; you are tracking thousands of different values simultaneously. You can see traffic density on the streets, delays at the airport, the physical con-dition of the bridges, the status of markets, the condition of the city's finances, the current agenda at city hall and the board of education, crime conditions in the parks, air quality, average bulk cauliflower prices and a huge list of others.

This high-level view would represent—if you could achieve it at all—the ultimate and only goal of the *hardware* city model. In the software version, it's merely a starting point. You can dive deeper and explore. Pilot your mouse over to some interesting point and turn the *altitude* knob. Now you are inside a school, courthouse, hospital or City Hall. You see a picture like the one at the top level, but here it's all focussed on this *one* sub-world, so you can find out what's really going on down here. Meet and chat (electronically) with the local inhabitants, or other Mirror World browsers. You'd like to be informed whenever the zoning board turns its attention to Piffel Street? Whenever the school board finalizes a budget? Leave a software agent behind.

Eavesdrop on decision-making in progress. Among other things, you will discover video feeds down here. When you dive into City Hall, one part of the display on your screen might be a (little) TV picture. You can mouse over there and enlarge the thing, if you want to hear the mayor's press conference or the planning board meeting. In some parts of the display you will find dozens of little TV pictures. TV cameras are cheap, and getting cheaper. But how will we *distribute* and (just as important) how will we *organize* a potentially huge mass and variety of video material—almost all of which is of absolutely no interest to anybody? Mirror Worlds are one obvious answer. Those odd times when you *do* care what the mayor or the local school principle or the police commissioner is holding forth about, you can find out. Inside of each little courthouse on your computer screen is a televised courtroom. Inside each City Hall hearing room, you will find the hearing. Or—attend a school board meeting, visit a museum, take in a lecture at the university. This is an archive as well as a "live" medium—an encyclopaedia as well as a dashboard; so you can always go back and catch anything you missed. (This all will require prodigies of communication, but no unforeseen technological miracles. Some of the issues are discussed in Chapter 4.)

You can use the Mirror World's archival propensities to discover the history or background of anything that concerns you. What has the zoning board been doing lately? How did the school board membership get to be this way, what is the history of a particular piece of pending legislation—what was the whole city like, this time last year? Last decade? Merely run the thing backwards through time, using your history key and the time-travel-velocity knob. You can restore this whole dense, multi-layered image-world to any point in its past. You're not guaranteed to get the *whole* picture in every detail; some details may have been forgotten. By and large, though, you can explore the past in the same way you explore the present, and make some attempt to figure out how we got here.

But you may want more. You may need to press the "experience" key. Its function is to answer some profoundly important questions: Where have I seen this before? When did it happen last? And what was the outcome? Using the mouse, the keyboard and (sometimes) pop-up menus, I indicate which part of the current situation I'm interested in. The city council is considering a bill about garbage dumping proposed by councilman Piffel and only the following two members have shown up. Or (if I am visiting the federal government Mirror World) the Senate Finance committee is considering a bill about X proposed by Y, the following members are present—what's the likely outcome? This patient was admitted with a suspected diagnosis of Y but is now developing the following new symptoms. Gold prices are up, oil is down, the dollar is stable, the yen is in orbit, there's been a big run-up in molybdenum futures, the White House wants the following new taxes. Where have I seen it before? Where is it all leading?

You will be presented with a collection of previous moments in time. These moments capture situations, incidents or cases that *resemble* what you've asked about. Your display is reset to each of the precedents in turn so that you can revisit them, explore them in detail and find out where they went. Experience is a neat trick, maybe the neatest of all. We discuss the underpinnings in Chapter 6.

When you've finished exploring whatever sub-world you've dived into, grab your altitude control knob and head back to the surface. The new knowledge you return with feeds your growing sense of a big picture.

§ "Eavesdrop," you said?

Where does all this information come from?

Nowhere special.

Granted, lots of new information-gathering devices have been installed. But the information they are gathering and feeding into the Mirror World is strictly *public* information—or information to which this particular Mirror World's clientele is entitled. And the Mirror World will discriminate judiciously among visitors. The public at large, for example, is entitled to enter the City Hospital Mirror World, and to learn a good deal about what's going on. Furthermore, anyone is entitled to see his own medical records. But very few people have access to anyone else's, although they are all *stored* down here. Access to *private* information is closely controlled.

The Mirror World isn't snoopware. Its goal is merely to convert the *theoretically* public into the *actually* public. What was always available in principle merely becomes available *in fact*. Organized, archived, spiffily presented, up to the minute and *integrated* into a whole. That's all.

But that's a lot...

The Significance of Mirror Worlds

Why would anyone claim that these Mirror Worlds are, potentially, immensely important?

I'll discuss three bunches of reasons. The first bunch has to do with control systems that are up to the job of maneuvering and reining-in our high-output, overpowered modern society. The second bunch involves the exchange of information and the making of person-to-person contacts—processes for which the Mirror World may be (in some ways) better suited than the real one. The last reason is the biggest, deepest and most important. It's also the most abstract. I will prepare the ground for this last motive by making the whole proposition as concrete as possible—by explaining what has been done so far, and by whom, and where the whole effort is going.

Significance, I: Getting a Grip

A parable: consider the modern, state-of-the-art fighter aircraft. It's so fantastically advanced that you can't fly it. It is aerodynamically unstable. It needs to have its "flight surfaces" adjusted by computer every few thousandths of a second or it will bop off on its own, out of control. Modern organizations are in many cases close to the same level of attainment—except that, when they're out of control, they don't crash in flames; they shamble on blindly forever.

It isn't easy for a hospital administration with the best of intentions to make sure that bad or inappropriate or newly outmoded or wrongly sequenced or mutually inconsistent or maximally expensive or unnecessarily dangerous procedures are never scheduled. A battery of software agents planted in a Mirror World can watch for bad practices full-time. You might face broadly similar issues if you were responsible (in full or in part) for a company, a school district, a factory, an aircraft carrier and so on. If you merely *work* for a company or *deal* with a government or *study* at a university, you face related problems. Why do so many local governments hover so close to the jagged edge of clique-ridden sham, engaging the interests of a negligible fraction of the voters? Surely *in part* because it's so hard to find out what your local government is *doing*, to dig the issues out of the minutiae and the trivia. Many voters will enjoy a quick, bracing dip in their local-government Mirror Worlds from time to time, particularly the night before an election. Employees: Does the latest twist on tax laws, benefit packages, interest rates, job classifications, investment possibilities and insurance deals mean that, once again, you are doing the wrong thing with your money? Students: You are, we assume, meeting school and departmental requirements, applying to all the applicable scholarship or fellowship or training or research programs, public and private, going to the relevant odd lecture or meeting or workshop on campus or nearby, monitoring job conditions or admissions requirements in your chosen field, ordering software at a discount and generally getting your money's worth? *Ad infinitum.*

The Hospital, for Example

Take the hospital Mirror World. In recent years, medical practice has grown more effective, more complicated and more expensive simultaneously and at dizzying speeds. "Software quality control" is one approach to the resulting problem, and a main goal of the hospital Mirror World, to be achieved by software agents. Each agent monitors one piece of the picture; each one executes a separate program. One agent, for example, might run a program that says "if a patient ever shows up who is suspected of suffering from X, and a W test isn't scheduled within twenty-four hours, let someone know."

Letting someone know might mean printing a comment on every terminal screen focussed on this Mirror World, or electronic-mailing a note to the physician who is responsible for this patient. The note might be a brief sentence or two, or more extensive. It might cite a recent study that shows why the recommended test is useful, or statistics gathered in this hospital, or facts from the patient's medical history.

This simple example hints at several crucial Mirror World facts. Software agents are independent, and we can create as many of them as we like. Each one can monitor whatever we tell it to, from serious problems to minor details. They needn't be mutually exclusive, or even mutually consistent: A note might say that "Dr. X's agent is surprised that you haven't tried W yet." Some agents are public (their comments are available to all Mirror World comers), others designed only for their creators. Potentially, there are large numbers of agents: We may have to screen their comments or organize them in some way so that Mirror World browsers aren't overwhelmed. Their behavior can be custom-tailored to an audience: An agent might print a short note to the Mirror World's public dashboard, then send a detailed explanation to a particular clinician. They run simultaneously and continuously: Constant vigilance to every possible source of screw-up, no matter how rare or complicated or subtle or outrageously improbable, is a principle Mirror World goal. If a particular hyper-specialized agent runs patiently for thirty years without so much as clearing its throat, and on Day 16,951 prints a message that prevents a serious medical mistake, we are satisfied. We are delighted.

A Mirror World agent might cite local statistics, I claimed, to back up its case. A Mirror World can remember the history of its institution with perfect accuracy, in exhaustive detail. We can use the experience key to ask concrete historical questions: "When we try A and then B on patients suffering from C, what happens?" We can do prospective studies as well, by designing software agents who will henceforth monitor and report on the results of some combination of circumstances.

The Ensemble

I've noted that each software agent is independent, that each one executes its own program, and that all are active simultaneously. It follows that the Mirror World *as a whole* isn't an ordinary "sequential" program that does one thing at a time; it is an *ensemble*, a "parallel" or "coordinated" program, a program that does many things at once. As a consequence we have two choices. Either the Mirror World executes on many computers simultaneously, or it executes on a single computer that is powerful enough to behave like many separate ones. Most Mirror Worlds will choose the first alternative. The industry is building more and more "parallel computers," machines that come equipped with many sub-computers packed in the same box, like tinned sardines. These machines are relatively cheap and (because they can focus many computers on one problem) blazingly fast. Computer *networks* are even more important than parallel computers. Most organizations that are good candidates for Mirror World monitoring own lots of computers, all connected together. It will be convenient for the Mirror World program to run on many or all of them simultaneously (like a far-flung mercantile empire with toe-holds in every interesting principality—were we talking about Venice?).

As usual in the field of computation, finding a hardware solution is no big deal. The real problem is software. Although a great deal of effort has been spent on coordinated programming—it has been our group's main research focus for years—this is still new stuff, *not* what the average programmer-in-the-street understands a "program" to be. Building this kind of program still presents some tricky problems. But they will be solved; coordinated programs are the future of computer science.

Now let's go beyond the obvious and immediate benefits and look at some others that are more subtle but just as important.

Significance, II: The New Public Square

The Mirror World isn't a mere information service. It's a *place*. You can "stroll around" inside a Mirror World. You can meet and (electronically) converse with your friends, or random passers-by, chat with a policeman or a teacher or a politician, discover like-minded fellow-citizens; form some idea of the public mood.

Well—so what? You can do the same thing in the real world, can't you? Sure you *can*, it's just that you don't. (All right, *I* don't. Lots of people don't...) For most people, the real world is just too big, sprawling, complicated, disorganized, intimidating, cold-and-wet or smoggy-and-smelly or expensive, unpredictable, inconvenient, dangerous, whatever. Of course, you're no hermit. But you associate with your own crowd. It just isn't possible to deal on a friendly basis (on *any* basis) with a whole good-sized town-full of people. You inhabit some limited sub-world of necessity, and so does everyone else. Do a million separate, barely-intersecting worlds make a polity? I don't think so.

The "small town," an institution where you actually *know* your fellow citizens—now *there* is an interesting idea. The Mirror World is a re-application of the same concept on a smaller *and* larger scale. Much smaller: the whole town fits inside your computer. You can do the Grand Whirlwind Tour, see everyone and everything, without changing out of your pajamas. Much larger: this small town might support a population of millions.

The Mirror World as public square has many implications. Here are some.

§ Elections...

in the United States are screaming rapidly downhill towards the utopian Fantasyland of every politician's dreams. Here, amid the picturesque photo-ops and succulent sound bites, each and every incumbent is guaranteed re-election unless he is in prison or certifiably dead, and every campaign takes one step closer to the Absolutely Perfect Campaign—not merely vapid and expensive, but *zero* content, *infinite* cost! A Mirror World offers another way to campaign. Every Mirror World neighborhood is equipped with a public message board. Candidates can post statements. Towards election time, we can set up a special political playground, where they can hold forth at greater length. Shoppers can send questions directly via electronic mail, and post the answers on Mirror World billboards where everybody (whether or not they feel like taking the trouble to send mail) can find them. Politicians can open Mirror World offices,

where browsers can catch up on what they've been doing and leave
questions that the staff promises to answer. This whole campaign
strategy will be dismissed as naive nonsense—after all, voters don't
care about issues, they care about media advisors. Everybody knows
that. And then one day, some nobody of whom no TV reporter has
ever heard will win in a write-in landslide.

The message boards aren't for politicians only, of course. If you
find something you don't like, you can post a note; you will soon
discover whether anyone else agrees with you. In these impersonal
days, it's difficult for a community to mobilize mere annoyance. Mirror Worlds will help.

§ The Public-Nuisance Level

This sounds like a small point, but it isn't. The basic principle
of toxicology is *the dose makes the poison.* Modern society would
rather ignore this principle, because it makes things complicated.
We have a wasteful, dangerous, perfectly understandable tendency
to go crazy over trivial doses of "poison" but to ignore massive doses
of "irritation," although the poison in this case is merely irritating
and the irritation is toxic.

Most people will go to some lengths to avoid any exposure to a
chemical (a pesticide, say) that is known to be poisonous in large
doses. The probability that a *tiny* dose will make you sick might
be minuscule, say a few parts per million, but what the hell—being
only human, we'd rather get sick with *zero* probability and live forever. Fair enough. Rational or irrational, it comes with the territory. Now, *irritation*—irritation is known to be absolutely harmless,
in small doses. Noise, rudeness, obtuse bureaucratic stupidity, pointless procedural obstacles, the wanton squandering of your time by the
worldwide confraternity of air-headed, brain-dead officialdom: stop
whining, it won't kill you. Yes, but the problem is, in *massive* doses,
it might. At least, it is quite as likely to contribute to real physical
illness (by way of stress) as those trace quantities of pesticide in your
yogurt. Maybe a whole lot *more* likely.

If life gets more and more annoying—well, people get annoyed,
and that's that. Individually, a million irritated people accomplish
nothing. And the slow-acting poison of loudness, callousness and
obtuseness that has leached so deeply into public life is clearly *not*

important enough to deserve attention from the politicians, TV anchors and movie stars to whom we have entrusted the Official Setting of the Public Agenda. *Have a heart.* These people are busy.

When was the last time you heard a politician call a news conference to reflect thoughtfully that "maybe we should enforce the noise ordinances after all? And by the way, are police sirens ten times louder than they need to be? Is it really, I mean *truly* important that you be able to hear them on Mars?" Or "collecting tolls is an idea that made sense when roads were a lot less busy than they are today. It was never intended when we installed these things that they'd cause backups stretching for miles—wasting fuel, fouling the air and squandering billions of hours of the public's time. This is a stupid way to collect money." (The Administration's new five-year highway plan calls for *wider* use of tolls.[1] How about more potholes, too, while you're up?) Or "maybe the people in government offices ought to be polite to the public." (Muffled guffaws from the back of the room. It's official, by the way: The Wall Street Journal has announced the virtual eradication of the private-sector apology. "Apologies have all but disappeared from America's commercial discourse..."[2])

Mirror Worlds will allow coalitions to accumulate gradually and spontaneously, around issues that are important not to the lobbyists and not to the deep political thinkers of Hollywood but to the (*huh??*) public, without fund raising, full-time staffers or histrionics.

§ Chatting with Passers-By

Which leads us to some of the broader implications of the Mirror World as public square. A Mirror World may have lots of visitors at any given time, and it's supposed to show its users exactly what the system looks like *right now*. It follows that visitors should be aware of each other (after all, they too are part of the system's current state). So each visitor is represented by a blip on the screen. Because the Mirror World presents its world-view in visual form, in the shape of an intricately detailed multi-level neighborhood, users of the program can rely on ordinary visual cues to find out where other program users are congregating. If you happen to be browsing around Piffelwood High one evening and you notice another visitor doing the same, you might strike up an electronic conversation. The other guy might be worrying about the same issues you are. Then again, probably not.

But, as many computer users already know, electronic conversations are a lot easier to start *and* to stop than real ones.

The larger the Mirror World, the greater the opportunity for chance encounters with interesting consequences. Browsers might run into other browsers from anywhere in the country (or the world).

§ **Business**

Business applications: a final Mirror World example that partakes of the public-square, information-exchange aspects of the operation. It should be clear that Mirror Worlds have many commercial applications, but one of the most important may not be obvious. Complex high-tech manufacturing requires teams of design, engineering, manufacturing-process and production specialists. Traditionally, new products wend their way back and forth among these groups, from one to the next and (if necessary) back again until an initial idea has been transformed into a buildable product. Nowadays we hear that this *ad hoc* process is too expensive. An integrated, *coordinated* design process is essential, with designers and engineers and production people working simultaneously on the same project. "Concurrent engineering" is the newly-hatched buzzword.[3] A competitive global economy means that companies have two choices: They will learn how to turn ideas into products *quickly,* or they will be squashed, mopped up and taken out with the trash (not infrequently by those past masters of coordination, the Japanese). The problems in coordinated design center on information flow. Everyone needs to be up-to-date. Everyone needs to know immediately if his own group's work has been jeopardized or in any way affected by another group's decisions. But we can't flood people with too much or irrelevant detail, or waste their time in hunting around for the information they need. The right people need to be told things promptly and automatically. The others need to be left alone. A Mirror World that captures the current right-now state of the entire project (allowing any participant to stroll around and take in the big picture), and a set of software agents charged with alerting participants to relevant developments, seems like a promising approach.

Building Mirror Worlds

Before I take up one last aspect of the Mirror World's reason for being, let's make the proposition concrete.

Building Mirror Worlds is a complicated but unmysterious proposition. There is nothing science-fictionish about these programs. They're built out of a few basic software components all of which are under active development, if they don't exist already.

A Mirror World is an ocean of information, fed by many data streams. Some streams represent hand-entry of data at computer terminals; they flow slowly. Others are fed by automatic data-gathering and monitoring equipment, like the machinery in a hospital's intensive care unit, or weather-monitoring equipment, or traffic-volume sensors installed in roadways. These streams may be so fast-rushing that they threaten to overwhelm the main program with information tidal waves. The solution is to connect Mirror Worlds to fast-rushing data streams via a sort of software hydroelectric plant. Such programs are designed to sift through complex floods of data looking for trends and patterns as they emerge. They are constructed as layered networks. Data values are drawn in at the bottom and passed upwards through a series of data-refineries, which attempt to convert them into increasingly general and comprehensive chunks of information. As low-level data flows in at the bottom, the big picture comes into focus on top.

One current prototype (designed in collaboration with clinicians at the Yale Medical School) is designed for patient monitoring in operating rooms and intensive care units. The same principles are applicable in many areas. A Mirror World dealing with a transportation network, for example, or a factory, powerplant or aircraft carrier might draw information from an elaborate array of automatic sensors *through* a datafilter. In every case, the filter program tries to answer the same basic question: What's going on here? What does this mass of small, individually inscrutable detail add up to?

The intensive care unit program encompasses on the order of a hundred "modules" or basic elements, but research points in the direction of vast million-module filters, with data values streaming constantly upwards as (perhaps) thousands of data-requests cascade downwards simultaneously, and a complex blur of information comes into focus.

Expert datapools are the programs that make the "experience" key work. They are crucial to Mirror Worlds and have enormous potential significance outside them as well. Users hand these programs the description of some problematic object or event, and it elucidates this thing on the basis of the patterns and likely outcomes recorded in thousands or millions of similar cases. In the course of doing so, it pulls from its massive files a few individual records that are especially pertinent to the case in hand. In effect, the expert datapool is a a huge case-library, expecting to be asked not "get me file 117," but "get me anything I can use."

This software technology, in combination with high-speed parallel computers and computer networks, makes it possible to envision enormous, intelligent information reservoirs linking libraries and databases across the country or the world.

These pools and filters are major building blocks of a Mirror World, in the sense that (say) geartrains and jeweled bearings are important components of a watch. But they also capture the two aspects of the Mirror World as a whole. A Mirror World is a two-faced duality. You can look at it as a datapool, as a detailed historical archive; or you can look at it as a datafilter, capturing and synopsizing the current state of a complicated system right now.

§ The Key Ingredients

Four key ingredients make up a Mirror World: a *deep* picture that is also a *live* picture; plus agents; plus history and experience. And then there's a fifth element: the basic idea that knits these all together.

All four "key ingredients" occur already in some form or other in the world of software or (at least) of imaginary software.

Deep pictures—pictures you can view at many levels, zoom into and zoom out of—bring to mind the software that electronics designers use to lay out their silicon chips. These packages can show you the design of circuitry at many levels, from a bird's eye overview to a detailed close-up of one small corner. Some computer games let you amble around imaginary landscapes. In a book about robots, Hans Moravec of Carnegie Mellon University describes a computerized library system in which you cruise up to interesting-looking items and then dive in.[4] And so on: There are lots of other examples.

The graphic-design aspect of the problem, the so-called *information visualization* field, is challenging and fascinating. There is a fair amount of work in the area. But what you see today is a drop in the bucket next to the dumpsters-full of research that will materialize soon. This is one big, neat problem, and in a few years, computer scientists will be thundering in like a herd of elephants. Today, Xerox's computer science research lab (a place I'll be mentioning again) has software that shows you images, on standard computer screens, of 3-D structures that represent abstractions like personnel charts. A few other software researchers are working on the problem. (Steven Feiner at Columbia, for example.) I'll discuss our own efforts in later chapters. The leader of the field is non-computer-scientist Edward Tufte of Yale, a statistician, designer and political scientist who wrote a classic book on the subject and has just published the sequel.[5]

Live pictures, which show you the state of a complex external system *right now* and change as you watch, are probably the most exotic item on our list. You don't encounter these often. The pictures that computer-driven flight simulators produce (or ship simulators, or the home-computer games that let you drive race cars) fall vaguely into this category. So do the graphs that medical instruments display, and a few other odds and ends.

Agents in one form or another occur in several contexts. Thomas Malone of MIT builds electronic mail systems in which agent-like entities examine a slosh of electronic letters and announcements, trying to pick out items that their human sponsors will find interesting. Robert Kahn of the Corporation for National Research Initiatives is the moving force behind a major effort to build a national computer network that will move data around the country at blinding speeds. Kahn talks about "Knowbots"—*agents* in our terms, software entities working on behalf of their human sponsors. These "knowbots" cruise around the network, ferreting out interesting volumes from network-accessible electronic libraries.

Then, there's experience and history. Any old database is history, in a sense. (Though not quite in our sense.) Other groups whose work is related to our Finding Precedents problem include Craig Stanfill and David Waltz at Thinking Machine Corporation and Roger Schank and colleagues at Northwestern University.

So all of our key ingredients either exist, sort of exist or clearly *could* exist. But then, finally, there's the "basic idea" that guides the knitting-together of these elements. Forget the details, if you like. The "basic idea" is what this book is about.

I will explain in detail how I think Mirror Worlds can and will be built. But obviously, I could be wrong. I think our tools and methods are great, but who knows? Perhaps I've simply failed to recognize better ones. The techniques and software architectures that strike me as beautiful and powerful might be small potatoes when all is said and done. Discount everything we've done and all the details, if you like; the *basic idea* stands. Before long, *someone* will start building Mirror Worlds *somehow*. You may be absolutely certain of that.

Why? Because the idea of this fundamental inversion in man's relationship to society is hard to grasp but too potent to suppress.

Significance, III: Seeing the Whole

Mirror Worlds are devices for showing you the big picture, *the whole*. Every Mirror World has the same goal, in the end: to show you the whole thing at once, the whole *whatever* this Mirror World is tracking. Yes, you can plunge in and explore the details. You can meet people and chat, transact business, hold meetings and go shopping inside a Mirror World. You can leave your software agents behind. But whatever your particular business, you'll be hard-pressed to avoid achieving something else as well: catching a glimpse of *the whole thing*. When you switch-on your city Mirror World, the *whole city* shows up on your screen, in a single dense, live, pulsing, swarming, moving, changing picture. This big picture is the "top surface" of the Mirror World. You can dive deeper to explore, but you *start out* from the big picture—with the big picture on your screen. When you're finished doing business in the depths, you return to the surface—to the *big picture*—on your way out. Whenever you use a Mirror World, the *image of the whole* is available, and inescapable.

Grasping the whole is a gigantic theme. Arguably, intellectual history's *most* important. Ant-vision is humanity's usual fate; but seeing the whole is every thinking person's aspiration. If you accomplish it, you have acquired something I will call *topsight*—and will discuss at greater length further on.

Mirror Worlds will contribute to whole-sightedness in many areas. The first Mirror Worlds will be nothing like entire cities. They will be focussed, most likely, on university departments or research projects, and possibly on single units of academic hospitals. A whole-university or whole-hospital Mirror World is an ambitious step beyond that. Then, commercial applications: fragments of businesses; eventually, whole corporations. Only then do we move out into the fully public world of governments, cities, countries. What might these systems mean *ultimately*, when they reach this point? What does *seeing the whole* mean—what might *Mirror Worlds* mean—to democratic government and society?

It used to be generally conceded that whole-sightedness—a due respect for what Madison calls "the permanent and aggregate interests of the community"[6]—was a good thing. Today, all sorts of angry factions are proudly dedicated to the methodical tearing-to-shreds of public life. Rapacious PAC lobbyists in Washington and multi-culturalists at Stanford are quite agreed that a little E Pluribus *Unum* goes a long way—

But whether they are in fashion or not, whole-sighted citizens are *the* prerequisite to sane public life. This is true on rational grounds and on spiritual ones.

You can't arrive at sound judgements and good decisions without a view of the big picture—knowledge of the facts in each particular case; but, still more important, a *habit of thought*. The habit of going beyond that narrow self-interested slice of truth that is dished out (with coffee) at every inform-the-public affair, no matter *who* is doing the serving.

Spiritually, the ant's-eye view means not only that your outlook is malformed, but that you are in a dangerous position: damned likely to get stepped on. You are caught inside a something you can't picture and can't fathom.

All this is obvious. But consider a few examples, for concreteness. *Why* (Mr. and Mrs. Joe Citizen) have you chosen to allow Independence Hall in Philadelphia to rot, nearly half the surrounding historic buildings closed for lack of money, while a hundred miles away you lavish your tax dollars on another federally supported park (in a politically better-connected district)—is "Steamtown National Historic Site," "a third-rate collection in a place to which it has no relevance," decisively more important to you than Independence Hall?[7] Where is your sense of *the whole*? If we ban polystyrene hamburger clamshells and force the fast-food industry to use all-natural, degradable cardboard instead, that's good for the environment, right? A number of especially virtuous cities have already done so. But those evil polystyrene shells cost 30% less energy to manufacture than cardboard containers, and cause forty some-odd percent less air and water pollution in the process.[8] Don't you need some sense of *the whole* before you make these decisions?

These are mere details; there is an endless list of others just like them. One slightly broader example. At a recent government-sponsored workshop near Johns Hopkins University in Baltimore, a distinguished medical researcher asked the following question: What are the costs of *not* adding five dollars a pack to cigarette taxes? That sounds *in isolation* like an outrageous tax, but maybe, if you look at the big picture, it's merely a modest attempt to recover a small piece of the yearly federal health care outlay that smoking costs us. Should we think of those health care dollars as federal career-support handouts, awarded annually to certain prominent southern politicians? How does it all add up? What's the big picture? Good policy *demands* a sense of the whole.

But even the largest policy questions don't define the edges of this topic. Beyond the political boundaries we enter the spiritual domain. Ant-vision isn't an acute crisis. It's a deep, subtle, gnawing problem, and moreover a problem that far transcends the details of American politics. Whole-sightedness, as I have mentioned, used to be regarded as a good thing. Edmund Burke thought so. The British Parliament should be an "assembly of *one* nation, with *one* interest, that of the whole—."[9] Robert Moses (New York City's leading urban planner during the middle years of this century) thought so. He was "totally without ideology, except for a basic belief that the whole was bigger and more important than the sum of its parts."[10] Moses today is reviled, for building public works on the ruins of private property. Today we have come to understand (many of us, anyway) that Moses was bad, that the "melting pot" was a silly idea if not outright offensive, that we are not a watercolor nation of smoothly-blending individuals but a Calder Mobile of disjoint hard-edged pressure groups circling each other warily, and that Independence Hall can rot—

It's easy to blame the special-interest lobbyists, the multi-culturalists, the whole crowd of *rip-in and tear-it-uppers*. Personally I blame them plenty. But in fairness, how can you value something of which you have no concept? How can you value the whole if you don't know what it *is*? Public life grows more intricate, diverse and simply *larger*. *Envisioning the whole* grows tougher and tougher. Sure, this sense-of-the-whole sounds great; but it's not easily achieved...

It never was; and it's getting much harder, harder all the time. *Galloping complexity* is the theme of modern society. "Ours is a complex age. It is much more complex than any previous age. Invention, machinery, industry, science and commerce are characteristic of today." These words were written by a schoolgirl in her Home Economics notebook in 1937.[11] Things were a lot simpler then. Her remark is dead-neutral in tone; it merely reports a fact. By 1981, the temptation "to believe that society has become too complex to be managed by self-rule"[12] was prevalent enough to be Officially Denied in President Reagan's inaugural address. James Marone's valuable description of the "dense environment of contemporary government"[13] in his recent, much-acclaimed *The Democratic Wish* is a litany of complexity: Nowadays, everything seems to be subtly and mysteriously connected to everything else. To build a dam, review a hospital's rates or set American trade policy you must pick your way over a vast sticky web (of laws, interest groups, technical problems) anchored in far-flung outlandish places. The big picture is a cypher. The *whole* is simply *too complicated to comprehend*.

Can we afford to go on this way? Who will accept responsibility for our ultimate achievement, the Incomprehensible Society? Is ant-mindedness our fate? What are we going to *do* about it?

Okay: political scientists first.

Marone, for one, sees the problem. But he understands it differently: not as a failure of vision, but as a failure of government. Fair enough. Things *look* chaotic, he says, because they are chaotic. We must reconstitute the American government on a new, more integrated and powerful basis. "America need a more powerful political center; we need to renew the public sphere."[14]

The only problem with Marone's plan is that it will never work,

and he knows it. "It is hard to imagine a more unlikely conclusion
to the story of American state building."[15]

All Right. Technologists?

Consider the peculiar idea that technology might help. Yes, we
could re-order, rationalize, *simplify* society to suit the viewpoint of
ants. Or we could sharpen our vision instead; fight progress with
progress. We could abandon the naked eye and look at society
through the wholeness-enhancing lenses of our Mirror Worlds.

It's nice to gaze up at the night sky, but if you want to *comprehend*
what's up there, gazing is not enough; you need *instruments* too. It's
too bad, but there it is. And we need instruments to help us now.
In the long term, ant-vision is incompatible with a free society. The
Mirror World is a wholeness-enhancing instrument; it is the sort of
instrument that modern life demands. It is an instrument that you
(*almost* literally) look though, as through a telescope, to see and
grasp the nature of the organizational world that surrounds you. To
see and grasp not in tiny pieces, but *whole*. An instrument not for
scientists but for citizens.

The Mirror World will not solve all your problems, answer all
of your questions, make you brilliant or teach you Japanese. It will
merely *rub your nose in the big picture*. It will foster a new way
of thinking—vividly, colorfully, intriguingly and relentlessly. And
society may be subtly but deeply different as a result.

You will still be encompassed by the defining institutions of modern life; but now, they will also be encompassed by *you*. They will be
objects in your hands. Literally: Whole organizational worlds will inhabit pint-sized computers. You can pass one around after dinner—
anything from the local school board to the federal government—
like a brandy bottle or a box of chocolates or a Hooka Pipe or the
golden Microcosmal Orb of kingship, the *sphere perfectly held in the
right hand*[16] symbolizing the whole world—inherited from Rome by
Byzantium, passed onwards to medieval kingship and into modern
times. The original Mirror World. Look at it and imagine (if you
cannot see) the world and your kingdom: the two being synony-
mous. Primitive technology. Opaque, but evocative. The Orb, a
perfect sphere: perfect; *whole*.

Sure, you might be too tired this evening to turn the box on.
Or you might have better things to do. Or you might be such a
bored and apathetic goofball that you *never* turn it on, never even

peek inside a Mirror World. Doesn't matter. The fact that *this box exists*, that the world is *right there* on your coffee table, makes all the difference.

Adding It All Up

Since the start of the technology age, previous generations have made their marks with iron and steel, aluminum, glass and concrete; software is our own distinctive building stuff. We think of modern software as fulfilling its destiny in the form of cute little shrink-wrapped boxes at the corner store—software for the people, cheap and universally available. The vision is attractive, but leaves something to be desired; as if the science and engineering that made everyday realities of steel, aluminum, plastics and electric power were all aimed ultimately at the realization of—say—the dishwasher. Dishwashers are useful. There is nothing ignoble about a dishwasher. But it would have been sad had railroads and airplanes, skyscrapers, bridges, highway networks and supercomputers never existed, and we had contented ourselves with kitchen appliances exclusively. Now the time has come to build some noble and inspiring public things out of software. And we surely will.

Is it an inadmissible stretch to refer to these Mirror Worlds as the Saint Marks' of their time? A Mirror World that encompasses a large hospital or university or a moderate-sized company is an enormous, complicated structure. A City Mirror World is immense. And such programs will blend as they grow, eventually encompassing many universities, or every hospital in the region, or all the somethings in the country or, conceivably, in many countries. These monumental projects will absorb great quantities of labor. And a program of this sort might see throngs of strollers on a busy day: Thousands, even millions of computer-windows might be thrown open on one Mirror World simultaneously. It's not hard to imagine the largest of these projects becoming the grand *piazzas* of their age. Such projects surely qualify as civil software-engineering on the order of rail systems or highway networks. Like all great engineering projects, they are potential artistic masterpieces as well. All that's required is a Brunel or an Eiffel or a Maillart to work in software. Apart from their structural beauty, the constantly changing, endlessly detailed pictures that these programs project might be beautiful and *will* at least be striking.

Still, some (many?) won't grasp the *structural reality* of Mirror Worlds. After all, if you turn your computer off, they disappear. You can't turn off Saint Mark's. Certainly these things are *peculiar* structures: invisible, built out of gossamer info-fluff, gliding silently through dozens or thousands of computers simultaneously, fed by quiet datastreams and raging datafloods to which they respond with billions of clock-work micro-reactions every second, host to visiting hordes—each member of the crowd sealed in absolute physical privacy. Pull the plug and it vanishes. This kind of structure does take some getting used to.

Where previous generations would have gotten excited, we— numbingly prudent middle-aged society that we have become—tend to get worried. In the face of huge, powerful and potentially abusable programs like Mirror Worlds, worry is in order. Exhilaration is also in order.

Chapter 3

Disembodied Machines

We begin with the central question. The answer forms the most important part of the Mirror World's intellectual foundation. It also forms, for that matter, the most important part of computer science's intellectual foundation; which makes it one of the central questions in modern engineering, and arguably the most important question in the history of technology. Despite which, it is a question that is rarely asked; and on rare occasions when it is, the answers you hear tend to be blatantly wrong. *What is a program?* What does "software" mean? Any technoglitz book that proposes to slobber on for hundreds of pages about software (there are plenty of them nowadays) should make you *acutely* uncomfortable unless it starts out by telling you *what software is.* And not many do.

Because (or at least *partially* because) the answer isn't simple. Or to put it another way, the answer is simple but it's also subtle, because it requires that we give a name to something that (like adolescent female pigeons or the sky just as a cold front is arriving) we are accustomed to seeing but not to identifying. I've said that a computer program is a kind of machine, which is true. But it's a funny kind of machine that must be defined with care, or we miss the whole point. I'll define a program as an example of something I'll call an "embodied machine"; this will place it roughly at the midpoint between a lathe and a symphony.

A Machine?

I need to say, first, what a "machine" is in general. (Arguing about
this definition used to be a fairly popular diversion. Machines are not
the sexy proposition they once were...) Let us say, for present purposes, that a machine is a man-made structure that converts energy
into value. This definition is vague on purpose, but it makes several
points. A machine is man-made (a cloud doesn't qualify), and it is a
structure—an object that occupies space and time. (An idea doesn't
qualify). A machine is the meeting place between physics and society: It converts energy, which has a precise physical definition, into
value, which doesn't. Value is whatever you say it is.

Embodied **Machines**

Suppose you visit an art museum and walk up to a painting. I say
"Ah ha! I see you're admiring some powdered pigments, mixed with
oil and smeared onto what appears to be a canvas panel." You say
"No, you moron. I'm admiring *a Rembrandt.*" Good. You're three-
quarters of the way towards a deep understanding of software.

How did this happen?

Well clearly we may, if we choose, regard a painting as a coming-
together of two separate elements. The paints and canvas—the physical stuff; and the form-giving mind-plan. I'll call these two elements
the *body* and the *disembodied painting* respectively.

Both are necessary to the finished product.   But they are
*un*equally decisive to its character. If Rembrandt had (while trying to shake out a tablecloth) accidentally chucked his favorite paint
set into a canal on the very morning he was destined to make our
painting; if he'd accordingly been forced to go down to the basement
and hunt up another set—the finished product would be the same.
But if he'd altered his mind-plan—the *disembodied painting*—before
setting to work, our finished painting would obviously have been different.

In fact, the disembodied painting *is* a painting *in and of itself*—
albeit a painting of a special kind, namely an *unbodied* one. Rembrandt is perfectly entitled to tell his wife "I have a painting in mind"
before setting to work. But plainly the mere *body* is no painting, not

in and of itself. If the paints on Rembrandt's table went around telling people "Hey look at us, we're a painting," no-one would believe them.

This distinction is the key to software and its special character. A running program is a machine of a certain kind, an *information* machine. The program text—the words and symbols that the programmer composes, that "tell the computer what to do"—is a *disembodied* information machine. Your computer provides a *body*.

Unlike Rembrandt's mind plan, a disembodied information machine must be written down precisely and in full. It's a bit like the engineering drawings for a new toaster in this regard; the machine designer leaves nothing to chance. Unlike Rembrandt's mind plan *or* the toaster drawings, on the other hand, a disembodied information machine can be "embodied" *automatically*. No skill, judgement or human intervention is required. Merely hand your text to a computer (it's probably stored inside the computer already); the computer itself performs the "embodying."

So: A running program—an *information machine* or infomachine for short—is the *embodiment* of a *disembodied machine*. In saying this, we have said a lot. A fairly simple point first, then a subtle and deeply important one—

Some people believe that, when they see a program running, the machine they are watching is a "computer." True, but not true enough. The *computer*, that impressive-looking box with the designer logo, is merely the paint, not the painting. When you say *I'm watching this computer do its stuff*, you are saying in effect *I'm admiring* not this Rembrandt but *some paint smeared on canvas*. Some people imagine the computer as a gifted actor (say) who is handed a program and declaims it feelingly. No: bad image. The computer itself is of the utmost triviality to the workings of the infomachine you are watching. It may decide how fast or slowly the thing runs, and may effect its behavior just a little around the fringes, but essentially it is of no logical significance whatever. It is a mere *body*, and bodies are a dime a dozen.

OK, agreed. But the second point is harder.

People often find it difficult to keep in mind that, when they see a program text, what they're looking at is a machine. The fact that, for the time being, the machine they're looking at *has no body* confuses them. With good reason: This is a subtle, maybe a confusing point. They leap to the conclusion that what programmers do amounts to arranging symbols on paper (or in a computer file) in a certain way. They look at a program and see merely a highly specialized kind of *document.*

This mistake is fatal to any real understanding of what software is.

Understanding software doesn't mean understanding how program texts are arranged, it means understanding what *the working infomachine itself* is like—what actually *happens* when you embody the thing and turn it on—what kind of *structure* you are creating when you organize those squiggles—the *shape* of the finished product, the way information hums through it, the way it grows, shrinks and changes as it runs, the look and feel of the *actual* computational landscape. *This* is where software creativity is exercised. *This* is where the field evolves, metamorphoses and explodes. Talented software designers work with some image of the actual *running* program uppermost in mind. Failing to see *through* the program text to the machine it represents is like trying to understand musical notation without grasping that those little sticks and ellipsoids represent *sounds.*

This kind of information is hard to convey. You can't directly *see* a running program. You can sense its workings indirectly, but you can't open the hood and look *right at* the mechanism. An ironic reversal of the Rembrandt experience: Here the mind-plan is tangible, but the embodied thing itself is not.

Nonetheless, there are good ways to understand, indeed to *envision* exactly what a running program is like. The rest of the chapter presents them.

Now let me backpedal a bit, by way of conclusion, to emphasize the trickiness of this game.

Say you're a toaster designer and you've just completed a brand new project. I see the finished engineering drawing sitting on your worktable and I ask you "what's that?" There are (at least) two possible responses. You could say "it's a drawing" or "it's a toaster." Maybe, if you're an accurate-minded guy, you'll say "it's a drawing" or "it *denotes* a toaster." Same thing, for our purposes.

I've just gotten through insisting, emphatically, that the *toaster* answer is the important one. When you see a program, you're not looking at a document; you're looking at a machine.

But it *is* true nonetheless that your engineering drawing is a drawing, and that your program is (among other things) a document. Your program text can be manipulated in the same way other documents can be. It can have spelling and grammatical errors, stylistic quirks; you can print it on paper, frame it, hang it on the wall; draw little daisies on it and send it to your mom.

We need to keep this duality in mind, but not be misled by it. The danger is acute. There is a whole school of computer science research dedicated to the proposition that "programming is mathematics." Why would anyone make such a fantastic claim? Well in fact a program *as a document* can be made to *look* a lot like mathematics. And of course a program *is* a document (among other things), and if it appears to be a mathematical document, you can treat it in a mathematical way—prove theorems about it and so forth. It may even be useful to do so, up to a point.

By the same token, you can learn a lot about music on the basis of the purely mechanical manipulation of symbols. You can *see* what good counterpoint looks like on paper. You can learn how to "compose" good counterpoint, even if you don't have the vaguest idea of what it sounds like.

But if you get carried away, and start asserting that "music *is* the mechanical manipulation of symbols on staff paper," "programming *is* mathematics," you have committed intellectual suicide. You've mistaken the means for the end. You've cut yourself off absolutely from all real inspiration, creativity and growth. And you have failed, profoundly, to understand the character of your field.

A dangerous mistake. Where software is concerned, an all-too-natural one.

The Design Process

Designing an embodied information machine is much like designing any other kind of machinery. First you need an idea; then you produce a specification; then you build a prototype.

Creative hardware designers often proceed by incremental tinkering. Build a mechanism of some sort, play with it, modify it, build another one. The same kind of thing goes on in software building. Many creative software engineers also proceed by incremental tinkering. They build a little program, watch it run, build an improved version. The two activities, hardware and software machine-making, are very similar in spirit. But the fact that the software builder never needs to go anywhere *near* a lab bench, never needs to fool around with cumbersome hardware, can merely hand his spec to the computer and see it embodied *automatically*, gives him an incalculable advantage. Alone at his keyboard he can improvise machinery of extraordinary power, brilliance and intricacy.

So: What kind of machine?

What does a working information machine look like?

Well *actually*, of course, it looks like nothing. It's a bunch of electrical signals running around inside of wires. But metaphorically, we can go into some detail about its appearance. (By the same token, I can say "this is what the organization of the company looks like," "this is what the reaction between two particles looks like," "this is what the division of resources in the U.S. economy looks like" and so on. The pictures I show you are arbitrary, but that doesn't make them untruthful. Once you learn the rules, such pictures can represent with great accuracy and faithfulness the "un-depictable" thing you're attempting to discuss.)

So let's envision an information machine. They're not all alike. But they're *enough* alike so that we can describe an idealized model that captures the most important features of nearly all of them.

The ideal model I'm about to describe is simpler and more uniform than you'll find in other books. It's the product of a research effort aimed exactly at that goal. The plan was to dump every infomachine everywhere into a large pot, fish out the especially weird or atypical ones and boil the rest down for a long time. Eventually, all the inessential distinctions evaporate, and you are left with the basic, simple, concentrated essence. What I'll describe below is the essence of the essence. (Another book goes into technical detail.[1])

It comes down to this: An infomachine is a landscape, divided into plots. As the machine runs, the landscape changes. It evolves, like the surface of a developing photograph; the stuff inside those plots changes; eventually it's done—the process is complete, you have what you want, and the evolution stops.

Now I need to define what's in the plots, and how it evolves.

The Computational Landscape

Picture a landscape, divided into plots, with a "command post" at the center. Each plot has a name, and each one may *contain something*—in the sense that a field contains wheat, or a building lot contains a building. A plot can contain three kinds of things: an *information chunk* (infochunk for short), a *procedure*—or more plots. (A plot can be subdivided, in other words.)

An *information chunk* is usually a number or an alphabetic character. It might also be a word or a phrase or a few other things. A *procedure* tells you how to accomplish something. If a software machine were an auto repair shop, the infochunks would be the parts department (infochunks are the stuff you work with if you are an information machine), and the procedures would be the library of shop manuals (e.g. "How to Fix 1977 Pontiacs" and so on).

By subdividing plots, I can group a set of infochunks together. For example, I might need a table of numbers with a hundred rows and a thousand columns. So my software machine has a single large plot (named "table of expenses per project by department," or whatever); the large plot is subdivided into a hundred thousand plotlets, one for each entry in the table. By sub-dividing I can also create "modules," discussed below.

The command post is walled with one-way mirrors. Whatever is in there can see out, but you can't see in. Pacing around inside, surveying the big picture through fieldglasses, is an automaton I'll call "the Actor." He's equipped at all times with "the script;" the script lists a series of operations for the Actor to carry out. (This isn't the "Actor" for which some people, I claimed, mistake the *computer itself*. This Actor is a software creature entirely, one element of the infomachine that gets created automatically when your program is embodied.)

What does the Actor do? Its objectives in the large are pretty clear: to respond to information. Information gets dumped into its regions like piles of sand outside a glassworks, for conversion into

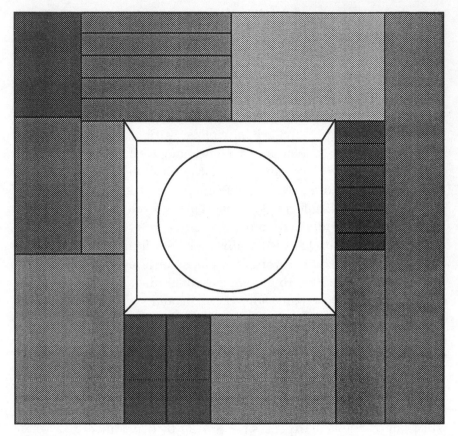

Figure 3.1: A computational landscape. The circle represents the
Actor.

some other form. The means at the Actor's disposal are limited but
powerful. It can make new information objects out of old objects. It
can use objects to make executive decisions. It can get new objects
from outside and dump them into regions ("input"), and it can cause
objects to be printed, displayed on screens, stored in files or whatever
("output").

(The one-way mirrors mean that you *think* there's an Actor pacing around in there, but sometimes you are wrong.)

We'll refer to the disembodied information machine that the programmer lays out as the *spec*. A complete spec includes a *map* of the
information landscape, and the aforementioned *script*, to be carried
out by the Actor.

When a spec is finished, it can be be presented to the computer for *embodiment*. ("Bodification"? "Bodying forth...") Whereupon the landscape is laid out according to the map, the Actor picks up his script and we're underway.

I've now covered all the basic stuff. I'll fill in a few details by discussing a simple example; then we're ready for the transition to "advanced infomachinery" and the key question, *how do you build these things?*

An Example

Making new infochunks out of old infochunks is the Actor's main stock in trade. This is accomplished primarily by plugging numbers into formulas, by gluing objects together to make bigger ones and smashing them apart to get smaller ones.

For example: You want to build an infomachine that, when it's handed the lengths of two legs of a right triangle, returns the length of the hypotenuse. There is an exceedingly well-known formula for computing the hypotenuse of a right triangle: Take the square root of the summed squares of the lengths of the two legs.

We lay out the following map: three plots, one named "First Leg," one "Second Leg" and one "Hypotenuse."

Now, the script. Here is what it says: (1) Input two numbers; dump one in the "First Leg" plot and one in the "Second Leg" plot. Now, prepare to create a new infochunk. (2) Grab the numbers that you just dumped into the Leg regions; square each and sum the squares; take the square root, and dump this number into the "Hypotenuse" region. (3) Finally, print the number that is now stored in the "Hypotenuse" region. That's it.

When the Actor has finished with the script, it takes a graceful bow, the curtain falls and the information machine disappears.

Although I need to say more about scripts and procedures, we've arrived at an important point: We can now say exactly and concretely what a *programming language* is. A programming language is a system for writing down information machine specs, or in other words, for creating unbodied infomachines.

There are, God knows, *many* programming languages. There is an awe-inspiring surplus of them. Serving Europe alone you will find, right next to the famous Wine Lake and Butter Mountain, the

less-well-known Programming Language Sludgepile. Here, old users'
manuals sit decomposing in gargantuan heaps dotted with wildflowers, visited only by the odd graduate student or Tyrolean mountain
goat. Large dump trucks make fresh deliveries daily.

There are only a few genuinely important languages. But these
few are *very* important: Although the oldest dates only to the late
1950's, these languages rank among the most heavily-used and influ-
ential engineering tools of all time.

Programming languages differ somewhat in the range of specs
they allow you to write down, and dramatically in the means of expression they allow you—hence, in the actual *look* of the blueprint
and in its style. But *every* programming language has the same
purpose—to allow you to spec out information machines—and, in the
final analysis, it's the information machine and not the programming
language that matters. Information machinery exists independent of
programming languages (as buildings exist independently of pencils
and straightedges). By and large, and neglecting a few subtle but
reasonably significant details, all languages allow you to express exactly the same range of information machinery. By the same token,
all architectural drawing tools, from the fanciest computer package
to a pencil and a straightedge, allow you to design exactly the same
range of buildings. Of course, some tools make it a lot easier to do
the job, and some make it harder. Nonetheless, the world of all possible buildings (and infomachines) is independent of the world of all
possible drawing tools (and programming languages).

§ Details: What the Program Looks Like

Concretely: We've described a software machine for computing hypotenuses. Here is what the spec looks like in a programming language called Pascal:

```
program(input, output);
var FirstLeg, SecondLeg, Hypotenuse: real;
begin
    read(input, FirstLeg);
    read(input, SecondLeg);
```

```
    Hypotenuse := sqrt(sqr(FirstLeg)+sqr(SecondLeg));
    write(output, Hypotenuse)
end;
```

The **var** stands for "variable", and it means "here are the names of some regions for holding infochunks." Three names follow. The "real" means that the chunks stored in these compartments will be "real numbers"—meaning, in Pascal's terminology, that they may have fractional components (as in 3.1415). The phrases that make up the script stand between **begin** and **end** (which mean precisely "beginning of the script" and "end of the script"). The details of the phraseology may be obscure, but they don't matter. (The phrase beginning "Hypotenuse :=" means "put the following thing in the region named Hypotenuse," as you probably guessed.) The big picture should be pretty clear. The script we outlined above had four steps; each step is described by one line of the formal script as it occurs in Pascal.

We might have used one of two dozen other programming languages to produce very different-looking specs. But they'd all create exactly the same information machine.

Aside from evaluating formulas, the Actor's other chief occupation is making decisions based on infochunks. The script can contain lines like "look at the infochunk in region so-and-so; if it's the number 1 do this, and if it's 0 do that."

Suppose you want a software machine to read a document and compile an alphabetical list of every word you have used. The spec creates a region named "Next Line," and another named "Word Use Table," which is divided into sub-regions. The Actor does the following, repeatedly: reads the next line *from* the document *into* the "Next Line" region. (When you drop an infochunk into a region, the old chunk disappears.) Then it looks at each word in this line. For each word in the line, it asks "Do I already have this word in my table?" If the answer is no, it looks for the first empty sub-region in the "Word Use Table" and drops this new word into it. If the answer is yes, it doesn't need to do anything.

When it's reached the end of the document it alphabetizes the table—once again, by making lots of decisions based on the values of infochunks or expressions. (Does this word come *after* this other

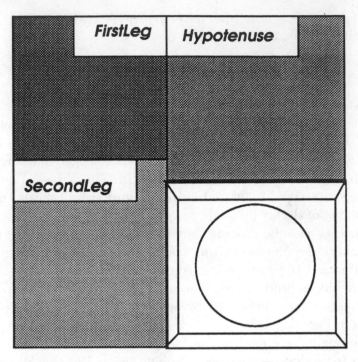

Figure 3.2: The landscape created by the Pascal program.

word in alphabetical order? If so, switch these two words...) Now it can print out the words in the table, and it's done.

Sounds pretty simple, I hope.

What I've described so far is sound and correct as far as it goes—but that's not far enough. We've been discussing how to saw a piece of wood, drive a nail; now, a big leap: Let's build a building. If you're building (let's say) a wood-frame structure, it's going to be based (no matter how large it is) on techniques like sawing and nailing. Without a grasp of these techniques, you'll never have a concrete sense for what the building process is like. But it's also true that "building a house" is not merely a *bigger* topic than "driving nails," it's also a *different* topic. It centers on issues of design, planning, strategy and organization that don't occur on a smaller scale.

So let's move on to this new and bigger topic.

Building Info-structures

First questions: What are the goals? What's the point? What do you design for? Yes, to put a roof over your head (if this is a house), to perform a computation correctly (if this is an infomachine). *Beyond* that. What guides the design process? If you're designing a car, for example, you design for reliability, economy, safety; speed, performance, good looks... When you design an *infomachine*, what are you designing for?

For two goals: efficiency and clarity.

§ Efficiency

Maybe "efficiency" doesn't sound like a very exciting topic but, sorry, that's the name of the game. Efficiency means: Do the job without wasting time or space. Your infomachine should run as fast as possible. It should occupy as little space as possible, so it will fit into small computers and not waste space inside of large ones.

§ Details: Efficiency and Algorithm Design

Although efficiency considerations have a lot to do with the way landscapes are laid out, they're more important to the script than to the map. For example: My lexicon program compiles a list of words. Should I arrange for this list to stay alphabetized *throughout* the execution of the program? Or should I let it accumulate in random order and alphabetize it only once, right before I print it out?

This might sound like a minor consideration, but in many cases it will be the decisive influence on your program's performance. If you need to handle large documents, your answer to this question may determine whether your program finishes the job in two seconds or two years.

Here's the issue: If I keep the list alphabetized throughout, I'll have to do extra work every time I stick a new word in the list. *Where* does this word go, exactly?—I have to figure this out, and then I have to make space for the new word, probably by shuffling a lot of other words around. All of this takes time.

On the other hand, every time I read a word, I need to check whether or not this word already appears in my list. If the answer is no, I'll need to add it; but whatever the answer, I *always* have to check. And for a long document, the answer will usually be yes. Most words I find, I've already seen at least once.

If I've taken the trouble to keep my list in alphabetical order, it's a lot faster to perform this check. Say the list is *not* alphabetized. To check whether some word is in it I will need, in the worst case, to look at *every* word on the list. This takes time. The longer the list, the more time. The average lookup time is proportional to the length of the list: If the list doubles in length, so does the average lookup time.

But if the list is alphabetized and I want to do a lookup, I will *not* need to look at every word in the list. I can take my new word and compare it to the middle word in the list. If the new word comes before this middle word in alphabetical order, I can forget about the whole bottom half of the list: My new word is guaranteed *not* to be there. If the list is ten thousand words long, I've just eliminated five thousand entries at a stroke. I repeat my procedure on the remainder of the list, the first half. Does my new word come before or after *its* middle word? If it comes before, I can throw out the entire second half of the first half. I repeat this procedure until I've found what I'm looking for, or concluded that it can't be there.

This second procedure is not merely faster, it's *astoundingly* faster than the first. The first procedure required time proportional to the length of the list. The second requires time proportional to the logarithm-to-the-base-2 of the length of the list. That is: If your list is 512 entries long, you can search it completely (using the second method) not in 512 steps but in 9. If the list doubles in length, the first method now requires 1024 steps in the worst case; the second method has shot all the way up to 10.

If you're dealing with a long list of words, or a word list that must be searched often, or both, this enormous gap in searching time can spell the difference between a program that runs well and one that is simply too slow to use. And this simple example is typical of what software designers worry about constantly: What's the most efficient way (the best algorithm, in technical terminology) for accomplishing what needs to be accomplished?

But algorithms are only part of the story.

§ Clarity

In fact, clarity is not an *ultimate* goal; it's the means to an end. The real end is something called "topsight." But first we need to get acquainted with the big monster problem, the leading killer of software:

§ Complexity

Information structures are, potentially, the most complicated structures known to man. Precisely *because* software is so easy to build, complexity is a deadly software killer.

The same problem exists for hardware machines, but it lacks comparable significance. Physical reality is the overflow valve that siphons off excess complexity before the whole system blows. If you're building a hardware machine, you reach a point where your device has so many parts that you can't afford any more, or the weight, size or power consumption of your gadget is untenable—it can't get any more complex, and so it doesn't. You don't worry about hyper-complex *hardware* because you haven't got any. Sure, there *is* the odd space shuttle, nuclear power plant and whatnot—there are *some* staggeringly complex hardware machines, but not many, because not many outfits can afford them.

With infomachinery it's a different story. Programs that amount to a quarter of a million lines of text (there are about 7000 lines in this book, so picture 35 volumes of program) are not in the least unusual. Many programs are much longer. 250,000 lines is enough to create an enormously complex info-landscape with many thousands of regions. How can you design, build and understand such complex landscapes?

Not easily.

It's very hard to make programs come out right. After a decent amount of effort they tend to be *mostly* right, with just a few small bugs. Fixing those small bugs (a bug can be small but catastrophic under the wrong circumstances) might take ten times longer than the entire specification, design, construction and testing effort up to this point. These are *subtle* structures.

If you're a software designer and you can't master and subdue monumental complexity, you're dead: your machines don't work. They run for a while and then sputter to a halt, or they never run at all. Hence "managing complexity" must be your goal. Or, we can describe exactly the same goal in a more positive light. We can call it *the pursuit of topsight*. Topsight—an understanding of the big picture—is an essential goal of every software builder. It's also the most precious intellectual commodity known to man.

§ Engineering Topsight

To manage software complexity, you must seek a deep and thorough understanding of the structure of your problem; and then you must transfer this understanding directly into software. Like studying a face carefully enough to achieve a deep understanding of what it *really* looks like, then transferring this understanding directly into a painted portrait. The goal of the exercise is to achieve something that is so universally important and yet so hard to come by that it doesn't even have a word to describe it. So I'll make one up: *topsight*. (I don't like this coinage particularly and would be glad to have a better one. If you can think of one, let me know.)

If *insight* is the illumination to be achieved by penetrating inner depths, *topsight* is what comes from a far-overhead vantagepoint, from a bird's eye view that reveals *the whole*—the big picture; how the parts fit together. ("Overview" comes fairly close to what I mean. But an "overview" is something you either have or you don't. *Topsight* is something that, like insight, you pursue avidly and continuously, and achieve gradually.)

It is *the* quality that distinguishes genius in any field. (What Newton displayed when he saw planets reeling round the sun and teardrops falling as two pieces of one picture; what Churchill showed when he grabbed for the Dardanelles to break an impasse in France; what Hamlet is transfixed by: the special providence in the fall of a sparrow...) It is the keystone of a beautifully transparent definition of *philosopher*: one who seeks "to transcend the world of human thought and experience, in order to find some point of vantage from which it can be seen whole."[2] But topsight is emphatically *not* a feat for philosophers and geniuses only. Every thinking person aims to achieve it—to understand how the parts relate, how it all adds up. It's not easily won. The fact that we don't even have a *word* for this vital commodity is evidence, more than anything else, of our reluctance (or inability) to teach it. Its significance is denigrated by the run-of-the-mill hacks, bureaucrats and cadres who swing chattering from detail to detail like monkeys in branches, never sensing or caring about the forest in the large. Such people more or less run the world. But all thoughtful people—*most* people, when all is said and done—are born with a powerful inclination to seek this thing—

If you're a software designer, at any rate, your task is hard and clear. When you're presented with a difficult problem, you seek topsight; you use whatever topsight you've achieved as your guide through the treacherous terrain of program building.

It's a tall order, but the alternative is clear-cut: to drown in complexity.

§ **Programs illuminated by topsight...**

have one unmistakable property: clarity. No down-directed gaze can penetrate an opaque structure. The software designer works *always with the aim of coherence and clarity of statement*. (I will return to this phrase...)

Clarity is marked by three major phenomena. Or, in operational terms, you *get* clarity by applying three principles. Perhaps you build software in a constant blaze of topsightful inspiration, and we're merely characterizing your handiwork: we recognize it by the presence of three attributes. Or maybe you're merely trying to achieve the same affect by humble, serious, meticulous work (good for you—give that guy a cigar); you follow three guiding principles. It amounts to the same thing.

§ The Three-Fold Way to Clarity

In software building, there are three ways. (Actually, I'm not sure whether this is an exhaustive list. I suspect it is, but maybe not. In any event, these are the three that underlie this book.) The three principles are *Recursive Simplicity, Uncoupling* and *Espalier*. I'll introduce the latter two in later chapters, and the first below.

The essence of all three methods is the same; it is *design sense.* This is where engineering comes down to *aesthetic judgement.* To impose clarity upon complexity through deep and careful design-thinking is *the* crucial achievement of the master programmer. I've just noted that the software builder works *always with the aim of coherence and clarity of statement*—this is George Henderson, Art Historian, imagining the unknown master architect of Chartres.[3] The software revolution balances ultimately on a fine point of aesthetics.

This fact bears investigating. I'll return to it.

§ Recursive Simplicity

An object is *recursive* in structure when the whole is structurally identical to its parts—or at least to some of them. You can build a large electronic circuit out of smaller pieces that are *themselves* electronic circuits. You can build a large algebraic expression— something plus something else, times something else—out of smaller pieces that are *themselves* algebraic expressions. You don't build a large toaster out of smaller toasters—recursive structures are un-common; but: The most important event in the history of software happened somewhere around 1959, when the designers of a program-ming language called "Algol 60" realized that *you can build a large program out of smaller programs.*

Break out the Dom Perignon!! Why? Because this principle rep-resents such an immense break-through for the *clarity* of information machines. I don't need to understand how a million different struc-tures fit together. I need only master a few, a small handful—for software machinery the grand total is *two*, a space-organizing and a time-organizing structure—and I can re-use these structures again and again *ad infinitum.* These two structures are in fact nothing less than our two most important simple infomachines. The space-organizing structure is what I've called the *map.* The time-organizing structure is the *script.* I can use them to organize an immense program, to organize each of this immense program's gigantic pieces, and the large components of the gigantic pieces, and the medium-size pieces and each small, tiny and minuscule piece down to the bottom. It's as if I could learn French by mastering a grand total of two phrases, and then relax in the assurance that, wherever I happen to find myself, one or the other is bound to be exactly right.

Recursive simplicity means: You have this capability in the abstract. Now *use it.* Don't build a large component out of a million tiny pieces; build it out of a few medium-sized ones.

Recursive simplicity as a structuring principle is not unique to software. I mentioned algebra and electronics; also, trees, mountains, coastlines... Benoit Mandelbrot discusses the ways in which "self-similar" natural structures re-use the same patterns at many scales.[4] We use another form of recursive structure in the numerical codes that impose organization in many domains (zip codes, library codes, phone numbers). As you decipher one of these codes, you repeat the *same question* (which geographical area?—which topic?) on a smaller scale for each number or group of numbers you encounter. This books is conceptually recursive: Topsight is the goal of Mirror Worlds; and topsight is the goal of one sub-effort that goes into the making of a Mirror World.

In engineering, recursive simplicity requires that complex machines be planned, organized and explained as a series of levels. At the highest level the big picture is clear, but the details are not. At lower levels, the details come into focus. Each level breaks a problem down into a manageable collection of parts or steps. Once I've assimilated the big picture—this nuclear reactor consists of five basic pieces—I can proceed to the next level of detail: The cooling system consists of eight basic components. And so on. In this way I can pilot my thought-glider gracefully downwards level-by-level towards the nitty gritty, assimilating detail gradually, *never losing sight of where each detail fits.*

This gradual playing-out of detail, the ability to intuit a bold, simple, multi-layered organizational framework for an immensely complex structure, is an art pure and simple, a manifestation of design sense. You don't have to be born with it; there are rules and methods that you can learn, as in any design discipline. But of course, innate predilection and the occasional flash of inspiration don't hurt. It will never be *called* "design sense," not by computer people, anyway; nonetheless, a roomful of advanced programming students at their terminals is less a laboratory than it is a studio.

There's nothing mysterious or novel about the hierarchical structuring principle I've described. Complex machines and activities have always been described in terms of layered outlines. Not, "in order to send a man to the moon, build the following twenty-three billion pieces of equipment and carry out these eighteen trillion steps." Instead, "in order to send a man to the moon, (1) design and build rocket engines, (2) design and build space vehicles, (3) find and train astronauts, (4) plan and organize space missions." Each of these steps can be subdivided in turn. Ultimately you get down to the nuts and bolts: "Issue Astronaut Piffel his jar of Tang." But you get there gracefully and gradually.

What's novel in computer science is the fact that the principle is applicable, not merely as an abstract thought-tool, but immediately and concretely: It's *built into* the machinery.

Organizing Space and Time—

—the worthy goals of *modules* and *procedures*, respectively. These tools allow you to build "recursively simple" programs.

If you notice that a bunch of regions are related, you can clump them together into a single super-region called a module. If you notice that a bunch of time-regions are related, you can do likewise: You can clump them into a procedure.

What is a "time region"? The Actor performs the steps specified in the script. Each step takes some time to perform. So we can say (if we feel like it) that each step *occupies a region in time*, just as each piece of the landscape occupies a region in space. We can clump a bunch of steps together, and give the clump *as a whole* a name. Such a clump is referred to generically as a "procedure."

§ Details: Modules and Procedures

Suppose some infomachine is designed to read data, do some calculations and then display the results as some kind of graph. Lots of infochunks and a large script might be required. We might start by building some time-clumps: We gather steps into procedures, some having to do with reading data (say a procedure called "get next data value"), some having to do with building the graph (say a procedure called "plot values"), and so on. When the Actor needs to plot some values, the script doesn't spell out all the steps; it merely says "now perform the *plot-values* procedure," or words to the effect. Then we build some space-clumps. Some of infochunks and procedures deal with reading data, some with the calculation, some with producing the graph and displaying it. Others might come into play at all three stages. If we choose, we can gather together the infochunks and procedures that are designed for reading data, and treat all these regions as sub-regions within a single large region, called the "Reading Data Module" (or whatever). Similarly we might build a *Calculation* module and a *Display Results* module.

Details: How Procedures Work

But there's more to procedures than this.

Plot-values is the name of a region; inside this region is a procedure. Whenever I need to plot some values, I grab this thing and set it to work. But what *is* it, exactly?

Two possibilities: It might be a script; or it might be an entire landscape with its own command post and its own Actor.

Say the Actor arrives at the line in his script where it says "Now perform the *plot-values* procedure." What does he do? In the first case, he reaches into the region named *plot-values*, grabs the script and starts performing it. When he's done, he puts the script back and continues where he left off. In the second case, he picks up his walkie-talkie and radios over to the Actor who is snoozing in the *plot-values* command post—the message he sends is "OK, do your stuff; let me know when you're done." He sits back and waits, very possibly sends out for a pizza; eventually a reply comes back: "I'm done; the answer is..."

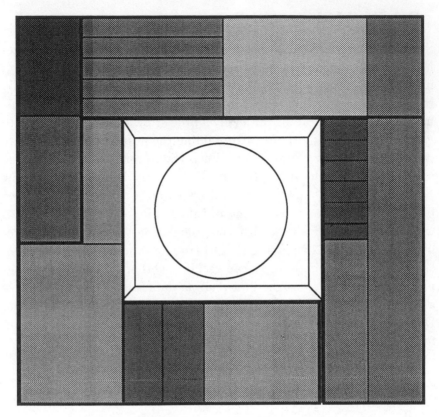

Figure 3.3: Gathering plots into modules.

Both of these possibilities are perfectly reasonable, but in general they are both wrong.

Actually, the object that inhabits the *plot-values* region is not a script, and is not a snoozing information machine. Instead, it is the spec for a completely *new* information machine.

So: When the Actor arrives at the "perform *plot-values*" line in his script, he reaches into the region of that name and grabs the spec that is lying inside. Following this spec, an entirely new information machine is constructed inside the command post: a new landscape, with a new command post furnished with its own new script, and a new Actor inside. This new Actor performs the new script. When the performance is complete, the entire purpose-built information machine vanishes—leaving only the answer behind (swirling around on a mysterious scrap of paper near the floor...So to speak) The old Actor reappears, finds the answer, and continues on his way.

This sequence of events has interesting implications. The new Actor inside the purpose-built information machine might *itself* decide to perform a procedure. Another new machine pops up inside the new command post. Inside, yet another procedure might be invoked and then another, on and on.

So this information machine is radically unlike a hardware one: It grows and shrinks. It may spiral deep into a recursive hole and then spiral back out again. The only ultimate limit on *how* deep it can go is the amount of real space inside the embodying computer.

Another thing about those one-way mirrors, by the way: The information machine *inside* the command post can see out. It can make use of the infochunks and procedures that exist within the surrounding landscape. But the surrounding landscape can't see in. Procedures in the surrounding landscape can't (for example) be defined in such a way that they grab infochunks that only occur inside the command post.

Why go to all this trouble? The first of our simple hypotheses about procedures—that they were mere scripts, to be picked up and played out by the main Actor—is no good in practice. Infochunks and procedures might be required specifically for the use of the procedure itself. A procedure (in other words) needs a landscape of its own. The second possibility—that a procedure is a separate, self-contained information machine with its own command post, waiting

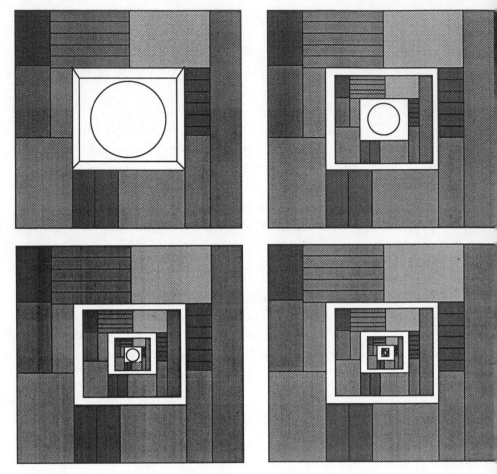

Figure 3.4: An inward-spiralling computational landscape. The "command post" is repeatedly replaced by entire new landscapes.

to run—works out fairly well. The programming language called "Fortran" operates in this way. Fortran, dating to 1957, was the first successful programming language; its lineal descendants are still in widespread use. But in most subsequent languages, a procedure is a spec—which gains you exactly one magical little power over the Fortran approach: You can build a procedure which invokes *itself*.

So what? To make a long story short, this ability allows you to express certain things very concisely. (It's a lot simpler to say "my brother looks like me, but with a beard" than to say "my brother has dark hair, brown eyes, fair skin" and so on through seventeen more attributes. It's useful to be able to refer to yourself.) It also allows you to improvise elegant, sinuous computing patterns round the unpredictable twists and turns of growing data structures. (Douglas Hofstadter expounds on these issues in his *Gödel, Escher, Bach.*[5])

§ **Details: Using Modules and Procedures**

Modules and procedures exist for a number of reasons, but recursive simplicity is the most important.

First, a simpler reason: If you package a bunch of related stuff into a single wrapper and give it a name, it's easy to *re-use* the whole bundle whenever you need it. Thus I can define *the plaintiffs* once (let's say, as a list of forty-seven names), and then recycle this one definition repeatedly by referring simply to "the plaintiffs" and not repeating the list. If I need to carry out the same set of steps repeatedly, I use a *procedure,* in the same vein. A cookbook may have sixty-nine recipes all of which require a pie crust. The pie crust procedure is spelled out once; all other recipes say merely "make a pie crust (page 12)."

But there's a more fundamental reason. A huge software machine may involve a landscape with thousands or millions of regions, a script with millions of steps. That's too many. I need to pilot my thought-glider *gracefully* downwards...

Hence, I use modules to play-out the complexity of the *landscape*, procedures to play-out the complexity of the *script*, gradually.

Instead of a million regions, I can have (say) five. Each of the five is a *module* containing (ultimately) hundreds of thousands of regions. But a hundred thousand is also too many, so I can structure each big module as a set of smaller modules, and so on.

Likewise, the script. Instead of a million steps, I can have three. The three might be "invoke the get-started procedure," "invoke the do-the-computation procedure," and "invoke the clean-up-and-go-away procedure." Each of these three is defined in terms of slightly narrower procedures, and so on.

The Shape of Computational Spacetime

Information machines are lovely to contemplate, so I'll conclude by doing so.

An infomachine bursting forth into the emptiness of computer-space is a fireworks chrysanthemum—intricate tracery drawn carefully on nothing, hanging in a void, un-graspable, unfolding automatically—but real, vivid and striking. It burns fast and bright, transforms galaxies of combustible data into information, then falls back into nothing and disappears. Designing this kind of—*whatever*—structure, *event*—is one the most inspiring challenges engineers and designers have ever faced; and one of the hardest.

The Embodiment (Mere Hardware)

Ultimately a piece of electronic equipment, an object built largely of metal, plastic and (for now) silicon—roughly the same stuff that goes into your average trash-strewn beach—yes, a (out with it!) *computer*—is responsible for embodying your software machinery. Intellectual thoroughness requires that we have a look at these things, even though they are mere hardware. You can have a deep and creative mastery of software with only the most rudimentary understanding of computers. But obviously—the more you know, the better. It certainly won't *hurt* to have a look at these devices. They are less interesting than software. Nonetheless, they are neat little items when all is said and done. A little respect, please.

(Skip this section if you're in a hurry.)

A computer has two basic pieces, the *memory* and the *processor*. It also has a collection of so-called "devices," which are responsible for input and output—for moving data into and out of the computer. Data values are dumped into the memory, they get transformed into more interesting values, and then they are pumped out of the memory (in one form or another) to the waiting public.

The memory represents space in this world, and the processor time. The processors' role is to *evolve the memory*, to transform the stuff that is stored in there, to push it step by puny step from the starting state to the finish line. The steps *are* tiny: Generally speaking, each step changes a single minuscule patch of memory. Acres and acres may need to be transformed *repeatedly* in order to get the job done. Thus a computer (mildly) resembles a painter who insists on attacking the Empire State Building with a makeup-daubing brush. But if you are a computer this strategy is sound, and you will complete the job much faster than an army of humans equipped with industrial-size paintblasters. *Yes*, you are only capable of daubing. But you daub *fast*.

The memory is like a huge blackboard divided (as if by neatly-ruled lines) into a fixed number of same-size boxes. Each box holds a number. The computer's worldview is inhabited by numbers *exclusively*. If a computer is dealing with words, those words are represented by numbers. (I can say that the number 1 means the letter *a*, 2 means *b* or whatever.) Pictures are represented by numbers. (I break the picture into dots or "pixels" and use a number to indicate the color, intensity and so on of each one.) Sounds are represented by numbers (as they are on a compact disk). Thoughts are represented by numbers—insofar as thoughts can be expressed in words, pictures, sounds and so on.

The memory is a sort of primitive *map*, in the special sense of the term I have used in this chapter. The regions of this primitive map are all the same (small) size. They may *only* hold numbers. They don't have names, merely numerical identities—"region 56,712". The processor is like a primitive Actor: Its basic task is to grab numbers from memory, transform them into new numbers and replace them. This Actor has a primitive script, which doesn't exist as a separate document. Instead, it's stored line-by-line in the memory. Some portion of memory, in other words, is devoted to holding numbers that *are* or that *represent* infochunks; another part holds numbers that represent the Actor's simple script.

A computer works in a simple, endless cycle, like a piston engine or a loom or countless other machines. The processor grabs the next instruction from memory, and does that instruction. The cycle repeats. That's all.

To find out what the next instruction is, the processor looks in a special memory region called the "program counter." The program counter has a number inside, just like every other region in memory. This particular number designates another region, namely the region that holds the next instruction. If the number is 3, the processor knows that (next) it should look in region 3, pull out the instruction and do it.

That *instruction* is also a number, of course. The actions of which a processor is capable are very simple, which makes it simple to *encode* these actions in the form of numbers. If you'd hired a horticulturally innocent gardener and you were directing his weeding activities from your back porch, you could use a simple numerical code: 1 means pull that plant out, 2 means leave it alone; 3 means move on to the next plant to your left, 4 means move on to your right. You could put numbers together to extend or modify the meaning of instructions: 11 means to pull the weed out and put it in the weed bucket, 12 means to pull it out and chuck it to the back of the bed, 13 means to pull it out carefully, because it's poison ivy. *Why* you would want to communicate with your gardener in this way is another matter, but it's easy to see *how* you could.

A computer's instructions are encoded in this way. Their range is very limited. They fall into a small number of classes. One class performs simple arithmetic on numbers: Add the number over here to the number over there and put the result here. One class makes simple decisions about what to do next, based on numbers. Other instructions move numbers from one region to another. Others have to do with input and output, and so on through a few more simple categories.

As the computer runs, the processor and the memory are in constant communication. The processor repeatedly checks the program counter, grabs the appropriate instruction and does it. In many cases, executing the instruction causes memory to be altered, one small piece at a time—the old contents of some region are eliminated, and replaced by some new number. Then the processor trudges onward to the next instruction. The cycle repeats.

Yes, it is, in reality, a *little* more complicated than this. The thing

I've called "memory" usually consists of several separate sections, called "registers," "cache" and the "memory" proper; the processor may be capable of working on several instructions at the same time (starting the next one before the current one is finished), and so on. But even the most complex of modern machines is, at base, just a processor plus a memory.

§ Information machines vs. computers

We're talking about *instructions*, but the alleged topic in this section is hardware. When we talk about *instructions*... aren't we talking about software?

Yes and no. The primitive instructions that the processor understands, that are arranged in neat rows inside the memory, *are* software of a simple kind. These instructions are called "machine language," and the program stored in memory is called a machine language program.

If you wrote a machine language program on paper, it would look nothing like Pascal. It might look something like

```
71522361
22310003
42218244
. . .
```

Catchy, huh? In other words, a list of numbers. These numbers *are* software: If you put them into the computer's memory and turn the computer on, these numbers will cause the computer to do whatever you want it to—calculate hypotenuses, draw pictures, hop up and down and shriek or whatever you'd like.

How do you get an orchestra to play what you want it to? Easy: Write a score, and hand out parts to each musician.

But in order for music to be generated by these people, some complex translations must take place. Each musician must convert the notation he sees into the series of strokes, twitches, taps or toodles that his instrument requires in order to generate the called-for sounds. Now it is possible, in principle, to imagine a musical score that bypasses standard notation and relies on direct physical instructions instead. "At this bar, each first violin presses his third finger to the A string and draws his bow at moderate velocity and a sustained pressure of .35 newtons per square meter from left to right," and so on. Is what you have written *music*? Is machine language *software*? No. Or at any rate, just barely.

A highly-trained computer can sight-read your Pascal program in (sort of) the same way that a highly-trained violinist can sight-read Paganini. Where the computer is concerned, "highly trained" means that you've gone round to the Corner Computer Store and bought a piece of software called a "compiler." The compiler translates information machinery into a form that raw hardware can understand. It reads the phrases that make up your Pascal program one by one, and translates them into the numbers that actually make it all happen.

Enough. Back to software.

Chapter 4

Space, Time and Multi-time

We move now to the world of *asynchronous ensembles*. We've discussed information machines. Now imagine a lot of them zipping around separately, each piloted by its own Actor—communicating occasionally, getting born and self-destructing spontaneously—all converging like a swarm of space-scooters or electronic piranhas on some lurking huge problem in the near distance. Now *this* is computing!

What is an ensemble?

A group of objects that *interact*; a group, accordingly, that is more than the sum of its parts.

If you assemble a hundred toasters side-by-side and turn each one loose on a slice of bread, what you've got is a hundred toasters, toasting their hearts out. If you assemble a hundred monkeys side by side, what you've got is *not* merely a hundred monkeys. You have a monkey *community* of some kind, an *ensemble* and not simply one hundred separate parts. Toasters don't interact, but monkeys do. One hundred information machines working on the same problem also form an *ensemble*, an entity that is more, in some sense, than the sum of its parts. Like monkeys, these information machines interact. They must communicate and coordinate with each other in order to make progress as a group on the same problem.

67

What is "asynchronous"?

An ensemble is *asynchronous* if each part is independent, ticking along at its own pace.

In the ensembles we're talking about, each information machine is encased in its own little piece of spacetime. The machines are *un*synchronized: No machine can predict exactly what any other machine is doing at any given time, because each Actor runs his own show, executes his own script. Nothing *outside* the machine beats time or constrains the Actor in any way: He barrels along at his own speed.

So what?

Asynchronous ensembles (ensembles for short) are a major topic for software in general. They are *the* crucial Mirror World technology. Mirror Worlds would be unthinkable without them.

But here's another interesting thing about ensembles: They are also the "crucial technology" of nature and mankind. That's a biggish statement. But a bit of thought makes it clear that physical, chemical, biological and sociological systems are virtually all asynchronous ensembles of one kind or another. Ensembles are *so* all-pervasive and fundamental that there's not terribly much we can say about them *per se* (although we will say a *few* things in this vein later on). But this all-pervasiveness also poses some subtle and fascinating possibilities for software specifically. Software ensembles can be *modeled after* natural ones (for their own benefit); or they can be *models of* natural ones, in order to serve as laboratories, software terraria, for the study of natural or human ensembles. Or they can *blend together with* natural ensembles—software ensembles can reflect natural ones, and then blend with the originals into an endlessly echoing mirror-maze of possibilities. Once we have mastered ensembles, the *people* shuffling their feet tentatively on one one side of the room will inevitably, inexorably approach the infomachines on the other side: They will mingle (because "mastering ensembles" *means* "allowing independent agents to mingle"); they will grow *inextricably* entwined. What happens next? A catastrophe of Biblical proportions? No: merely new kinds of structures, new organizations and new programs, of which Mirror Worlds are one highly significant example.

Concretely...

We're talking about one infomachine built out of many. The simplest way to think about this is in terms of one multi-part program running on many computers at once. These computers might be packed into a single box, in which case we have a "parallel computer" or multi-computer; or, they might be a collection of separate machines (let's say two dozen IBM PC's, or whatever), connected into a network.

It's important to keep in mind, though, that you can build ensemble programs even if you have only a *single* computer at your disposal. The programs that make up the ensemble can all inhabit *one* computer *simultaneously*. The computer can execute a little of one, than switch to the next and then to the next so fast that it *appears* to be running them all simultaneously. The effect is something like a motion picture. A machine can project still pictures one after another so rapidly that the image appears to move. Computers can switch their attention from one program to another so fast that they appear to be executing them all simultaneously.

Ordinarily this is not what you *want* to do; you've built an ensemble precisely because you want to be able to focus lots of computers on a single problem. But as we'll discuss, there are important reasons to build ensembles even if you have only one computer.

Ensemble programs (as we will sometimes call asynchronous software ensembles) pose serious problems and open remarkable vistas. I'll get to the problems later. First, consider the possibilities. There are several important ones.

The Bottom Line

Throughout human problem-solving history, complex engineering and organizational problems have been attacked and mastered by using ensembles. Complex organizations are managed, large buildings built and formidable enemies defeated by bunches of workers, not by isolated actors. A watch, a steam engine or a factory is built up out of many simultaneously active components.

Ensembles are the norm. *Sequential* problem-solving—the one-step-at-a-time approach—is the anomalous restriction. Consider our top-level description of the space program in the last chapter: In order to send a man to the moon, (1) design and build rocket engines, (2) design and build space vehicles, (3) find and train astronauts, (4) plan and organize space missions. These four sub-problems can be attacked *simultaneously*. No-one wracked his brain to come up with this kind of solution. It was the obvious thing. There are innumerable examples.

Ensembles, then, are the *natural way to approach hard problems*. So it's not surprising that they are the natural way to approach hard problems using software.

Our major fixations in building information machines were (you'll remember) *efficiency* and *topsight*—or in operational terms, *clarity*. There are two reasons why ensembles recommend themselves again and again as the *natural* thing. Conveniently enough, one has to do with efficiency and the other with clarity. These two are *speed* and *uncoupling*.

§ Speed

For many problems, modern, conventional computers are simply too slow to be useful. *Many?* Yes: We are talking about important problems in science, engineering, making pictures, handling databases, building Mirror Worlds. The fastest single computer you can build is simply not fast enough to cope with them.

Once you've tuned an information machine for maximum performance, once it's running on the fastest conventional computer you can find, ensembles are the obvious and *only* way to get more speed. An ensemble program runs on many computers simultaneously. In other words, it allows you to focus many computational energy-beams on a single problem and blast it away fast. There's nothing deep or tricky about this policy; it's the obvious thing to do. What's a speedier way to demolish James Bond, one piranha or a thousand piranhas?

Of course, if you are merely dealing with James Bond, a thousand piranhas are nice but one will do the trick. For the massive computing problems we're talking about here, one computer will *not* do the trick. The world's fastest conventional computer progresses so slowly as to make the effort pointless. If you're designing a machine part, for example, you might be able to wait 24 hours in a pinch to have the computer simulation tell you whether your latest design will work. If you had to wait three months, you'd chuck the computer because, in practical terms, it would be useless. The gap between one day and three months is roughly a factor of one hundred, and it's not at all hard to build machines with one hundred separate computers inside. If you're working on a problem of real scientific significance—you want to understand the shape of a molecule, the formation of a galaxy, the life-cycle of a star—you might be willing to wait patiently for the results of a computation that runs for three months. But would you wait twenty-five years? (Another factor of one hundred.) One final example: A large military program needs to simulate a sequence of complicated events at "realtime" speeds— simulating a minute of actual goings-on must require (at most) one minute of computing. On the fastest supercomputer the military can buy, it now takes about thirty hours of computing to simulate about thirty *minutes* of reality. No good. Bring on the ensembles. (Just what they're doing, in fact.)

It's impossible to describe these extremely-hard problems in general. There are many oddball cases. Mathematicians, for example, occasionally like to chew up huge quantities of computer time in the search for some huge number's prime factors—the collection of indivisible numbers that yield this huge number when they are multiplied together. In June of 1990, people were hopping up and down in excitement: After a mere two months of computing on various machines, a 155-digit number (the largest ever factored) was disassembled into its three prime components.[1] All right, maybe *you're* not impressed enough to take the rest of the day off and go party, but you have to remember that, *technically* speaking, mathematicians are pretty strange people. No, strike that, I mean that after all, you're not a number theorist or a cryptographer, but if you were, you'd be duly thrilled. (Actually, some of my best friends are mathematicians.) Number-theoretic results of this sort are of real practical value in the ongoing attempt to develop better encryption schemes, and break them.

Many super-tough problems do, nonetheless, fall into a single important category: using mathematics to model physical systems.

To understand why we need much faster computers, it's essential to grasp what this means, at least in a general way.

Take a simple case: I climb up a step-ladder and drop a tennis ball to the ground. How fast is it traveling when it hits? I can write down an equation that will tell me. (If you have inexplicably forgotten this formula and are dying to know what it is, look in any first-year physics text.) This equation is a model of the falling tennis ball. A model is a likeness that captures some aspect of the thing modeled. A plastic toy model of a car captures the car's shape; the equation captures the falling tennis ball's velocity.

Vastly more complex systems than falling tennis balls can be modeled mathematically. The models may involve thousands of equations instead of one, but the point is the same: Plug in numbers you know; get out numbers you want. You may know the height from which you dropped a ball, and want its speed when it hits the ground; you may know the size, shape and composition of each part of a car, and the car's speed when it hits a wall, and you want to know the shape of each piece after the collision. In both cases, you can get the answer (or a reasonable approximation) by solving equations.

You can write down equations that model all sorts of interesting things—the behavior of molecules in chemical solutions, fluids flowing, galaxies forming, steel frameworks flexing, soundwaves propagating. *Solving* the equations—plugging in the numbers you have, getting out the ones you want—is another matter. Solving large sets of equations efficiently and accurately, without wasting time on unnecessary steps, may entail a highly complex and tricky game-plan. But *carrying out the plan* inevitably comes down to performing huge numbers of *simple* operations— "multiply each of these ten thousand numbers by this other number; then multiply those other ten thousand numbers by this number; then..." Your computer may perform many millions of multiplications per second, but for problems like these, that's laughably slow.

In the final analysis, a single computer can only go so fast. Computer speed has shot up so staggeringly in recent decades that you may have gotten the impression that this is a permanent unlimited Bull Market we're dealing with here. Unfortunately, no. When you start brushing up against hard physical limits, the party is over. Signals can only travel so fast, we can only pack so much stuff into so much space and dissipate so much heat. Never mind *where* the limits are; we're not there yet. But in the end, there's no way to evade or overrun them. We are talking death and taxes here—death, taxes, physics.

Thus the future belongs, in logical terms it can *only* belong, to ensembles. When we turn to ensembles, the limits nearly vanish. One computer can only be so fast, but the aggregate power of a *group* of computers is limited only by the size of the group. Such groups can and will grow *very* large.

§ Clarity, Principle Two: Uncoupling

The go-fast aspect of ensemble programs speaks to the *efficiency* side of the house. The other major attraction of ensemble programming has to do with *clarity*. Here we encounter the second of our Big Three Clarity Principles: *uncoupling*.

Uncoupling means to pull a complex problem apart into separate components; solve them separately; *minimize* the interactions between these separate solutions. Instead of handing one agent a complex jumble of responsibilities, use an ensemble of agents; now, each agent's job can be clearly and simply defined. If some agent's job still *can't* be, uncouple him too—replace him with another ensemble. And so on.

I discussed *modularity* in the last chapter, and modularity is related to these issues; modularity is a *passive* form of simplification-by-pulling-apart. Uncoupling is the *active* form.

Let's say some businessman opens up a supermarket and he decides to label every aisle "food," with everything randomly jumbled together. He is making a mistake. The "statics" of his system are too complicated. He needs a fruit "module" (a.k.a. department), a meat module, a bread module and so on. Modularity can clarify things.

Suppose his next project is an office building. The floors have to be swept, the telephones answered, the computers and the building maintained and every visitor welcomed by a sweetly smiling receptionist. Let's say it's a small office building, and none of these jobs is especially demanding. So he does the economical thing, and hires exactly *one* person to do it all.

Once again, he's doing things wrong. (Evidently he's not all that bright.) His new mistake is related to his first one, but it's not the same. This time the *dynamics* of the system are too complicated. How exactly will he explain to his one employee that she's supposed to act like a receptionist except when the computers need fixing, but to drop that and go answer the phone when it rings, except if a pipe bursts, in which case, forget about the phones? And also sweep the floors in her spare time? Even if the total demands of this job don't exceed eight hours a day on average, the dynamics of the situation are too complicated to handle. To clarify things, you need to *uncouple* them. Five people is a larger workforce than one person. But for this problem, it's also simpler.

This explanation has a negative spin: To avoid getting hopelessly messed up, use uncoupling. But the real implications are positive and formidable. There's a hard limit on how complex any *single* information machine can get (just as there's a limit on how fast any single computer can run). But there is no limit on how big a machine *ensemble* can grow. Ensembles allow us to outstrip the speed limit, *and* (just as important) the *complexity limit*, that ultimately bound any single infomachine. Once you have mastered ensemble-building, you have smashed right through the major barrier in the way of continued unlimited expansion in software's power. You can even contemplate something as dizzyingly, stupefyingly complex as a Mirror World.

Ensembles are the only natural, indeed the only *possible* way to build Mirror Worlds. We've described throngs of independent software agents who operate *while* rivers of data are pouring into the system, *while* information filters are processing the data, *while* visitors are hovering around and through it. The natural approach is to allow each software agent to be a separate information machine, to use a network of information machines to build an information filter, to assign each visitor his own separate information machine as a guide. No single infomachine could possibly master such a complex assignment.

Ensembles, then, are natural and they are inevitable.

Uncoupling by the way, like recursive simplicity, is by no means only (or even mainly) a software phenomenon. The behavior of natural objects is usually the combined result of many separate influences. Uncoupling these influences, analyzing each one's contribution separately, is the right way to understand this kind of behavior. A simple example: You throw a ball, and you want to understand its flight path. To do so, you uncouple its up-and-down motion (fighting gravity as it rises, sped-up by gravity as it falls) from its forward motion (at a speed that remains the same—except for the effects of air resistance—throughout the flight). This style of analysis is fundamental throughout science. Closer to software, uncoupling is the basic tool of the "organization engineer" (otherwise known as a "manager"). If you are running an army, a corporation, a firehouse or whatever, your skill at uncoupling complex behaviors into manageable pieces goes a long way towards deciding your success or failure.

What do ensembles look like?

We now pose for ensembles the same questions we discussed in the context of ordinary, single-shot information machines: What do they look like? How do they work?

These questions have more possible answers than the earlier ones. Researchers have proposed many ways to build ensembles. My plan is to describe exactly one and studiously ignore the rest.

The one I'll describe is (of course) *our* system, the one we designed and built in our lab: a system called Linda.[2]

In focusing on Linda exclusively, I don't mean to suggest that nothing else exists, or that Linda is the consensus solution to the ensemble problem. No such thing. There *are* other possibilities.

On the other hand, basing this kind of discussion on Linda isn't mere egotism either. After the knock-down battles of the last decade, Linda is one of the few contenders left on her feet. There are perhaps half a dozen systems on the Contenders list, as of today. Linda has been taken up by a number of large companies, gets used at labs and universities all over the world and has inspired computer science research projects in North and South America, Europe, Asia, Africa and Australia. In short, most continents.

The system is too radical for some people's tastes. It doesn't extend earlier well-established approaches; it veers off in another direction, and whatever community you belong to, there's always hell to pay when you do that. Today, some people still can't stand Linda, and some people love it; at any rate, it's a contender.

Linda is, furthermore, not merely a *plausible* basis for our discussion. It's essential to Mirror Worlds as I'll describe them. The
Mirror World *concept* is wholly independent of Linda, but the Mirror
World *strategy* I will lay out depends on Linda not merely in passing
but fundamentally.

Okay: So you have a group of infomachines...

How do you knit them together into an ensemble capable of attacking
hard problems *en masse*?

Let's reach for our space-scooter analogy. Picture a bunch of
information machines, each piloted by its own Actor, converging on
a hard problem. *How do they communicate?* That is the nitty-gritty
question.

You can't have an ensemble if you can't communicate. The machines in our ensemble must be able to assign tasks to each other.
You take this part and I'll do that; or *I'm handling this; somebody—
anybody—take care of that*; or *I have a problem with Blah Blah Blah—
anybody understand Blah Blah Blah? Please help me out*; or *you're
the expert in this, please solve it for me and let me know what the
answer is.* And they must be able to send information to each other.
*Here's a new problem to solve, let's get to work you guys, the in-
put data is...*, or *I've just figured out that the answer to so-and-so
is such-and-such, anyone interested?*, or *I'm willing to do that job;
send it over here*; or *I'm too busy, bug off, get someone else*; or *here's
the answer to that problem you asked me to solve. Communication* is
the life-blood of the ensemble, and communication is the very thing
that *doesn't exist* in an ordinary programming language. An ordinary language allows you to create exactly *one* Actor, one machine,
one scene of activity, so what's to communicate? But when we move
to ensembles, communication becomes our major question. How to
do we do it? How do information machines talk to each other?

The obvious answer: They merely grab their Cellular Space
Phones and call each other up. I promised not to discuss anything but Linda, but there's one important exception: *the* simple
and obvious communication strategy, the technique that pops immediately into every undergraduate's head, the Big Idea behind your

typical WizzoTek computer company's Revolutionary New Product announcement—it's called *message passing*. Message passing is one answer to the communication question; it is, in effect, the Cellular Space Phone answer. Under message passing, if one machine has something to tell another machine, it sends that other machine a *message*. The message gets delivered to a software mailbox (or, it gets left on a software answering machine if you prefer, whatever, same thing); when the recipient-machine is in the mood, it opens the mailbox (or turns on the answering machine) and gets the message. That's it. Simple. Obvious. Easy to understand. One lousy idea.

Here is the problem. We might describe communication as, in general, a matter of three separate questions: where, when and who. The answers to any one of them may be, broadly speaking, *this*, *any*, *every*. When you mail a letter or send a software message, you're sending it to *this place* (the place to which it's addressed), at *this time*, to *this person* or *this machine*—i.e., the specified one. When I say *this time* I don't mean instantaneously, of course. There's some leeway for the time it takes to find the recipient, and a letter can sit around in a mailbox for awhile. But you're sending the thing to a mailbox that exists *now*, to a person who exists *now*. You can't mail a letter to the four hundredth president of the United States or to your great-great-grandchildren.

§ Communication, Liberated

The problem is that *this*, *this* and *this* aren't the only useful answers to our Big Three questions. You might want to send a letter to *this* person, *any* place: You don't know where the guy is, or you don't care; maybe, for that matter, he moves around unpredictably. But you still know *who* he is, and you have a message for him. Or let's say you have a message for *any* one, *any* place, *any* time. This is a vital species of communication when you're building software ensembles: you constantly confront the need to communicate with *anyone who's willing to do this new task*. There's no way to send a message to "*any* information machines willing to do this," any more than you can place a phone call to "Any Plumber Who's Interested in Fixing My Sink." Note that the *any time* is important. At the time you create the message, everyone may be busy; no-one may be interested; it's not merely that you *don't know* who the recipient is, there *is* no recipient. Your communication must hang around somehow until someone *is* free—or, maybe, until some new Actor arrives on the scene.

We've just said something decisive: Your communication must *hang around*. It must *persist*. It can't be a mere spacetime ripple— your phone call passing over the wire and then vanishing; your letter that either gets delivered or thrown out. Communication must be based on *persistent* objects.

Software ensembles often require *every*-type communication as well. *Here's new information for everyone, everywhere, every time, who's working on this problem.*

Again, the every *time* is important. A Super-Deluxe message passing system might allow me to *broadcast* a message to everybody: I pick up my space phone and *everybody's* phone rings. I talk to everyone at once.

But that's not what we need. A broadcast is a *this* time event; we need something that holds good at *every* time. This means, for one, that you get the message when *you* decide you need it, not when I decide to send it. You might broadcast something at four o'clock; my phone rings, I write down the message, I think it's irrelevant and I throw it out. At four-thirty I might be doing something completely different; I want the data *now*, but I've already chucked it. The only safe thing is for me to archive every broadcast, but this is a nuisance—ninety percent of them might *in fact* be pure junk mail so far as I'm concerned. Every *time* communication means that I can go shopping for information exactly when I need it—again, communication must *persist*.

It may even be the case, to extend this argument, that when you picked up your phone and did your broadcast, *I* didn't exist. In a genuinely *useful* communication system, communication is possible between two Actors whose lifetimes are completely separate—the sender is dead when the receiver is born. We need communication through *time*, in other words, not merely through space. Infomachines are born and die out at a much brisker clip than (say) people. Communication through time is an important requirement.

Linda is a communication system designed specifically to overcome these limitations—to allow every communication to write its own ticket. Maybe this sounds complicated, but actually it is, in many ways, a lot *simpler* than message passing.

§ So, when infomachines need to communicate...

They don't pick up their Cellular Space Phones; instead, they write down whatever it is they need to communicate, and set it adrift. They generate a new landscape and heave it through the air lock into outer space. The new landscape consists of a bunch of regions, like any landscape; these regions hold the substance of the communication. Usually, the first region holds a phrase that acts like a name tag. The phrase might be *Here's a task that needs doing,* or *New Information about Blah Blah Blah,* or *Attention: Machine Schwartz.* These jettisoned floating landscapes are called *tuples.*

When I need information, or I'm in the mood to take requests or get messages, I don't punch a button on my answering machine. Instead, I peer out my windshield, where lots of jettisoned landscapes (lots of tuples) are floating around among my fellow infomachines. When I've located the one I want, I have two choices. I can reach out and grab it, or I can copy down the stuff it contains and leave the tuple itself floating around out there.

In a message-passing system, there are two basic operations: Send a message; receive a message. In Linda, there are three: *Jettison* a tuple; *grab* a tuple; *read* a tuple. It's important that floating landscapes can either be grabbed or (merely) read. A *here's a task...* or *Attention: Schwartz...* tuple ought to be grabbed. If I'm willing to do some task, it's a waste of time for some other infomachine to start work on the same thing. The tuple *must* be removed, so that other machines don't duplicate my efforts. But a *New Information about...* tuple might be of interest to lots of machines. If I'm one of them, I can *read* this tuple's contents, but the tuple itself must remain adrift and accessible.

§ Have I solved my "this, this, this" problem?

Yes. I can now customize any communication event in any way I choose. I can communicate with someone who might be *any*where. When I jettison an *Attention: Schwartz...* tuple, machine Schwartz will pick it up wherever he happens to reside at the moment. I can

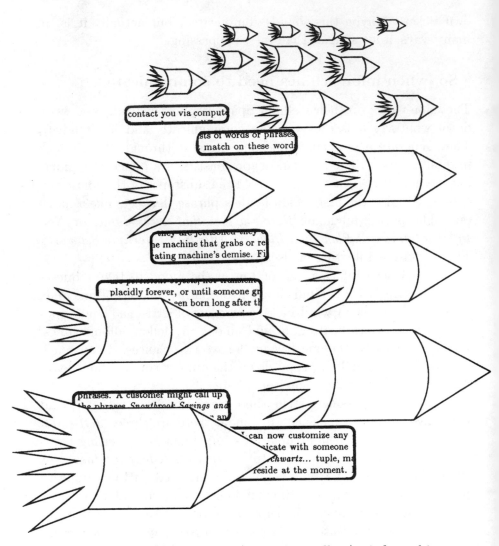

Figure 4.1: A Linda program (metaphorically...): infomachines at work among jettisoned tuples.

communicate with *any*one who might be anywhere. When I generate a *Here's a task...* tuple, I don't know and don't care *which* machine will grab it. I can communicate with *every*one, *every*where. When I generate a *New Information about...* tuple, everyone who chooses can read it. And I can communicate across time, not merely across space. Tuples are *persistent objects*, not transient ripples. Once they are jettisoned they drift placidly forever, or until someone grabs them. The machine that grabs or reads one may have been born long after the tuple-generating machine's demise.

§ What does it look like?

Fine, but maybe this is a little abstract. Let's consider something concrete, two different kinds of problem.

First, let's say you run a research service of some kind. You maintain a huge database of news stories; your customers come to you with lists of words or phrases, and you get back to them with a bunch of stories that match on these words and phrases. A customer might call up (for example) and ask for stories containing the phrases *Snoutbrook Savings and Loan* or *Robert Piffel* or *Bob Piffel*, or the phrases *federal bank deregulation* and the word *Arkansas*, and so on. I'll discuss a strategy for a much more sophisticated kind of search in a couple of chapters, but people *do* make use of this simple searching scheme today. You have a lot of customers, we'll assume; they call you on the phone or contact you via computer network, and you need to respond quickly.

Let's consider another very different kind of problem as well. You want to build a computerized market. It deals in barrels of oil, tons of grain, stocks, bonds or what have you. Anyone who's interested can enter the market via computer and make a deal. We imagine a series of blackboards, one for each commodity traded on the market. If there's no action in some commodity at the moment (no-one selling or buying), the current price—the price that the stuff was last sold for—appears on the blackboard. If I enter the market and want to *buy*, I grab the appropriate blackboard and write "bid," the price I'm offering, and something that identifies me (let's say a phone number to call, once a deal is set). Then I replace the blackboard. To keeps things simple, let's say that all transactions are for equal-sized chunks of stuff: 5 tons of this, 100 shares of that or whatever. If I want to *sell*, I look at the blackboard. If someone wants to buy and I'm satisfied with the price he's offering, I grab the blackboard, write "sold" and call the guy up (or send him a computer message). If the price he's offering is too low, I grab the blackboard, write down *ask* and the price I'm willing to accept. And so on.

In the first problem, we'll build an ensemble program in order to get *speed*: We want to search the database quickly. In the second, we need to build an ensemble because those are the facts of life. The real-world system I'm dealing with (a bunch of people making deals) *happens to be* an ensemble whether I like it or not. My software will merely reflect that fact.

Here are the strategies we'll use.

In the first case, a Primal Machine (PM for short) creates a bunch of "worker machines"—say a couple of dozen. The number doesn't matter. The PM starts out by announcing "we are looking for articles that meet the following criteria." It announces this by heaving a tuple out the air lock into outer space, otherwise known as "tuple space."

The tuple might look like

```
(LookingFor, "Snoutbrook Savings and Loan OR ...")
```

In other words, a tuple is just words (or numbers or other kinds of data) put together into a kind of list. This is a two-element tuple. The first element identifies the tuple in a way the workers will be able to understand ("this tuple announces what we're LookingFor"). The second element provides the actual information ("I want you guys to scan some stories for the phrase Snoutbrook Savings and Loan or the phrase...").

The PM is merely an infomachine. There is a script that specifies what this infomachine is supposed to do. The script is written out using a programming language (like Pascal, or whatever). When the PM reaches the point where, having set everything up properly, it's *ready to start communicating with other infomachines*—at that point, it executes the instruction

```
out(LookingFor, "Snoutbrook Savings and Loan OR ...");
```

When the PM executes this instruction, a tuple goes sailing *out* the air lock into tuple space.

Each worker machine has a script too. At the start of the script, there's an instruction that causes this worker machine to *read the "LookingFor" tuple.* If there are 100 worker machines, *each one* reads the "LookingFor" tuple to start out—and now, they all understand the goal of this particular search.

The PM now proceeds to rip apart the database of newspaper articles. It grabs each article, puts the article in a tuple and heaves the tuple out the air lock. In other words: if there are twelve million and one articles in the database, the PM executes twelve million and one instructions that look like

```
out(Article, 114,
    "Passaic, June 21 (AP): Today, Robert Piffel...");
```

In other words, the 114*th* article reads `Passaic, June 21 (AP)`.... Of course, we don't write twelve million instructions separately, one-by-one, in the PM's script. Instead, the script says "For *each article in the database,* however many there are, execute the instruction `out(Article,` *next article's number, next article's text...*)."

So: The PM is busily heaving tuples into tuple space, and they're starting to collect. Each worker machine repeatedly does the following. It reaches out and grabs an *Article* tuple. Doesn't matter which one; any one will do. Note that, if *I* grab a tuple, no-one else can grab it; I haul it onboard, and it disappears from tuple space. I check the text in the tuple against the search criterion. Do the specified phrases appear in this article? If the answer is yes, I heave a tuple like:

```
out(Checked, 114, Yes)
```

If the answer had been no, the tuple would have looked like

```
out(Checked, 114, No)
```

Notice that it doesn't matter *in what order* the articles get checked, nor does it matter which worker does what, so long as every article gets checked eventually.

Now, the PM merely gathers up these answer tuples and collates them. When every element has been checked, the PM prints a report and the ensemble evanesces.

If there's a single worker, it plods through the database article by article, and eventually gets through the whole thing. But if there are five workers, the ensemble (at any given point) is checking five articles simultaneously; if there are a thousand workers, it's checking a thousand simultaneously, and so on. The more workers, the faster the search goes.

This *particular* example might or might not be realistic, depending on characteristics of the search criteria, the database and some other factors. (Technical aspects of this sort of problem are discussed in a parallel programming textbook.[3]) But in fact, there are many ensemble programs in many domains that *do* solve problems fast and efficiently using *precisely* this kind of approach.

Now, let's glance at the second problem, the software market.

The basic idea is extremely simple. Every commodity has a tuple. That tuple represents its blackboard. For example,

```
(Cauliflower, BID, 1522, 12345)
```

(where the 12345 is a number that identifies the bidder). Or

```
(USZipper, ASKED, 154, 54321),
```

or

```
(SweetTexasCrude, CURRENT, 22.545, 0).
```

(The zero at the end means "no-one"—there's no buyer or seller at the moment.)

If I'm interested in a current price quote, the infomachine that's acting on my behalf executes an instruction that *reads* the tuple of interest. If I want to sell or buy, my infomachine *grabs* the appropriate tuple, updates it, and then heaves it out again—for example, by executing an instruction like

```
out(SweetTexasCrude, BID, 22.545, 12345);
```

meaning that I, number 12345, am now ready to pay $22.545 a barrel for Sweet Texas Crude.

This sort of market is oversimplified as it stands; but it's not hard to add details that make it more realistic. The result is more complicated—but represents exactly the same general idea. Using this sort of market, two mutually unknown people can make a deal.

Or, a person can make a deal with a program (that is merely acting in auto-pilot mode on someone's behalf)—or two *programs* can make a deal; it's all the same story.

§ Grabbing Tuples

How does a machine grab or read a tuple? How does it specify which one it wants? How does it *describe* the longed-for tuple? By specifying the contents of *any* regions it chooses. It announces "I want to read the tuple whose first region says *New Information about Blah Blah Blah*", or "the tuple whose second region holds the number 3 and whose seventh holds the word *Puce*," or whatever. Machines may (in other words) grab or read a tuple based on the name-tag in the first region, but they may specify more or different regions as well.

So, concretely: I'm interested in the current going price for cauliflower. My infomachine executes an instruction like

```
rd(Cauliflower, ?status, ?price, ?dealer);
```

which means "read the four-element tuple whose first region says *Cauliflower*." After I've executed this instruction, the current price (or more precisely, the number that happens to occupy the third region of the tuple, which is *supposed* to be the current price) has been stored in a region named *price*—I merely look in this region, and there is the price, copied out of the floating tuple.

Suppose I've bid on cauliflower, and I'm waiting for a buyer to show up and specify an *asked* price. In other words: I've set the status of the cauliflower blackboard to *BID*; I'm waiting for its status to be *reset* to *ASKED*, which means that a seller has materialized. As soon as this happens I'll grab the blackboard; if I'm happy with the price, we have a deal; otherwise, I'll flip the status back to *BID*, with (perhaps) a new, revised offer for the seller to think about. So: My infomachine will execute an instruction like

```
in(Cauliflower, ASKED, ?price, ?dealer).
```

This instruction means "grab a tuple (haul it *in* from tuple space) whose first region says *Cauliflower* and whose second region says *ASKED*."

In other words, I can be as specific as I choose about *which* tuple
I'm looking for. I can specify merely a name tag, the contents of
the first region: "I'm looking for a tuple whose first region says
Cauliflower." Or I can be more specific: "Not only does the first
region have to say *Cauliflower*; the second region has to be *ASKED*."

This flexibility is important, because it allows you to build *data
structures* out of tuples. A tennis ladder or a tournament tree exists,
sometimes, in the form of little name tags on hooks. A tennis ladder
is a *data structure*: each name tag is a datum; the *structure* in this
case is an ordered list. Data structures are important for the same
reason that tennis ladders and tournament trees are important: They
allow you to locate things quickly and to keep track of the big picture.
It often makes sense to arrange tuples into data structures—into
ordered lists, trees, other shapes. In principle we might tie them
together with software Space Rope, but that doesn't work out well
in practice for a number of reasons. Instead, we rely on our ability
to ask for a tuple by naming *several* regions. For example, we can
build a list of tuples by putting the name of the list (say *Task List*)
in the first region of each tuple, and the tuple's position-in-line in
the second. The first tuple on the list has a 1 in its second region,
the next tuple has a 2 and so forth. To read the seventeenth tuple
on line, we ask for *the tuple whose first region says "Task List" and
whose second is 17.*

§ The Rest of the Story

Two more points and the Linda story is complete.

Point one: We've been talking about *passive* tuples, but a tuple
can in fact be a full-blown infomachine. Instead of heaving a passive
bunch of regions out the air lock, we can send a *new infomachine*
streaking outwards. The new machine does some work, computes
some values—then *turns into* an ordinary passive tuple, whose regions hold the values it just computed. The new infomachine (in
other words) flies around for awhile and then blows up: an exploded
moon whose asteroid-trail of space junk is a brand new tuple.

In fact, you have just learned the origins and the fate of *every*
infomachine in a Linda ensemble. *Every* infomachine begins life by
streaking out of some Mother Machine's air lock (except for the one
uncreated "primal machine" who starts everything off). Every info-

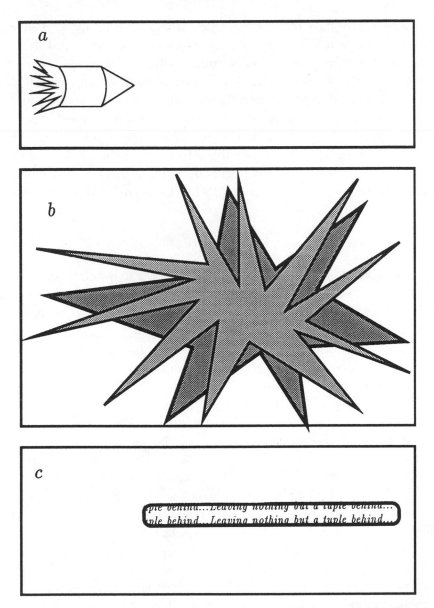

Figure 4.2: Life cycle of an infomachine in a Linda ensemble: begins by streaking out the mother-machine's air lock (*a*); eventually blows up (*b*), leaving an ordinary tuple in its wake (*c*).

machine is destined to blow up when it's done computing, leaving
a passive tuple in its wake. During its lifetime it may give birth to
more infomachines, or to passive tuples only, as it chooses.

Concretely: I discussed a simple ensemble to search a database.
There's a Primal Machine, and then a collection of worker machines.
When I turn the ensemble on, the Primal Machine is created automatically, *ex nihilo*. Where do the worker machines come from? The
Primal Machine's first responsibility is to *create* them. If we want five
workers, the Primal Machine begins by sending five brand-new infomachines streaking out of the air lock. It executes five instructions
like

```
eval("Worker", WorkerProcedure()).
```

By executing five such instructions, we dump five new things into
tuple space—but these five things aren't *passive* tuples, mere lists of
values; each one is an active, live infomachine, doing its own computation *simultaneously with, and independently of* the Primal Machine
and its fellow workers. So we now have *six* things going on at once:
The Primal Machine keeps chugging along, and we have five worker
machines as well.

Now, for the obscure-looking *eval* instruction itself. The word
eval is short for *evaluate*. The phrase following "*eval*" means: Create
an infomachine that is destined, when it blows up, to leave a two-
element space-junk tuple in its wake. The first region of this tuple
will say "*Worker*". I don't know what the second region will say; to
figure it out, find the procedure called *WorkerProcedure* and execute
it. Whatever value *WorkerProcedure* computes—*that's* the value that
goes in the second region of the space-junk tuple.

Now: *WorkerProcedure* is the name of a map somewhere, and
in the map there's a script that spells out exactly what a worker
is supposed to do. Namely, read the search specification, and then
repeatedly grab *article* tuples and check them out.

By executing the *eval* instructions, in other words, we've created
some new infomachines, and each one will devote its entire life to
figuring out *what kind of space-junk tuple it should leave behind*. To
figure this out, each new infomachine dutifully digs up the *WorkerProcedure* and starts executing it. We've created five new infomachines and turned them into workers. We accomplished this by

telling them "your goal in life is to bequeath a space-junk tuple to the infomachines you leave behind, and in order to do this—you've got to execute a *worker* procedure"; or in other words, turn into a worker.

The final point: As I've mentioned, this collection of infomachines and passive floating tuples is called a *tuple space.* (The objects it contains are either *tuples* or incipient tuples: every infomachine will be a tuple eventually...) Tuple Space differs from Outer Space in (at least) one highly significant way. There's only one Outer Space, but there can be lots of tuple spaces; in fact, one tuple space can have lots of others *inside it.* And of course, each one of those can have many tuples spaces inside *it*, and...

How? A tuple consists of regions; each region holds a value. That value may be another whole tuple space.

Picture it this way: You pilot your machine over to a floating tuple, dock alongside and peer in. The first region has a phrase inside, let's say; the second has the number 17; the third holds an entire new world. When you look inside, you see thousands of infomachines, clouds of tuples... Beaming your flashlight off-handedly down the fissure in a mossy outcropping, finding a huge domed, pale-glimmering cave chamber underneath—waterdrops faintly hollow-plunking into a still pool far below—must be similar, I guess. Vaguely.

Does this remind you of Command Posts with whole new landscapes popping up inside? *Recursive hierarchies*, worlds within worlds, one structure with many of the same *inside* it—this is the primal landscape of the Infomachinery Universe.

Disclaimer: Putting tuple spaces inside of tuple spaces is a tricky business, and not all Linda systems can do it. At the moment, only a few research versions can. The Linda system you buy this afternoon from Scientific Computing Associates in New Haven (the General Motors of commercial Linda) won't have this feature. But eventually, every Linda will.

Simple Machines for Coordination

The most important simple infomachines are the ones I described in the last chapter: the *map* and the *script*, basic structures out of which you build all infomachines.

But maps and scripts allow you to build *single* infomachines; and we need ensembles. The four basic instructions that Linda provides— exactly the four I've presented above, *out* (heave a tuple out of the air lock), *in* (grab a tuple), *rd* (read a tuple) and *eval* (create a new infomachine)—are a set of simple *coordination* machines. You can use these instructions to build any kind of ensemble you need.

Down to Earth

We aren't talking about science fiction stuff; this is a practical way to solve hard problems fast.

I described a database search problem involving news articles. The problem *in general* amounts to the following. You have a big database and you want to search through it quickly: You need to check many records to find the "best match" against something or other. In one example we work with a great deal, the database holds information about genetic sequences. Biologists need to search through it to find good matches between newly-discovered sequences and already-known ones. But the database could just as well hold images, descriptions of chemical reactions, customer records or whatever. You want to *check* every element in a large pile selected from the database. *Check* could mean a lot of things, but generally speaking, it means "find out how close this element lies to some target." Is it a news article that's "close" to whatever I'm interested in? An image that's close to some ideal template? You can determine each element's "closeness" by doing some kind of computation that compares this element to the target. The simple ensemble I described is a good starting point for attacking any of these problems.

A simple program; many ensembles are a good deal more complicated. Mirror Worlds are a radical example. But there are plenty of important problems that can be treated in more or less this same straightforward way. Two instances, for the hell of it. You're some kind of finance house and you have a "bond pricing model" that tells you how much a certain kind of bond will be worth, depending on circumstances. You're interested in the worth of this bond under lots of different scenarios. You can distribute these computations to Worker Machines in the same way we handled database elements. Workers grab a tuple, which specifies a bond and a set of interesting circumstances; the worker does a computation that predicts the bond's value, dumps an answer-tuple and repeats. One more example: You're using computer-graphic techniques to make pictures. You compute your picture scan-line by scan-line—the pictures will be displayed on computer screens, and a computer's screen (like a TV's) displays images in the form of many horizontal lines. Again, you create a bunch of Worker Machines; workers grab tuples instructing them to compute some scan-line or other. They dump the results back into tuple space. The PM collects and collates the results.

Pretty simple, but it works. This is *reality* we are talking about. If you were at the Guggenheim Museum in New York in April 1990, you saw some spectacular pictures produced by (among other people) Ken Musgrave, a graduate student who works at Yale with Benoit ("Fractal Curves") Mandelbrot. Musgrave's images were computed using a Linda ensemble that was almost as simple as the one we just described. Nowadays, significant problems are solved by ensemble programs all over the place, every day.

Hypercomputers

We've been talking pure software—unbodied machines, unbodied ensembles. How does the "embodiment" take place?

Take the examples we've discussed; let's suppose, for concreteness, that you want to run them on an office network. The network consists of a bunch of desktop computers wired together in the usual way. You *might* execute an ensemble on a multi-computer, one box (recall) with lots of sub-computers inside. But multi-computers are still just a tad esoteric. Networks are not, so let's talk about a network.

During normal working hours, the computers in an office network often have little or nothing to do. If you're reading mail or typing words into a file, your computer is doing next to nothing, not even working up a sweat, stifling yawns. If you are staring at the screen and thinking, or talking on the phone, or doodling, napping, flirting or having lunch—and these are all activities in which (yes) people *continue* to indulge, in *flagrant disregard* of the powerful computers sitting on their desks—believe it or not—well, under these circumstances, your computer is fighting back tears of boredom. Most times, in other words, you could go round an office network discretely borrowing chunks of computing power from everyone's desktop machine, and no-one would ever know the difference. Should a user actually *need* his machine all of a sudden, you'd give it back immediately.

We refer to the computing resource that emerges from all this idle power as a "hypercomputer." If we take all the unused power in a network of computers and lump it together, we have an excellent home for ensemble programs.

Let's say I have a difficult problem to solve—maybe it's a database search or a bond-pricing calculation or a graphics program of the sort we've been discussing. Let's say the program would run for an hour and a half on my desktop machine, but I'd rather solve it in ten minutes. Clearly, I need to focus ten computers on it at the same time.

Say I'm in an office with a hundred-computer network. Chances are that virtually any time of the day or night, I can find ten computers that are doing either next to nothing or *absolutely* zero. And if you had an enormously hard problem and you were willing to stay late, you would find it easy to grab all one-hundred machines (or almost all) and focus the whole skein on your program. Depending on the efficiency of your ensemble, you thereby stand a good chance of solving your original one-and-a-half-hour problem in about a minute. Instead of creating six pictures in a nine-hour shift, that's more like six hundred. Or you can stick with the same six pictures, and make each one a hundred times better. And you did this trick not by investing in fancy new hardware, but simply by using what you already had. Another name for "ensemble computing on a network" is "getting what you paid for."

Let's go back to the ten-computer case. Let's say you're searching a database. You create an ensemble that has nine workers plus the primal machine. (The unbodied ensemble doesn't care how many workers you create on any particular run. The score has a "worker machine" part, and you can decide from run to run how many workers should perform it.) In the "bodying" process itself, each of your ten infomachines takes up residence on one of your ten computers, like falcons settling on fence-posts. They start work. The PM generates tuples and heaves them into tuple space. The workers grab them. Tuple space (which already contains your ten infomachines) is knit together using pieces of each participating computer's memory. When I add a new tuple, characteristics of the tuple determine (automatically) in which computer's memory this new tuple should be billeted. When I scan tuple space for some particular kind of tuple, my attention is directed automatically to the memory of the appropriate computer. So there's no single box anywhere in which tuple space resides. It's an all-enfolding vapor, so to speak.

The Linda *programmer,* of course, couldn't care less where tuple space is. He just heaves stuff in and pulls stuff out.

Does it work?—running an ensemble on a network? The standard approach to ensemble computing still assumes that you have a multi-computer to work with, not a mere network of ordinary machines. It's easier to get good ensemble performance on a multi-computer than on a network. A multi-computer is *designed* for this sort of thing. As a consequence, communication (for example) is likely to be much faster on the multi-computer; and the multi-computer will have other nice properties as well.

But in fact the network approach *does* work very well. Not for every ensemble, but for many significant ones. For example: Not long ago, a Linda graphics program (similar to the one I mentioned before) was set upon by forty mild-mannered desktop computers in the Yale Computer Science Department. These are reasonably powerful machines, but not in the last racey or exotic. They sell for well under ten thousand dollars a pop. The forty of them produced an image *fast.* Ten times faster, in fact, than a fifteen-million-dollar traditional supercomputer, running a non-ensemble version of the same program. (The Linda program was written by Craig Kolb of the Yale Mathematics Department, and tested on the network by Robert Bjornson of the Computer Science Department.)

Not a fair test, completely. We made no effort to coax good performance out of the supercomputer, and you damned well *better* make an effort if you own that kind of equipment. You *expect* to make an effort. Nor is this kind of almost-embarrassing triumph (or anything close to it) guaranteed on every problem.

In other words, if you are already halfway out the kitchen door with your fifteen-million-dollar supercomputer, lugging it down to the sidewalk in anticipation of the next bulk trash pickup in your neighborhood—come back. You're overreacting. But if you do any kind of serious computing at all, and you haven't scheduled some intensely serious pondering about this Network Linda business and the enormous, explosive computing potential lying two inches beneath the surface of any garden-variety computer network—you're underreacting. Which is a lot worse, I'm afraid.

§ Piranhas, and the Out-of-Body Future

I've described the Linda-based hypercomputer of the present. One word about the hypercomputer of the near future: forget about space scooters and falcons; back to good old down-home piranhas. A few years from now, there are still plenty of one-computer desktop machines, but desktop multi-computers are commonplace as well. (Once you've paid for all the other stuff that goes into the computer, the processor chip—the little item that does the actual computing—is a relatively minor expense. So you might as well throw in a handful. Cheap "parallel PC's," so-called, are already starting to appear.) Desktop machines are interconnected using fast fiber-optic networks. (Again, fiber-optic networks are no big deal technologically—you can buy one this afternoon—but they're still pricey. Not for long, though.)

Now, full-blown Piranha Parallelism takes hold. Computations of all sorts are routinely constructed as ensembles. Not that *you* care, necessarily; you buy programs shrink-wrapped, and you don't care whether they're asynchronous ensembles or conventional programs or ruffled potato chips. But you notice that they run fast. At any rate, when you turn one on, it releases a cloud of task tuples into hypercomputer tuple space. Each separate computer in the network (lots of them might be crammed into your desktop box, remember) harbors an infomachine that has been trained to behave like an info-piranha. An info-piranha cruises around tuple space looking for a task cloud to attack. You have first claim on your *own* pet piranhas, the ones who reside on your desktop. But your task cloud might easily attract other marauding infomachines who are bored and hungry. The more piranhas you attract, the faster your task cloud gets demolished and your computation completes. And your own info-piranhas, when you don't need them, will go cruising around with their low-life friends looking for computational trouble elsewhere in the network. Not a pretty picture perhaps. But these boys get the job done, and what's so bad about that, *huh?* All right.

Of course, the computer sits where you put it. It doesn't *actually* cruise around; it cruises in spirit. You might come back from lunch to discover that your computer has slipped out of its box ("spiritually") and is working on a problem in the next building. But, needless to say, it comes romping right back the minute you call.

Our prototype Piranha system, now up and running, is the work of David Kaminsky, who is a graduate student at Yale. He recently ran a gigantic physics program in this way. The program ran in two stretches, one fourteen hours long and one six hours. Roughly forty computer-piranhas participated at one point or another. Only six stayed for the whole party; the rest zigged in and out, darting over for a snack whenever the opportunity arose.

There's more to be said about Linda, its characteristics, and what Linda ensembles look like. But I'll postpone further details until we need them, in the Building Mirror Worlds chapter. One final point: What *is* Linda? Answer: a *coordination language*. Using a *programming language*, we build unbodied infomachines; a *coordination language* is the glue that allows us to clump infomachines into ensembles.

Implications I: Nature

Asynchronous ensembles and their behavior are a bright thread running the length of the modern mind. It's striking how often and how wide-rangingly the answer to the question *what are you studying?* turns out to be, ultimately, *an asynchronous ensemble*. These ensembles differ so hugely among themselves that there's no science of asynchronous ensembles *per se*, and there never will be. Regardless, a due respect for topsight demands that (at a sheer minimum) we *notice* this common theme.

I'll glance in passing at three instances outside of software. Then we'll take up the *interface*, those fascinating tidal marshes where natural and software ensembles swirl together in subtle and far-reaching ways.

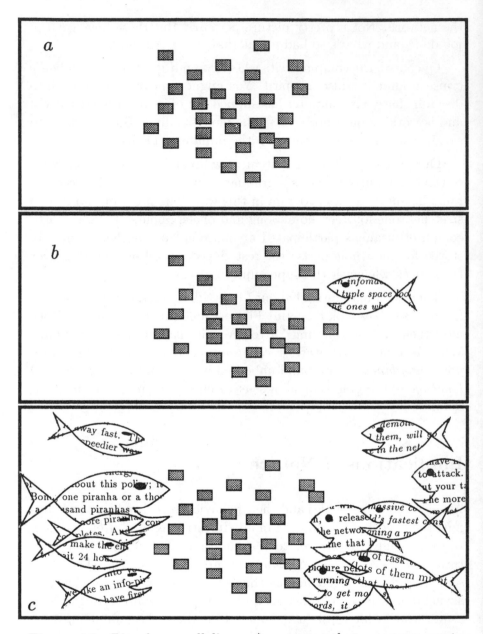

Figure 4.3: Piranha parallelism: A program that someone wants
to run takes the form of a task cloud full of crunchy morsels (*a*).
The program is complete when every task has been consumed. Each
computer on the network acts like a cruising piranha. The more
piranhas attack your task cloud, the better. (*b*) is okay; (*c*) is a lot
quicker.

§ Ensembles in the Wild

Let's go on a field trip, but (due warning): It all comes down to software in the end.

Consider your favorite gas: the classical asynchronous ensemble. A gas is an ensemble of atoms or molecules, each charged with a fairly simple mission: *bounce around*. The temperature and pressure of the gas are properties of the *ensemble*, not of any particular individual within it. It's the *ensemble itself* that has a pressure and a temperature. Pressure reflects lots of randomly bouncing objects slamming into the walls of your container. Temperature reflects the mean kinetic energy of these objects, which has to do with their masses and velocities *on average*. Indeed, the scientific basis of "temperature," and its intimate association with the idea of "asynchronous ensemble," may have penetrated your thinking more deeply than you know (see further)...

Consider Darwin's twin processes of speciation and evolution. *Ensembles* evolve; *ensembles* develop species. Individuals don't. An atom has its mass and its velocity, an individual its genetic makeup and a marked tendency to mate. When you gather a bunch of such individuals together and allow them to interact, evolution and speciation emerge. What Darwin accomplished was the discovery of a new class of "ensemble properties"—attributes that are properties of ensembles and *only* ensembles.

Consider Adam Smith. He discovered another fascinating ensemble property—the tendency of free market economies to develop in the direction of greater over-all wealth. Economic productivity is an ensemble property, obviously. It emerges out of the interactions of oblivious individuals. The fact that an economy is an asynchronous ensemble is something of which most people are aware. I would guess that they are aware, too, of the fact that *temperature* is an ensemble property at base. After all, we say "the economy is heating up," not "the economy is turning purple" or "gaining weight," although in the abstract, rising frequency or weight might have worked out just as well in the metaphor department. (And after all, "metaphor is not just a matter of language, that is, of mere words,"[4] as Lakoff and Johnson point out. Metaphors structure our thinking and reveal much about the underlying thought processes. Vico argued along similar lines in the seventeenth century.[5])

Well, fine. So what does all this have to do with software?

The three natural ensembles we've described form a sort of hierarchy based on the complexity and predictability of their members. Bouncing molecules are (in the relative scheme of things) simple and predictable, walking two-legged Genomes in pants or skirts are medium, full-fledged Economic Man is complicated, with a wide range of behaviors.

Statistical computing models like "neural networks" and computational techniques like "simulated annealing" are the software analog of a gas-type ensemble. These approaches work well, and are increasingly applied in practice; they seem to be effective on a somewhat narrow but important range of problems. "Genetic algorithms" for the construction of certain types of artificial intelligence programs attempt to harness a kind of simulated recombination and evolution in the service of steadily-improving program performance. More broadly, "adaptive behavior" in software systems is a topic that has been attracting a great deal of attention recently.

These topics are interesting but off the point so far as Mirror Worlds are concerned. But the third type of ensemble, the "Smithian ensemble," hits home. The ensembles I'll discuss in the rest of this section are all Smithians.

Software ensembles, we said, might be patterned after "natural" ones either for their own good, or for purposes of studying, modeling and understanding human or natural ensembles. A small but growing research community is attacking the first of these two possibilities. The second remains largely unexplored.

A promising body of research focuses on the use of markets and quasi-biological organizations as models for smoothly, efficiently running software ensembles. Bernardo Huberman of Xerox writes about the development of a "community of concurrent processes which, in their interactions, strategies, and competition for resources, behave like whole ecologies."[6] Huberman has gathered a bunch of technical papers that address these issues into an uneven but intriguing book called *The Ecology of Computation*; the quote comes from its opening chapter.

I mentioned Tom Malone earlier. He's attempting to make "coordination" *per se* a topic that you can study. The *coordination* he's talking about is a goal that software ensembles share with certain kinds of business organizations and with whole economies. Malone hasn't yet settled on a precise definition for this effort or a sharp delineation of its boundaries. But the character of this research is stimulating and promising.

There's much less to report with respect to the companion proposition. The fact that software ensembles can mimic "real" ones gives us a new kind of laboratory. Consider what a college course on "experimental ensembles" might be like—

You might build some simple mock ecosystems to begin with: creatures of a few different sorts (each population represented by a separate infomachine, perhaps); macro-features of the landscape; add weather and let her rip—see how your creatures do. Tinker with the mechanism and see what it takes to make the whole thing unravel. (Do *not* leap to the conclusion that you've proved anything about nature; your experiment is far too simple. But you *have* learned a lot about each component of your ecosystem as you've tried to model it accurately, and you've started to understand the dynamics of such systems in general.) Build a population of infomachines which "mate" in a genetically (if not anatomically) convincing fashion— see if you can observe speciation or evolution. (There has actually been a fair amount of work on a topic called "Synthetic Life" by its practitioners. Experiments by Thomas Ray at the University of Delaware, in which small programs make copies of themselves inside a computer memory, experience "mutations" and compete for resources, are an interesting example of the work in this area. In these artificial and abstract environments, you can observe evolutionary processes that resemble natural ones. The emphasis in this research community is rarely on ensemble programs, however. An ensemble of creatures is simulated by a conventional program.)

Next, something simpler: Build a market (each trader is a separate infomachine) and watch prices bob around. Create a boom and a panic. While you're at it, build an entire economy. Raise and lower interest rates, trade barriers, consumer confidence and so on. See what happens. Build a "public" out of infomachines, one machine per person. Each person has a certain level of information, willingness to talk and listen to other people, gullibility: See if you can start some fads or rumors or political movements. Take a poll every now and then. (Some of these experiments are outlined in a bit more detail in a textbook about ensemble programming by Nicholas Carriero and myself.[7])

And then, the fun begins: experimental history. You've already built an economy, studied public opinion; can you trigger the global economic collapse of the thirties? (Study the role of tariffs carefully. Send the results to your congressman. Of course you may have to explain what a "tariff" is, when the "thirties" took place and so on, but please be patient...) By tuning-in the proper incendiary mix of public and governmental attitudes and assumptions, treaty obligations and general cussedness, can you start the First World War? Can you reproduce the aftermath of Tet, Alexander's victories in Persia, the rise of feudalism *ad infinitum*? Maybe not. Don't expect it to be easy. But the attempt could be highly illuminating.

Computerized war gaming, as it is studied, developed and practiced *very* seriously by the military, comes closest to the sort of exercise I have in mind. But the differences are significant. My claim here is that understanding ensemble behavior is an indispensable part of being educated. And there is a further claim, rather a large and sweeping one: *Students should build working models* whenever they can. When you can see and feel *directly, immediately* how each part works and how they all come together, you've achieved something important.

Software ensembles may be a new modeling medium of significant power and promise. The goal is emphatically *not* to asphyxiate book learning under a heap of color graphics and technoglitz. It would simply be nice to foster a deep, intimate knowledge of the facts and processes behind ecosystems, economies, history and so on. The act of fine-tuning individual infomachines *and* the grand organizing strategy that knits them together will rub people's noses in this sort of knowledge. If students pick up a bit of topsight in the process, so much the better. And these exercises will be fun too, dammit. Why *not* give it a try?

Why not? Because, by and large, scholars, social scientists and biologists are unaware of the capabilities of software ensembles. And many computer scientists would sooner take out the garbage than think seriously about history. My own research group, accordingly, declares itself ready and willing to talk to all serious comers about experimental ensemble-izing in *any* field.

(Eventually, I'd expect to see a brisk ancillary trade in "working textbooks," monographs and articles, by the way—I capture my particular understanding of the dynamics of this or that historical factor in a disembodied machine that can be dropped into anyone's ensemble.)

There's a final issue we need to consider: the intermingling of software and human ensembles. We start right now, and carry this theme through the rest of the book.

Implications II: Communication

"What's good for software is good for humans." Talk about a stupid proposition... But there *are* a few specialized areas in which this principle holds, and communication (up to a point) is one of them. Infomachines in a Linda ensemble enjoy far more flexible, far freer communication than people usually do. Let's fix this anomaly: We'll conduct a little thought experiment—

This is a small-scale dress rehearsal for Mirror Worlds. The topic is not unrelated, but it's more limited and far less important. This is a useful exercise, though, not merely for its content but for its form as well. The essence of what software researchers do is to dream up crazy new structures, climb aboard them and shove off for extended thought-cruises through strange new territories. So let's try it.

§ The Tuplesphere

Suppose that (essentially) all non-face-to-face communication, between people and not merely infomachines, went through an all-encompassing "Tuplesphere." There are Tuplesphere sockets all over the place (home, office, hotel room, airport waiting lounge...). Whenever you're in the mood to communicate, you simply plug your laptop computer into the nearest Tuplesphere socket. Or you might forget about the cord, and tune your machine to Data Radio.

When you have something to communicate, you drop it into this world tuple ocean. When you need information, you pull it out. Usually you read it; sometimes you remove it. Pretty simple.

Mail-type communication can now be directed anywhere, not just somewhere. Drop your electronic mail messages (containing either text or fax-type images) into the Tuplesphere; each message is labeled with the recipient's name and (probably) some kind of identifying code. The receiver can pull it out wherever he happens to be. You don't have to know where he is, and you don't have to care.

Telephone communication works in the same way. A phone conversation is converted into a numbered series of tuples, like the streams I discussed earlier. As you talk, software breaks your conversation into a series of discrete chunks, translates each chunk into numbers, puts the numbers in a tuple, drops the tuple into a tuple stream. At the receiving end, software grabs the first tuple in the stream and translates the numbers into sound, then the second tuple and so on.

Again, this can be "anywhere" communication. Forget about phone numbers; you "call up" a person by using his name and code, the same way you send him mail. This information doesn't designate a particular telephone, not even a portable one; it designates a *person.* Two people make phone contact in exactly the same way whether one is in Ulan Bator and the other is in Lusaka, or they are both at home in Passaic. (Some phone companies are already talking about this sort of "personal id" system. But let's integrate this service into a big picture, an entirely new communications approach—not just slap it onto the current obsolete jumble of features.)

We've provided "everyone" communication, too. What holds for phone conversation also holds, in principle, for video. What used to be called "broadcasting" is now obsolete. TV presentations—images and sound—are translated into numbers, hacked up into tuples and formed into streams, just like phone conversations. Assuming your laptop machine has the appropriate numbers-into-pictures hardware (and why shouldn't it?), you can watch TV using the same machine that handles your mail and your telephone service.

Notice that all conventional bandwidth and geography limitations have just been torn up. To be a TV station, you don't need your own broadcast frequency or cable slot. All you need is a label that you can stuff into each of your tuples, to identify what you're putting out, and keep it all together. That label can be anything. In particular, it can be a large number. Luckily, there is absolutely *no* shortage of large numbers. They are in plentiful supply nearly everywhere. We should easily be able to provide every inhabitant of the earth with his own—it can be the same one, for that matter, that serves as the identification tag on your incoming mail and phone calls. And there you have it: You're a TV station. Congratulations. Geography also goes away. I tap into the same World Tuplesphere wherever I am. If I'm vacationing in Düsseldorf but can't get to sleep without watching the local news from Paramus, no problem. Any and all TV feeds, worldwide, are accessible from my local machine.

To be fair, some agency needs to move this information around, and moving information *costs* something. I may pay more to watch the Paramus news in Düsseldorf than I'm accustomed to paying back home. There might even be a brief delay in getting the video feed in place—a few seconds, maybe. But the service is available if you want it. And the cost, my guess is, won't break you. (Of course, we are talking *eventually* here.)

The disappearance of bandwidth limitations as such means, by the way, that you can generate your TV pictures with seventeen different sound tracks if you want. The customer chooses a picture that looks interesting, then dials up his favorite language to accompany it.

While we're at it, we might as well take the world's libraries, digitize them and dump them into the Tuplesphere as well. And the Tuplesphere is a good publishing medium for newspapers, periodicals and so on.

All Tuplesphere communication is (of course) trans-time and not merely trans-space. Once a TV presentation has been dumped into the Tuplesphere it *stays* there, until someone insists on removing it. I can watch today's TV programs, yesterday's or something from the last decade. "Broadcasters" can dump an entire season's worth of shows into Tuplesphere *en masse*.

Notice that I haven't merely replaced the phone lines, TV cable and so on with a single master-wire. I've unified things *logically*; all these communication modes work in the same way. I can begin by typing words, then switch to voice, then back to text and so on. And it all takes place within the Linda "free communication" zone.

So, let's say I need to call someone in Korea. I place the phone call. Then I remember that, alas, I don't speak Korean. I need a translator. I put the Korean on hold and type a message: "anyone willing to translate between English and Korean?" Let's say that one such individual *is* logged on somewhere. He mouses on your message, picks up the phone and says "sure, patch me in." You ask him what his rates are, you make a deal, and you add him to the conversation. You've now got both the Korean and the translator on the line, and you can proceed. You don't care where the translator is. He might be in Korea, or he might be in the office next door.

In short, you've got "anyone" communication, too. How did it work? Organizations that are willing to accept anonymous phone calls have installed a software monitor on their lines, designed to filter out most irrelevant calls and display your introductory query once they've caught something that seems plausible. If the introductory query looks interesting, the customer rep answers the phone. The same holds, obviously, for a free-lancing individual. The World Tupleshere encourages the proliferation of free-lance infoservice suppliers. Do you need someone to correct the lousy grammar in your reports, supply them with executive summaries, reorganize them according to federal format 71538q(4), translate them into French, check the facts, fill in the missing citations, reformat them for a new computer-printing system, supply classical references or redo them in rhyming Alexandrines? Just ask.

Of course, you can also place that phone call you've been wanting to make to "any plumber who can fix my sink by the day after tomorrow," "anybody's who's got an oil filter for a 1979 Buick Riviera" or whatever. You type this description into your machine, then pick up the phone and wait for a response. If several people from different companies pick up, you can talk to them all simultaneously. Why waste time repeating your problem? Let them bid against each other. If no-one answers and you get tired of waiting, hang up and check later—perhaps no-one is interested or available at the moment, but your request will (of course) hang around. Plumber Jones who was out on a job, and Plumber Smith who is destined to show up in town and open shop for the first time tomorrow, will both find your message hanging around out there when they look around.

Let's say that you and Fruitford need to have a conversation, and Piffelini in the Tokyo office would also be interested, but he's asleep at the moment. You and Fruitford have your chat, and "copy" Piffelini; he can replay the conversation whenever he wants, interpolate his own comments and send the results back to you. Trans-time communication also means that you can communicate with future versions of yourself. You can pick up the phone and dictate a reminder message that you'll get next Tuesday, next year or whatever.

People and infomachines cooperate smoothly in this environment. You might want to have your phone conversations transcribed; in a few years, software will be good at this sort of thing. You can patch a software transcriber into your conversation as easily as you can add a human translator. And people might want to communicate using the same data structures that infomachines find useful. Let's say that the X department is generating a lot of work for the Y department. X people might want to task the work out to Y people through the Tuplesphere: dropping each task description in a "bag" (when a Y person is free, he reaches in and grabs any task); arranging tasks in a stream (an unoccupied Y person grabs the first task in line); and so on.

The Tuplesphere will need to be cleaned up from time to time, so it doesn't get clogged up with uninteresting junk. But its capacity will be large, particularly if we use the standard computer science techniques of "caching" and "hierarchical memory." These techniques allow rarely-used data to be automatically elbowed aside into out-of-the-way corners; the convenient, easily-accessible locations are reserved for widely-used material. Massive data warehouses are cheap to build. So long as you're willing to wait a while for the information you need to be trundled out of deep storage, tuple oceans can have enormous capacity.

All this stuff needs to be organized somehow—here is where tuple spaces-within-tuple spaces are important. (I'll pursue this point in a couple of chapters.) And the best way to find your way around this info-ocean is *visually*. Sophisticated images on your screen, to begin with; "virtual reality," images projected onto little eyeglass-style TV screens, putting you *inside* a three-dimensional synthetic landscape, will also be nice.

There are loads of difficult problems here—privacy, security, reliability, charging schemes and accounting, all sorts of things. But the basic design is clear. The most important requirement is simply *raw communication capacity*. Our available reserves of this crucial resource are on the rise. Robert Kahn's project, the one I referred to in the second chapter, aims at a large leap in data communication capacity. We need to turn this raw hardware leap into real, usable communication services, not just for scientific data- and computer-sharing (obviously important), but for *everyone's* tangible, immediate and continuing gain. A family of fast data-network projects is being funded by federal research agencies (to the tune of fifteen million dollars or so, which—unfortunately—counts as a lot where computer science funding is concerned); research on transcontinental billion-bit-per-second fiber-optic networks is well underway. Is a billion bits per second enough? Probably not. But it's a start.

What's the net result of our Tuplesphere thought-experiment? Freer, easier, more improvisational communication—more like neighborhood face-to-face chatting, less like the typical phone, mail and so-on communication of today. Space and time—*where* someone is, *when* he's available—more or less don't matter. The boundary between speaking and writing is easily and repeatedly hopped over. Language differences fade somewhat in significance when translation services are easy to hire on the spot whenever you need them (and TV shows come in many languages routinely). Most portentous, people and software work hand-in-glove—sometimes, hand-in-hand.

We'll have more to say about these mixed marriages.

Chapter 5

The Deluge

We've installed the foundation piles and are ready to start building Mirror Worlds. In this chapter we discuss (so to speak) the basement, in the next chapter we get to the attic, and the chapter after that fills in the middle region and glues the whole thing together.

The basement we are about to describe is filled with lots of a certain kind of ensemble program. This kind of program, called a *Trellis*, makes the connection between external data and internal mirror-reality. The Trellis is, accordingly, a key player in the Mirror World cast. It's also a good example of ensemble programming in general, and, I'll argue, a highly significant gadget in itself. The hulking problem with which the Trellis does battle on the Mirror World's behalf is a problem that the real world, too, will be confronting directly and in person very soon.

The Problem

Floods of data are pounding down all around us in torrents. How will we cope? What will we *do* with all this stuff? When the encroaching electronification of the world pushes the downpour rate higher by a thousand or a million times or more, what will we do then?

Concretely: I'm talking about *realtime data processing*. The subject in this chapter is fresh data straight from the sensor. We'd like to analyze this fresh data in "realtime"—to achieve some understanding of data values as they emerge.

Raw data pours into a Mirror World and gets refined by a data distillery in the basement. The processed, refined, one-hundred-percent pure stuff gets stored upstairs in the attic, where it ferments slowly into history. (In the next chapter we move upstairs.)

Trellis programs are the topic here: how they are put together, how they work. But there's an initial question that's too important to ignore. We need to take a brief trip outside into the deluge, to establish what this stuff is and where it's coming from.

What **data?**

Data-gathering instruments are generally electronic. They are *sensors* in the field, dedicated to the non-stop, automatic gathering of measurements; or they are full-blown infomachines, waiting for people to sit down, log on and enter data by hand. Electronics are getting cheaper all the time—a revelation? Maybe you've noticed? And since humans have always been insatiable collectors of data (even if they are rarely inspired to *do* anything with it once they've got it), data-gathering instruments are proliferating, and the world's fresh-data supply is going through the roof.

Start with something simple. Cars are fitted with a handful of sensors today; in a few years they'll be fitted with lots more. The sensors gather data about the state of your engine and the rest of the apparatus. Today, this data is converted instantaneously into small tactical adjustments, for example to keep the engine burning efficiently. In the future, there will be enough of it to present a complete, detailed picture of the status of the whole machine. Will you need new brake linings on the front (at your present burn rate) in three weeks, and a front-end realignment while you're at it, but the tires are okay? Are you about to run into a tree? These are interesting questions, and ample data will no doubt be on hand to answer them—if we can *interpret* the data effectively.

Of course a car, even the macho Data-Car of the future, is a small potatoes operation. Speaking of cars, traffic is supposed to double over the next three decades, and in case you hadn't noticed, it isn't moving all that well right now. In some areas, complete breakdown is in sight. The *New York Times* mutters darkly about the need to "stave off a paralysis on the nation's highways."[1]

No problem, you say, build some new roads. Nope, sorry. No

room, too expensive, too much arguing, too many lawsuits, too slow, too smelly, too much of a nuisance. The hell with it. Want an example? In the early seventies, Manhattan's heavily used West Side Highway collapsed. In the early nineties (August 1990, to be precise) the Federal government politely requested of the City the return of some eighty-one million dollars that were supposed to have helped pay for a replacement. In almost twenty years, New York hadn't even managed to decide *what kind* of highway it wanted, much less started (however timidly) to *build* anything.[2] As a society we *are* growing a bit ornery as we age, aren't we? *Don't bother us with yer dang construction projects! Who the divil needs all that fuss and dirt? We got enough dang roads already*— Yeah, okay...

And so we have an important data-deluge impending. In many areas, sensors are being installed to monitor traffic; virtually every non-residential street in the country will be wired within a decade or two. The goal is to *sculpt* traffic flow instead of allowing it to blunder stupidly down the first blind alley.

An experiment in Los Angeles involves twenty-five cars with on-board navigation systems and congested-traffic information feeds. It deals with a fourteen-mile chunk of several parallel roadways. A fascinating start, but fourteen miles won't do it for us. We need *end-to-end* trip-planning and congestion-avoidance. We need to fine-tune urban traffic grids continuously (using traffic light programming, lane redirection and so on) for decent flow; we need to deploy repair trucks exactly where they'll be closest to potential breakdowns (a problem very much like deciding where to store tuples on a hypercomputer); we need to target maintenance for maximum effect, and anticipate catastrophes. This is a massive data-handling problem. We can lay down the sensors; fine. But what does it all mean? How are we supposed to respond? The data needs to be interpreted, *quickly.*

So much for roads. Many of the same issues recur, often on a huge scale, in air traffic control. Rising volume; insufficient capacity; plenty of sensors telling me exactly where everyone is—but so what? How does that help me? What should I do *right now?*

A blizzard of scientific data descends from space. Earth-bound experimental installations generate data of all sorts in ridiculous quantities. "Data volumes generated by [*whatever...*] currently overwhelm the available computational resources"[3] according to one federal study. "Data too cheap to meter" reads a news-item head-line in *Science,* the leading weekly in the U.S. scientific community.[4] "Learning to drink from a fire hose" reads another, about the same phenomenon.[5]

Finance, commerce and economic activity in general create huge quantities of data. The world is full of markets, of banks setting rates, companies and governments issuing reports, international agencies making pronouncements. The data is almost all available online; you can subscribe to all sorts of private services, and wind up with dozens of primitive non-integrated stand-alone systems, each focused on one little pieces of the picture. But what's really happening, and what does it mean? Another massive data-handling problem.

In operating rooms and intensive care units, clinicians must inter-pret and react to a complex, diverse collection of unstoppable data streams. What do these multiple blood pressure, heart rate, temper-ature, fluid inflow and outflow and many more numbers mean about the real condition of the patient? Is he basically OK? Is he about to die? What can we do to improve things? Which crises can we stave off by acting now? (More or less the same questions we'd like to pose about the economy...)

In the intensive care unit, unless the correct interpretation is available *fast,* it's useless. The *WizzoTek Post Mortem Pontifica-tor/Perfect Diagnoses While U Wait (Indefinitely)* is a tough sell. And technological trends are making this hard problem harder. They increase the volume, diversity and accuracy of the data that can be gathered, and the range of available responses to any given prob-lem; they do nothing to lessen the urgency of the required response, or to increase human data-processing capacity. Clinicians face the obvious difficulties of processing and interpreting masses of data cor-rectly. They also face the more subtle problem of "fixation" — the natural human tendency to become biased towards an initial hypoth-esis and to ignore or misinterpret data to the contrary. A massive data-handling problem.

Aircraft control involves similar issues: masses of data, time-critical decisions, a hard problem getting worse.

Offices are computerized; computers and their networks grow steadily more central to discussion, development and decision mak-ing. Computers are capable of noticing and remembering lots of details. Computers eavesdropping on their users (with the user's consent) are a major source of the data streams that feed Mirror Worlds.

And what about sensors in powerplants? Factories? Trains, submarines and aircraft carriers? Police-gathered and security data? Weather data? Marketing data? Data about the far-flung status of phone networks, water and power grids? World oil supplies?

We're talking a lot of stuff here.

§ In sum...

Look out your window. That just-faintly-visible pall blanketing the landscape to the rooftops, congealing in the valleys and climbing at some points up past the clouds is the worldwide info-smog. A dense clinging fog of information, full of the numbers and images that are emitted in crazy profusion by our burgeoning swarms of info-gathering devices.

And for what? What do we *do* with all of this information?

Some of it is studied seriously, squeezed hard for whatever knowledge it contains. Much of it is used in simple, primitive ways and then thrown out. A great deal of it is simply ignored. The info-smog is dense with numbers that have been glanced at, scanned superficially or never examined at all.

The problem is, in part, that our current-generation computer plant is simply not up to the task of digesting it all. There's too much of it. A state-of-the-art organization like NASA, which runs a whole collection of fancy labs full of very fast computers, keeps libraries-full of magtape that no computer has had time to analyze. But today's data-flow is a puny trickle compared to what these people have in mind. In the late 90's, for example, one project alone, the so-called "earth observation system," should be generating one trillion characters of data a day.[6] That's sort of a lot. Picture a third of a billion printed pages—ten thousand massive encyclopaedias—seven some-odd miles of shelf space; you get the idea. And they can't keep up with what they are getting *now*.

Parallel computers will be a major help in fixing this problem. They'll deliver the raw computing power that's called for...

§ The Basic Problem

But there's a more fundamental factor at work here. Throughout human history, mankind has been a lot better at gathering data than at thinking about it.

There were *annales* long before there were *annalistes*. It's much easier to be a bureaucrat than a scientist. It's easy to organize a data-gathering project, and you can count on a rush of neo-Victorian curatorial satisfaction as your collection grows. But *analyzing* data requires at least a measure of topsight, and topsight is a rare commodity.

We need to get a grip on this tendency, though. There's a great deal at stake. On one level, we'd like traffic to run more smoothly, patients to get better treatment, markets to function more effectively and so on. In other words, we'd like to accomplish a grab-bag of basically unrelated good things.

At a deeper and more general level, *power requires control.* The power and complexity of our technical infrastructure is exploding, and our control systems have not kept pace. When you double an engine's horsepower, you'd better improve your brakes, tires, suspension and steering as well. Interpreting this data instead of ignoring it is our main chance of beefing up the brakes and the steering. Without adequate control systems, we face real danger. With them, we can turn our new-found power to great advantage. We can put the top down, step on the gas, enjoy life.

Instead of venting all this data into the info-smog, we could treat our data sources as plunging waterfalls waiting to drive software powerplants that convert data into knowledge. I'll refer to such installations as Realtime Knowledge Plants. Clearly a knowledge plant will be built out of software. The kind of plant I will describe must in fact be realized by a software ensemble, of a very particular kind.

Software Architectures (*Architectures?*)

A *software architecture* describes a program structure—how parts can be assembled into a whole. The parts may be modules or entire infomachines. The whole will be (obviously) a single infomachine or an ensemble respectively. Software architecture comes into its own in the second case. Modules are mere passive sacks. How you modularize your program doesn't effect its dynamics: One infomachine means one actor, and that's it. But the way you *uncouple* your program into separate infomachines, or (looking at it the other way) glue infomachines together into an ensemble, decisively affects the behavior and dynamics of the whole.

I'm about to describe a software architecture for ensembles: a recipe for gluing infomachines together into a certain kind of structure. The recipe tells you how to determine what kind of infomachines and how many you need, and (the crucial datum) how exactly the infomachines coordinate their activities. Ensembles that are built according to this particular architecture can be (and are) built using Linda. Programs in lots of other shapes can also be built using Linda. Linda is a general-purpose tool; this architecture is a template for one significant *class* of programs.

Now, back to a prime fixation:

When we talk about "architecture" that's a term we've stolen, obviously, from its rightful owners. Computer scientists *do* talk about architecture a great deal, mainly "machine architecture" (how to design computers), but occasionally "software architecture," exactly as I'm doing here.

The term has been purloined for convenience, but the theft says a lot. The shape and structure of the ensemble programs I'm about to describe are almost palpable. Software architecture bears a deep resemblance to the real thing. Not to "real architecture" in strictly conventional terms, but to the Eiffel Tower (let's say) as architecture. Spare and stark: but possessed of *the particular shape it's got* and not some other one *in part*—not wholly but in *significant* part—because of the sheer aesthetic *power* of that shape. There is a strong, vibrant feedback loop between engineering utility and aesthetics, whether you're discussing iron towers or software ensembles.

I'm not making this up. David Billington, who is a Professor of Civil Engineering at Princeton, writes about Gustave Eiffel beginning to shape his structures "not only to carry loads but also to please himself." He writes, in discussing the "best structural engineers," of the "intimate connection between the quality of the technical work and the quality of the visual result."[7] In software there is no visual result, but there is a *visualizable* one, if you turn on your imagination.

Software architecture is no medium for untrammeled whimsy. It imposes ironclad discipline on the designer: The point is to solve a hard problem efficiently, not to make art. But good designers in any medium make art despite themselves; whether they work in steel or concrete or software or silicon, that's precisely how you recognize them. Some of the best art being produced today is "applied art" in exactly these tough media—because art, after all, *requires* discipline. You can't push if nothing is pushing back. The popular belief that you get art by pushing against society's assumptions and expectations used to make sense but is now quaintly obsolete, because after all, these expectations and assumptions—about content *and* form—collapsed years ago. You can *offend* people, sure, but you can't surprise them. (Attention Connoisseurs: If you fling yourself in a screaming massive assault at a supposedly locked door that turns out, in the event, to be wide open, what you get is called "slapstick," not "art.") Technology, on the other hand, still pushes back.

Damned hard, too. You'd better believe it.

The Design of Real Time Knowledge Plants

Here is a different kind of ensemble—not the dynamic, rowdy bunch of infomachines zigging in and out that we've considered thus far. A far more disciplined group.

Consider an upward-stretching network of infomachines tethered together, rung-upon-rung (billowing slightly in the breeze?) No two rungs need have exactly the same number of machines. But often, many rungs will have *roughly* the same number, giving us a kind of upright rectangle populated by running programs. There might be ten rungs in all or hundreds or thousands, and the average rung might have anywhere from a handful to hundreds of members. This architecture spans a huge range of shapes and sizes—and when we talk about thousands of rungs at hundreds of elements per, we are talking about something immense.

So, these things are "tethered together"—meaning? Those lines are *lines of communication*. Each member of the Trellis is tethered to some lower-down machines and to some higher-ups (except for the bottom and top rungs, of course). A machine deals *only* with the machines to which it is tethered. So far as it's concerned, the rest

Figure 5.1: The Trellis.

don't exist. It deals with inferiors in a certain way and superiors in a certain other way, and that's it. Those inferiors and superiors define its universe.

Information rushes upward through the network, and the machines on each rung respond to it on their own terms. The higher you rank, the more general your view of the world. Infomachines at the bottom focus all their energy on particular, narrow streams of data. Are these numbers *good* numbers—which ones are noise and garbage, which are decent data? On a slightly higher rung: are these numbers trending up or down? Stable or unstable? As we move upward through the Trellis, each rung concentrates on wider, bigger problems. Putting this trend and that one *together*, what do I get? Suppose (moving higher) I factor in this stuff and that stuff too?

To put it another way, data values are forwarded from the bottom rungs upward for *more elaborate analysis of their information content and for combination with signals from other types of receptors...* (I'll return to this phrase.)

Each machine focuses on one piece of the problem—on answering a single question about the thing out there (the traffic network, the patient, the financial market) that is being monitored. Each machine's entire and continuous effort is thrown into answering its one question. You can query a machine at any time—what's the current best answer to your particular question?—and it will produce an up-to-the-second response.

Raw data pours in at the bottom. The machines at every level study the work of their inferiors. Based on what their inferiors are doing, they develop a new, higher-level, bigger-picture view of what is going on. The top-most level produces big-picture information: *Part X seems to be malfunctioning because of a problem in part Y. Traffic flow in the north-west sector is normal. The patient is developing congestive heart failure.* In short, raw data flows in at the bottom; the big picture comes into focus on top.

Thus a knowledge plant is precisely *a machine for generating topsight.*

So data flows upward through the ensemble; there's also a reverse, downward flow of what you might call "anti-data"—*inquiries* about what's going on. A high-ranking element might attempt to generate a new value, only to discover that it's missing some key datum from an inferior. It sends a query downward. To wit, *what the hell is going on?* The inferior tries to come up with some new data. But it may fail, for the same reason the superior did: One of its own key inferiors may have failed to report. So the query gets bucked downwards another level. It may finally reach rock bottom, where there *are* no inferiors to needle. If a bottom-level machine is missing data, it can't pass a query downward, it can only pass one *outward*: It can ask the outside world directly for information. The system might print a message on a computer screen (*When did you last give this guy aspirin?*), or nudge an external sensor.

The fact that data flows up and anti-data flows downwards means that, in a certain sense, a Trellis can run either either forward or backwards, or both at the same time. There's more to be said about this, further on.

The Noisiest Ensemble

The Trellis is a lion-tamirg act. It's also the noisiest, most intense software operation we will describe—

A pounding rush of data thunders into the machine; to sight down a Trellis from the top is to stand on the upper roadway seeing, hearing and feeling the spillway at the base of a concrete dam, billowing mist. This outpouring of raw numbers is tamed and transformed, as it flows upward, into the nuanced silence of a carpeted room. *This patient may be developing hypovolemia. Watch closely.*

(Why these far-flung images? Because whatever helps you to *imagine* software helps you to understand it. And this imagery conveys something significant: It tells you where Trellises live inside the mind—)

Why do it this way?

What's the point of all this? What does the Trellis have that other architectures lack?

Point one: The Trellis is an ensemble. It didn't *have* to be; in principle, it might have been a single program (with lots of modules).

But for this problem, the ensemble is vital. First, consider *speed.*

If these knowledge plants are going to operate in "real time," they must respond quickly. To do so, they must assimilate, analyze and interpret data quickly. We have a fairly stringent definition for what this means. The Trellis deals with *streams* of values: a stream of blood pressure value, market transaction values, air pressure values or whatever. There are a number of possible definitions for when a Trellis is running "fast enough." We'll use the following one: A Trellis is running fast enough if *each* new data value is *fully analyzed* before the next one in its stream shows up. Suppose a bottom-rung element is wired to a sensor that produces new readings once per second. The Trellis program has to run fast enough so that this piece of data has made it through every rung, all they way to the top, in one second. During this same period, of course, lots of other data values will be percolating upwards through the structure; we need to make the same guarantee to *every* data stream. If there's lots of data or many rungs or both, this may be a stiff requirement to meet.

But luckily we're dealing with an ensemble, and ensembles can do many things at once. Each member of the Trellis is a separate infomachine. They can all run simultaneously. If a *single* infomachine (running on a single computer) were trying to do the whole job, it might have to either implausibly or impossibly fast. Focusing lots of computers on this problem is the way to achieve the speed we need.

Now, consider *clarity*: this is an obvious case for *uncoupling*. The Trellis as a whole has enormous, wide-ranging responsibilities. Its low-level machines worry about numbers—throwing out garbage, finding trends; to do so they might use (*do* use in our prototypes) mathematical techniques borrowed from signal processing. The high-lying machines may be radically different. They might reply on artificial intelligence techniques to simulate human-like expertise. Again, our running prototypes *do* work this way. Forcing all these complex responsibilities into a single script would be crazy. The ensemble is a radically *clearer* approach.

These arguments are decisive, but they have to do with ensembles generally, not (in particular) with *Trellis*-shaped ensembles. To deal with the Trellis itself, we need to introduce the last of our big-three clarity principles.

Figure 5.2: Espalier: A tree trained on a trellis.

Espalier

Take a complex, powerful, far-flung structure; train it on a regular grid. Bend (but don't break) it to the rules of an external framework. What you have is still a complex, far-flung structure, but now you can find your way around it.

Espalier is a vital software-clarity principle. We've already met it, surreptitiously. The Tuplesphere is a hugely complex jumble of stuff, but it's easy to conceive—and in a fairly concrete, detailed way at that—because the whole thing is espaliered onto the simple and regular Linda framework. Everything in there has been added in the same way, can be read in the same way, can be removed in the same way. Without an underlying simple framework of *some* sort, the Tuplesphere would make no sense even as a thought-experiment.

Like our other two principles, espalier isn't merely a software principle. It is, in one sense, the most widespread and profoundly important of our clarity devices.

It has manifestations in nature, like the other two. Think of a crystal—a neat lattice-work of randomly quivering particles.

It is a competitor of recursive simplicity, in some ways. An ordinary address uses recursive simplicity. I send a letter to (reading backwards) the U.S.A., the state of Connecticut, the town of New Haven, Prospect Street, number 51. At each stage I answer the same question (where?) on a smaller scale. But in principle, I might have addressed the same letter to 41°, 15' north latitude, 72°, 50' west longitude. No recursive levels: no resolution of a single problem repeatedly. Rather, the imposition of a single uniform, system-wide pattern.

But the most important manifestation of this technique is elsewhere. Espalier is a defining principle of art.

Good art consists almost by definition of *inspiration* squeezed into *an external framework* that (in some ways) confines and limits it—but in return allows us to *find our way around inside it*, to follow and comprehend it. Espalier imparts strength, energy and muscle tone. Espalier is that "wonderful opposition to wrench against and revise with" that Robert Lowell champions, defending meter to William Carlos Williams.[8] The clarity *and* the tension of wild ideas espaliered onto neat frameworks practically define we call great art. Rhymed or metered verse, and the standard forms of classical music, are espalier's most striking achievements. (So all right, this has nothing to do with software...)

Tom Wolfe and Al Bloom are Dead Wrong to suppose (respectively) that there is no good abstract expressionist painting or rock music. As some ancient proverb presumably notes, it's hard not to lop off a few flowers, if you weed your garden with a machete. But even a died-in-the-wool admirer of fifties slash-and-burn de Kooning or sixties Beatles (such as, say, your author) has trouble denying that the *greatest* paintings accept the external discipline of *depicting something* and, obviously, the greatest musical compositions are fugues, variations and classical sonata movements; not free fantasias.

Espalier is a principle of applied art as well. Just one example: Midtown Manhattan is a complicated place, but wherever you are, you know where you stand. The city was organized early in the nineteenth century into a regular grid of rectangular blocks. Anyone can figure out how to get from Thirty-second Street and Seventh Avenue to Ninety-first and Fifth (at least in theory). Espalier is a reasonable way to organize a city. But more than that: Throughout this century, Manhattan's most widely-remarked attribute is usually called *tension* (if you don't like it) or *energy, intensity* (if you do). My hypothesis: The Triumph of Espalier represented in Manhattan's street plan feeds this triumph of ferocious pizzazz. Squeeze a huge, dense, complicated, overflowing city into a square unrelenting corset-grid and the very buildings scream (if you are attuned to this sort of thing) and the energy flows. No wonder some people can't stand it.

Language itself is built on principles of espalier. Learning a language is do-able insofar as new words follow, by and large, the old patterns. People seem to reach for an espaliered life—a monastic rule, political autocracy, street gang—in times of disorder; naturally enough.

Back to software.

In the Trellis structure, our dependence on espalier becomes explicit. With all this stuff going on at once—all those data streams rushing in, all those analyses in progress—I'd have mere turbid chaos without a simple organizing scheme to find my way around.

Espalier allows me to make sense of what's going on. Inside the Trellis, an infomachine's connections to other machines are always the same: Each element must be prepared to receive data from its inferiors, and queries from its superiors. So long as it does this properly, it can do whatever weird things it wants the rest of the time. Connections between the infomachines in the Trellis are like modular phone jacks. I can buy all sorts of strange phones with many combinations of funny features, and still plug them into the standard wall outlet. The connection between the phone network and each telephone is simple and uniform. If it weren't—if each new phone required its own kind of connection—it would be impossible to support any real variety of telephones. Likewise, Trellis components.

A customer walks up to a Trellis machine: We need to explain to him what it can do (and importantly, what it can't). The Trellis framework is a way to show him. We don't need to tell people "the program can perform the following twenty-three thousand kinds of analysis." We can *show them a picture* whose structure mirrors their own concept of the problem, their own *mental* picture: a low level, a medium level, a high level. The lines in the picture show you what depends on what. Again, they mirror your *thinking*: Sure, diagnosis of an engine problem clearly has something to do with the state of the exhaust gasses, but nothing to do with how clean the windshield is. Once you've learned the rules, you don't have to relearn them for every segment of the picture.

The regular framework also means that you can work on one piece of the structure without having to understand the whole thing. In the espaliered Trellis ensemble, an infomachine needs to know who its inferiors are, who its superiors are, and that's all. In building (or changing) a machine, I don't need to worry about the ensemble as a whole (which might be enormous); I can restrict my attention to my own neighborhood. This is crucial when we talk about big Trellises built by a bunch of separate experts. In fact, even fairly small Trellises may be constructed by many hands. For example:

The Intensive Care Unit Prototype

This is a Trellis program of 150 some-odd elements. It was built by Mike Factor (then a graduate student at Yale, now at IBM Haifa, still the undisputed world Trellis-building champ). He collaborated with researchers from the Yale Medical School, notably Doctors Perry Miller and Dean Sittig.

The medical side of the team had medical goals, of course. They looked at the modern intensive care unit and saw a massive data management problem. I outlined this problem earlier. They chose the so-called "hemodynamic monitoring" problem to focus on, as it occurs in the intensive care units where patients recuperate from cardiac surgery.

The details aren't germane here, but I'll sketch out the structure of this program, in the interests of a concrete example.

The hemodynamic monitor is still a research vehicle. It continues to grow. When it's finished, it will be slotted into place for a clinical trial. Don't look for this kind of software gadgetry at your local hospital any time soon. The medical establishment is conservative (understandably), and it takes awhile for systems like this to propagate. And there is still work to be done before the prototype itself is complete. But the eventual unconditional victory of this *sort* of technology (whether or not in Trellis guise) is guaranteed. Our medical collaborators differ quite a lot about *when*, not at all about *whether* it will happen.

Figure 5.3 shows an excerpt from the structure of this program.

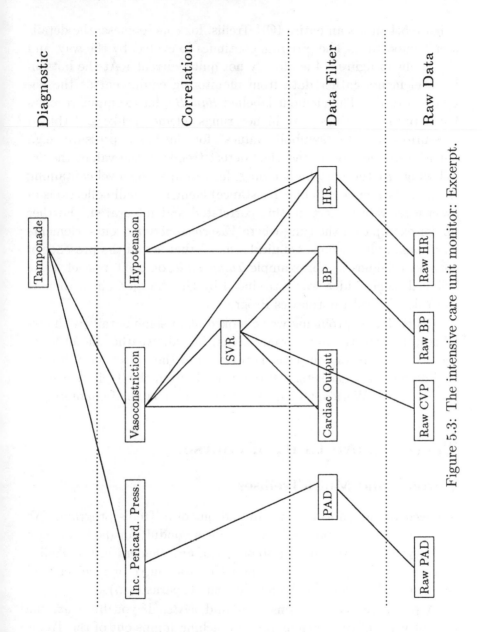

Figure 5.3: The intensive care unit monitor: Excerpt.

(Figure 5.4 shows an entire ICU Trellis, for concreteness; the details aren't important. The program continues to evolve, by the way, and the Trellis in figure 5.4 is already not quite current.) At the bottom level, elements gather data from monitoring equipment at the patient's bedside. The element labelled *Raw Bp*, for example, receives blood pressure values. At higher rungs, elements like *BP* (blood pressure) calculate "symbolic values" for the blood pressure (e.g., "high" vs. a number); and they detect trends in the values they're following. At the next-higher rung, for example the level containing the *SVR* (systemic vascular resistance) element, small collections of lower-level values start getting correlated and integrated. Further up, for example on the rung where *Vasoconstriction* occurs, elements start looking for various "clinical scenes" that signal the presence of complete diagnoses—for example *Tamponade*, on the top level. (The "clinical scenes" idea was introduced by Dr. Aaron Cohen, then at the Yale Medical Informatics Program.)

Other Trellis problems we've looked at in some detail (with collaborators from the appropriate areas) include weather monitoring, the management of computer networks and the detection of insider trading on stock markets. All this is aside from the Trellis's central role in Mirror Worlds, which I'll take up in a couple of chapters.

There's more to it, of course...

§ Probes and Multi-Trellises

We need to get information into and out of a Trellis program. We do so by means of "probes." A probe is a conduit for data. Using a probe, you can pump data into or out of any element in the Trellis. You connect one end of the probe to a data source or receiver, and touch the other end to a Trellis element. (Sparks fly...)

A probe has two buttons, *read* and *write*. If you hit *read*, the current value of the element you're touching jumps out of the Trellis into your data-receptacle. If you hit *write*, motion is reversed: a new value flows over the probe into the Trellis, resetting some element's current value.

Probes represent the (only) connection between the outside world and the Trellis. Each bottom-rung Trellis element is wired, via probe,

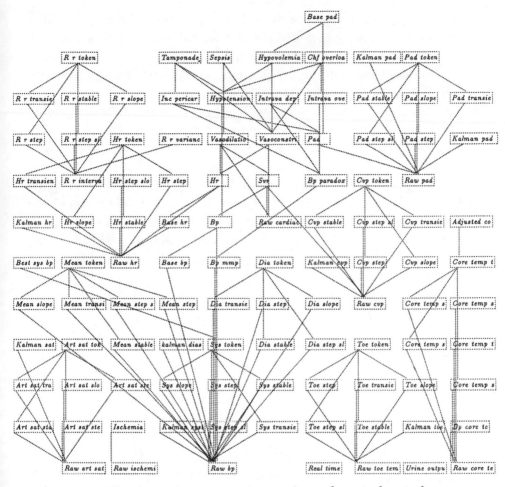

Figure 5.4: The intensive care unit monitor: forget about the details...

to the appropriate sensor or data terminal. ("Wired" metaphorically. Probes are realized by software, not actual wires. But a software probe behaves in essence just like a hardware wire.)

Probes are also useful for stringing lots of Trellises together into a multi-Trellis ensemble.

There are several reasons to build such an ensemble. For one, you might want to attach custom-built "personal" Trellises to the main public one. You have your own way of analyzing data, and you'd like to feed your data-analysis approach off a public Trellis. You may want to tap into the public Trellis at many levels. Some of your routines may need raw data; others may build on top of the partially-analyzed data that emerges from mid-level elements; others may superimpose new, super-general levels above the topmost rung of the public Trellis. You can use probes to tap into the public Trellis at any point you like.

There are other reasons to build multi-Trellis ensembles, having to do with *frequency*.

§ **Frequency**

A Trellis, it turns out, is a lot like a crystal (or at any rate, it's more like a crystal than some other software structures are...). When you turn it on, it vibrates at a certain frequency.

Meaning? In concept, each Trellis element is an infomachine. All these infomachines run separately and simultaneously.

In practice, we do things somewhat differently. We create a group of "worker" infomachines, just like the workers we described in the last chapter. We parcel out Trellis elements to these workers. Each worker is responsible for embodying the Trellis elements it's been handed. Thus the amount of parallelism in our ensemble—the number of things that are *actually* going on at once—is decided not by the size of the Trellis, but by the number of workers. If we have a thousand-element Trellis and a hundred workers, each worker will probably be handed around ten Trellis elements. When we turn the whole thing on, we get one hundred activities going on at once.

Workers collaborate to make the whole thing work *predictably*. Predictability is crucial: We must be able to guarantee that the Trellis fully digests each data value before the next value shows up. This is what our "realtime" requirement is all about. We need to be able to make assertions like "given this Trellis and those data streams, you need at least eighteen workers to meet your requirement." As before, our ensemble won't care how may workers it's running with on any particular run. If it's too slow with seventeen workers, we add an eighteenth, and the thing runs faster. Nothing else changes.

But: How will we make this kind of assertion? How can we tell exactly how many workers we need?

Imagine that each Trellis element generates a kind of stock-ticker. Whenever a Trellis element gets pinged by a new upward-flowing value, it performs its standard computation and then prints a new number on its ticker. The new number reflects this element's current, up-to-the-minute view of the world. It might be the same as the previous number on the ticker—the state of things might not be changing—but whatever it is, it's up to date.

Suppose we feed a single value to each bottom-rung element. In response, they each print a new number on their tickers. Reacting to the new data represented by these new numbers, elements in the next rung up print new numbers, and so on upwards through the whole structure.

Now: We run the Trellis in a series of sweeps. During the first sweep, each machine gets a chance to print one number on its ticker. During the second, each prints a second number, and so on. No machine prints a second number until every tape has a *first* number recorded.

To achieve this kind of behavior, we instruct each worker to run through its list of Trellis elements, sticking with each one *just* long enough to produce a single ticker entry. Each worker (in other words) is responsible for a bunch of tickers: It advances *each* of its tickers by one number. When it's done, it waits until all the rest have finished. Then, all workers proceed together into the next sweep.

Hence, the "frequency" of a Trellis. Given a Trellis and a squadron of workers, we can figure out how long (at worst) it will take the slowest worker to advance all of its tickers. This is exactly the amount of time that the squadron *as a whole* will require to execute a sweep (when the slowest guy is finished, all the rest will also be done). The frequency of a Trellis equals the number of sweeps per second. In a "fast" Trellis, sweeps are short; the frequency is high; the tickers spew out numbers quickly. In a slow Trellis, the opposite.

So what? This scheme allows us to figure out how many workers we need in order to meet our realtime requirements. To restate these requirements with our sweep model in mind: A Trellis must be at least as fast as its fastest data source. "Fast" means *frequency*. So long as a Trellis beats faster than its fastest data source, we're guaranteed that each new value will be fully digested when the next arrives. We can say exactly *what the frequency is* for a given Trellis and a given number of workers; we use a mathematical model to figure this out. If the frequency is too low, we add workers and check again.

So, a Trellis has a frequency. And one reason to build multi-Trellis ensembles is to accommodate some fast Trellises and some slow ones. There may be a handful of ultra-fast data streams, and many slower ones. Instead of running the whole Trellis fast, it might be better to *uncouple*. We build a high-frequency Trellis for the ultra-fast streams, and a "regular" Trellis for the rest. Top-level machines in the fast Trellis might pump data straight into the bottom of the slow Trellis: We string probes from the top of one to the bottom of the other. (Nowadays the ICU Trellis is built this way, as it happens.)

§ Dashboards

Any running Trellis has a natural companion picture, showing the elements and the way they're arranged. We can treat this picture as the Trellis's dashboard. Each element uses its own part of the picture as a display case for its current value.

Designing this dashboard is a research problem in its own right. Any decent-sized Trellis program is apt to know too much for its own good. This is certainly true of our intensive care unit prototype— which is pint-sized, when you consider the possibilities (as I'll do below). A Trellis must be able to draw your attention to what's *important*, to what may need *immediate* attention. If it buries you under all the verbose details, it's a failure, no matter how smart it may be in the abstract.

The current Trellis dashboard looks like a receding plane. Every Trellis element has a corresponding tile or paving stone. When the condition tracked by some element is normal or uninteresting, its tile

Figure 5.5: The Trellis dashboard: current model. The display is still evolving. The original is in color (of course); flat-lying tiles are blue. They turn yellow-orange-red as they tip upright.

lies flat. If conditions start looking noteworthy, the tile tips upward toward the viewer, turning more-alarming colors as it goes. (This display was built by Craig Kolb, who is a research programmer in the Yale Math Department.)

Implications

No decent research project stops short at any pre-conceived boundaries. The Trellis (like the tuple space) has implications beyond its original charter. I'll consider three below. In the course of doing so, I'll arrive at an alternate, arguably simpler, description of this architecture's basic mission.

Nerves

Data goes up, anti-data comes down. "Anti-data," we've said, means "inquiries." But it might also mean *commands*.

In other words, we might imagine a Trellis that is wired at the bottom (using ordinary probes) to sensors and *also* to actuators. Data flow upward from the sensors, seeking the first rung where the elements know how to react—how to change things in the real world in response to this data. Instructions flow downward to the actuators: either directly or (in some cases) through a descending series of elements that decide which actuator should receive this command, or how exactly a command should be carried out.

This kind of Trellis might monitor but also *control* a complex external system. It might reprogram traffic lights and dispatch emergency vehicles, retarget, zero or recalibrate experimental equipment, fine-tune the steering or engine or support services on a boat or a plane—

It's natural to envision Trellises in which simple data are handled quickly by low-level elements. Complex or ambiguous reports move higher. They need more processing and refinement and topsight-extraction before they can be translated into action. And after all, adjustments that need to be made fast and continuously aren't the sort that require careful analysis (we hope). Large, strategic adjustments—of which high-level Trellis elements would take charge—don't crop up as often, and don't usually need to be accomplished instantaneously.

§ The New Look

One way to describe a Trellis, I mentioned, was in terms of signals "being transmitted to higher centers for more elaborate analysis of their information content and for combination with signals from other types of receptors." The quotation comes from a book called *Medical Physiology*; it describes the human nervous system: "The spinal circuits involve very little delay and ensure rapid responses when speed is essential... While this immediate response is occurring, the same signals are being transmitted to higher centers..."[9] The sensor-actuator Trellis and the human sensory-motor system revolve around similar kinds of hierarchies: immediate "low-level," local responses at the bottom; more elaborate, global responses at higher levels.

Now, the Trellis starts looking a bit like the nervous system. In a Trellis-style "nervous system," a dense lattice-work stretches downward from the "brain centers" to the outside world beneath. Signals snap up and down in the lower regions in response to the normal ebb and flow of events. The odd unusual signal climbs higher; dramatic changes outside send floods of signals flowing upward and new commands pouring down.

We now understand the Trellis's mission is simpler terms: to *complete* a factory, traffic network or power plant by equipping it with a synthetic nervous system. To take a dumb lumbering pile of stuff and add the crucial ingredient that turns the whole thing into a functioning *organism*, "alive" metaphorically in the sense of being *able to cope*; able to *react* and not merely *be adjusted*; able to respond to the changing shape of the outside world. Or: to supply the recovering patient (who already has a nervous system) with another, supplemental one, one that "understands" instead of merely experiencing his disease.

§ Found Robots

We're accustomed (*getting* accustomed, anyway) to thinking of robots as self-contained humanoids, filling in for humans in tedious or physically-demanding jobs. Robots weld, paint, fetch computer tapes, explore contaminated areas and so forth. This intuitive feel for the subject is echoed in the research community, where robotics is a field that focuses on movement, simulated vision and the manipulation of physical objects.

On the other hand: Why can't the building you work in be a robot? Or the car you drive? One way to understand what we're actually *doing* when we install sensor-actuator Trellises in factories and so on is "turning this thing into a robot." The intent is to transplant not the physical aspect of humans or animals but an abstract version of the nervous system and, in some primitive low-level sense, the brain.

This is a matter of perspective as much as (or more than) of software technology. Cars have lots of electronic control circuits already, and they will get a lot more; but the circuits aren't integrated. They don't come together into a single electronic version of the whole car. If your car is a *robot*, on the other hand, it ought to know how to do things as a unit, and we should be able to interact and "converse" with it *as an integrated whole*. Consider the office building-as-robot. It's got sensors and data feeds of all sorts powering a fairly simple Trellis. The building fine-tunes its own heating and air conditioning system, as all reasonably bright buildings already do today. It watches current stockpiles (and maybe the price of oil), and orders more as needed. It knows who is where: If you need to move people around, you ask the building. "These three guys need to move from this group to that group. Suggest a plan." "I need to put four computers in there instead of three. Network implications?" If you want to know who is in what office, what's going on in the fourth-floor seminar room at the moment, which computers are up—you ask the building. There are no fancy software tricks here. There is merely a simple idea: A "robot building" can be put in charge of tracking its own status *as a whole*.

Factories could be robots; so could powerplants, airplanes, subway systems... A "found robot" is aware of its current status (from the details up through the big picture) and capable of reacting to it. Any set of physical machines, plus a synthetic nervous system—a Trellis that touches them all—equals a found robot. And these found robots could be just as significant in the long term as the "humanoid" ones.

§ **By way of comparison...**

Some readers might be thinking "Ah ha, we are now talking about *neural networks*." Nope, sorry. The Trellis has nothing to do with this particular hot research topic. Neural network research generally focuses on exquisitely abstract simulations of the brain proper, not of the brain-to-nerves-to-muscle hierarchy.

But the sensor-actuator Trellis does broadly resemble another research project. One of the most fascinating of all ongoing artificial intelligence projects is being carried out by Rodney Brooks at (of all places) MIT. He and his group have built a collection of "insect robots" that are capable of getting around a room—avoiding walls, clambering over obstacles—in surprisingly realistic, insect-like fashion. They've done it by abandoning the quest for simulated cognition that some "traditional" robots pursue. Instead of attempting to think things over, these robots wing it using simple, seat-of-the-pants reactions to the conditions they encounter. Thus the goal is, in a sense, to simulate *instinct* instead of cognition. Simulating cognition is tough, because who the hell knows what cognition is anyway? Simulating instinct is easier, and turns out to be surprisingly rewarding. You can go a long way on instinct.

The bottom levels of the sensor-actuator Trellis resemble these "instinct simulators" in a sense. (Higher-rung elements attempt to ferret out the big picture, as always.)

Turingware

I introduced software-human mixed marriage ensembles in the last chapter. Here it makes sense to push things a step further—to explore these collaborations in a formal context, and see where we get.

Specifically: It's easy to imagine a Trellis that includes human elements alongside the software ones.

The great mathematician Alan Turing devised what is now called the "Turing test"; Turing declared himself willing to concede intelligence to any machine that passed. Basically, the test hinges on posing a series of written questions to a hidden human and a hidden computer. If a human observer is unable to figure out which answers come from the human and which from the computer, the computer passes. (Or the human fails?)

In our group, we've used the term "Turingware" to designate mixed marriage ensembles; particularly, ones in which ensemble members don't know or care whether the other members they deal with are software or human.

The Trellis architecture is a good example of where and why this might be useful.

In a sensor-actuator Trellis, lower rungs act "instinctively." Higher levels look for the big picture; but in some areas, people are rather better at this than software. In these areas, we could use *people* to realize some of the higher-rung elements. Every element (whether software or human) has the same assignment: to respond to information from below, and to queries or instructions from above. Software-generated and human-generated information is passed to each element over the same channels, in the same envelopes. Human "elements" receive data from inferior elements, inquiries or instructions from superiors, in the usual way. They respond to read or write probes. Their inferiors (or superiors, I suppose) might be human *or software*—but who cares which? (Unless you want to get touchy about this thing. A touchy element has blown its cover, in any case. It is pretty likely to be human.)

Thus you might imagine a submarine, for example, being operated by a piece of Turingware, a mixed human-software Trellis. The routine fine-tuning necessary to keep the thing on course and the machinery running efficiently might be purely a low-level software matter. If a machine starts to malfunction, higher-level software elements might look the problem over. They might issue actuator-commands themselves, or they might pass their problem diagnoses upward for integration with other information sources. At some level of the hierarchy, human elements start to intermingle with software ones. For example, software elements might mull things over and decide that it would be a good idea to fire a torpedo; other software elements might carry out the actual firing. But the Trellis element that makes the "fire torpedo" decision itself should probably be a person.

§ Concretely

What does this mean in concrete terms? When a human is acting as a Trellis element, a computer terminal will be his window to

Figure 5.6: A Turingware Trellis: software and humans intermingle.

the rest of the ensemble. Data will percolate up from below in the form of messages on his screen: *Engine room reports that X pressure is trending above 4000 Y's. Response?* If this human "element" changes his own viewpoint as a consequence, he types a response, and the response is forwarded automatically to higher-ups. Questions or instructions flow downward in the same way. This particular element doesn't know or care whether the engine room report he just saw was human- or software-generated. Nor does he care what kind of elements see *his* reports. If his response takes the form of an ordinary English sentence, it may (of course) be hard for a software element to understand it. But if he responds in a stylized way (filling in a template displayed on his screen, for example), people *or* software might be equally capable of accepting and dealing with the new datum.

(Once you've added human elements, frequency is out the door. Mixed-mode Trellises don't hum: We can't guarantee that humans will perform within strictly predictable limits. But we can always build a multi-Trellis. A fast, predictable, low-level software-only Trellis might be patched into a higher-level mixed ensemble.)

What have we gained? People and software are now working together to impersonate an ideal model of the machine's nervous system. Their hierarchy—lines of communication, chains of command—precisely reflect the problem they are trying to solve. We have neatly dissected-out those sub-problems software can manage, and handed them to software. (One of these sub-problems is providing the common framework into which every element plugs.)

The mixed Trellis makes an opaque system transparent. In static terms: You can see at a glance how responsibilities are divided and where decisions are made. In dynamic terms: By glancing at the dashboard, you determine the current status of every element.

A transparent system is open to outsiders. (At any rate, to outsiders who know where to look.) If a technical expert needs to diagnose a submarine problem from a thousand miles away, he can look at the dashboard and tap into a detailed information-stream by affixing probes. In fact he can *become* an element of the Trellis temporarily, if need be. Likewise, an admiral or random bigshot who is monitoring and coordinating operations can watch the Trellis diagram, attach probes as he likes, incorporate himself into the structure if need be. For that matter, he can use probes to tie all of his Trellises together, and display a multi-Trellis dashboard that captures the state of the entire fleet. Relaxing with a drink on the official Admiralty Sofa, he can watch the large-screen computer display on the other side of his room and, with remote-control laser-mouse in hand, inspect his entire operation from highest pinnacle of rarefied topsight down to the nitty-grittiest detail.

Forget about submarines: The point is, of course, a general one. Complex operations are controlled by complex logic. Some of this logic is automated in software and some will remain, for the foreseeable future, in human hands. But we can knit the whole thing into a harmonious whole anyway.

§ In Sum:

The Japanese revolutionized car production by embedding workers, factories, suppliers, truckers, dealers in a tightly run ensemble where everything shows up just when you need it.[10] Nothing (not supplies, not information, not advice) collects in stagnant pools. Everything *flows*. Customers are coupled to dealers, dealers to factories, factories to suppliers... The Turingware Trellis is something similar but much more "intimate"—people and software can work far more closely, after all, than people and stamping presses. The Trellis allows us to restructure a piece of sprawling random chaos into a tight-knit crystalline whole, where the parts aren't rigidly tied together but are *coupled* and in synch. A whole corporation might in fact be structured this way (it would be an interesting experiment...).

True Bigness

Bigness is fascinating, where ensembles are concerned. How big could a mega-Trellis get? How far can we push these structures before they run out of conceptual steam? How many elements might you (could you *ever* realistically) want to tie together in this way?

When you're tying separate Trellises together with probes, there seems to be no practical limit. The whole-fleet multi-Trellis is immense. And suppose it's merely one element of the whole-armed-forces multi-mega-Trellis, and so on—

It's interesting to ask, too, how large an *individual* Trellis might grow.

The answer: pretty large. If you're monitoring a traffic network, weather or a complex experimental set-up you might easily want tens of thousands of elements; very possibly more. They won't all be distinct in design, of course. You might replicate the same basic, low-level structure thousands of times if you're monitoring (say) thousands of separate regions in a transport Trellis. But the net result is still many thousands of elements. Will it all hang together? Will it be possible to operate such a huge ensemble? Our largest prototype is a drop in the bucket next to these huge structures. But the evidence suggests that we *can* build mega-Trellises. We've built and operated a "synthetic' Trellis of more than twenty thousand elements. *Synthetic* insofar as it didn't do anything. It was an empty shell—a mere framework; while the program executed, the individual Trellis elements sat around twiddling their thumbs or napping as the spirit moved. But the experiments are suggestive. (A conclusive demonstration awaits experience with a *real* mega-Trellis.)

Mega-Trellis contemplation turns the discussion back to an earlier topic. We mentioned that, in a certain sense, a Trellis can run either forward or backwards, or both at the same time.

If we walk up to some Trellis and rip out all its information feeds, we can still ask it questions—"Is the patient developing congestive heart failure? Does all traffic need to be rerouted off the XYZ Bridge? Shall we mobilize the eighty-second Airborne?" One possible response is "don't ask me, Bozo," but in fact, even a disconnected Trellis can do better than that. It can take your query and disassemble it into primitive components, by merely sending inquiries downward in the usual way. The congestive heart failure element sees that it has no data and passes a query to the relevant inferiors. They pass it downwards in turn. Eventually the system can respond: *You want information about the following high-level condition? Then you must provide the following low-level data values.* If the user complies, the new data courses upward through the system and the high-level question eventually gets answered.

Here the system ran backwards, in a sense. Action was triggered by the arrival of a high-level inquiry, not a low-level datum. The query took root and branched downwards, seeking information. In computer science terminology, the Trellis became "demand-driven" instead of "data-driven."

Now, plug everything back in. A mega-Trellis is particularly likely to run forwards and backwards at the same time (although any Trellis is capable of this trick in principle).

A big Trellis is especially apt to have out-of-the-way, high-lying elements that rarely see enough data to jolt them into action one way or another. Such elements are designed to keep track of the esoteric, the peripheral or the bizarre. A driving force behind the whole mega-Trellis effort is the urge to *burn up* computing power, to throw it in bulk against hard problems. In the near future, after all, we will wish to be as enterprising with computers as a frugal fifties housewife with Ritz Crackers. These dandy little items are cheap, so why not use *lots*? If some Trellis element fires off every five months (or every five decades), but it tells us something interesting when it does, that's fine. If it spends ninety-nine point nine nine nine percent of its time doing *nothing*, who cares? Give it a raise.

So: *While* data pour into the mega-Trellis and course upward through the main shopping districts, users might walk up to the dashboard and lodge high-level queries about unusual or highly-specialized topics. These questions trigger a data-seeking downwards cascade. The same Trellis is running forwards and backwards simultaneously.

In Sum

Are we engineering knowledge plants here, or nervous systems? In either case, it looks promising.

Chapter 6

Simple Mind Machines

We plunge now into the deepest, trickiest, most treacherous and remarkable undersea cavern in the whole coral reef, the question of simulated experience. When we get to the bottom we will be face to face with the fundamental question of artificial intelligence (henceforth AI). We won't know how to solve it, but we will be shining a flashlight in its face. *What does it mean to think?* How does thinking *work*?

Not "how does the brain work," but what does the thinking process consist of, in logical terms? We don't need to understand lungs to realize that respiration has something to do with grabbing air, letting it soak in somehow and then pushing it out. Thinking is (one suspects) just as basic a physiological process as breathing; how does it work? Presumably it's not mere random helter skelter scurrying about. There is some system at work, some *process*, presumably. Even when you are not hard at work solving a math problem, planning a strategy or wracking your brain for the name of someone's daughter, there is something ticking over in there, as steadily (maybe even as rhythmically) as breathing. What is this process?

As usual, we have a particular, concrete problem and a software solution in mind. The problem is crucial to Mirror Worlds: How do we make the *experience* key work? In answering we will (again) be addressing a major problem in the non-Mirror World as well. In the last chapter, I discussed the extraction of information from fast-flowing data streams at the source. We turn now to oceans of data that have accumulated in databases. What can we do with *this* stuff?

All those multi-billions of records on file? *Here*, the focus is different. You don't worry so much about extracting information fast, as the data values fly by. You focus instead on the problem of *comparing* many stored incidents or situations.

In pursuing this concrete problem, I'll keep the deep questions and long-term implications at bay, for the most part—but they do have a tendency to wind their tendrils around the subject matter in this chapter. I will be describing a "simulated mind" designed for a well-defined, utilitarian purpose. But the simulated mind is inhabited by two simple machines, two raucous little yippers that *do* have a tendency to run away with things...

Our simulated mind is a very simple affair. It relates to a real mind the way a child's puppet theater relates to a real theater, only a lot less so; it's a far coarser approximation. Its only purpose is to allow "past experience" to shed light on the present, in the limited Mirror World sense: "Past experience" is the enormous historical Mirror World archive, and we want to *use* those archives to shed light on what is happening right now.

But—in tackling this assignment, we will build two little machines that seem to have bigger ambitions.

The Goal: Finding Precedents

We want to describe a "new case" to the program. The program should respond by *commenting about the new case* and by *citing relevant precedents*. In a Mirror World, a "new case" will be a list of features describing whatever *current situation* the user cares about. A committee in mid-deliberation (who's present, what's being argued, when and where it is all taking place, the political context); a hospital patient; a business plan; some particular state that a complex machine has gotten itself into, and so on. Outside the Mirror World, the new case is anything you care about. For example, you're a doctor making decisions about a patient. You describe the patient; you get *comments* and *precedents* in response.

What Precedents? What Comments?

You want to hear about earlier cases that are *relevant* to the new one. Lots of implications are packed into this spring-loaded word.

The database might be enormous. There might be millions of cases in there. The program must dig out a small handful that shed light on the new case—that relate to it in a substantial way. An earlier case might be relevant although it resembles the current case only a little—but the *significance* of that resemblance is large.

What about comments? In making comments, the system's main job is to *fill in the blanks* in two ways, with *conclusions* and with *speculative guesses*. You know certain things about the new case, but you don't know the whole story. You can describe a patient, but you don't know what the diagnosis is. You can describe the committee hearing, but you don't know what the final vote will be. The program will attempt to answer this key question.

But the system's attention isn't *restricted* to the key question. It may conclude or guess the value of *any one* of the new case's unknown attributes. In describing a new case, there is information you don't know (tests that haven't been done, results that are unclear); there's also information you simply haven't mentioned yet (or forgot to mention, or didn't intend to mention, because you didn't realize it was important). The program might attempt to fill in *any* of those blanks as you go along, describing the case.

This activity is crucial in digging up relevant precedents. The system will be lowering the new case as bait (so to speak) into a memory pool, attempting to lure the right cases out of the database. The juicier the bait, the more likely that the right precedents will be attracted. And obviously, by filling in the blanks, the software is also attempting to shed light on this new case *directly*, by telling you something about it irrespective of specific precedents.

(Wait a minute though, what is this *speculation* stuff? The program will fill in blanks by making "*speculative guesses*?" You want a program to *speculate*? Maybe you'd also like it to philosophize, reminisce, do a little tap dance and then have a nervous breakdown into the bargain? Speculation is *not* the sort of activity in which we ordinarily expect software to indulge. We want software to *figure out the answer* and *tell us what it is*, not take off on contemplative excursions.

Usually...)

For Example—

This is a *non*-Mirror World example of our software. The Mirror World as an integrated whole doesn't exist yet. Again, we are looking at a key software component in isolation, doing its stuff and attempting to be useful *on it own*, as if Mirror Worlds didn't exist. Which they don't, yet.

Consider a special kind of conversation with a computer. You're a clinician of some kind, and you're describing an x-ray image. For now you're describing it via keyboard, but we are working on a voice-recognition interface that will allow you to talk into a microphone or a telephone. (This is important so far as radiology is concerned, because radiologists it turns out don't like to write, and they certainly don't like to type; they like to talk, *over the telephone* if you don't mind, to their secretaries. None of this face-to-face stuff.)

You use standard, ordinary medical lingo to describe what you see. Currently, the language you use is sharply constrained by the fact that you're talking to a computer—like talking to a person who just barely understands English. You have to go slowly and choose your words carefully; you would never mistake the resulting interchange for ordinary conversation. Yet information *is* exchanged; at any rate, the software is getting better at this sort of thing.

You tell the program "The patient's age is 42. The mass density is high." (You're describing a breast x-ray, trying to determine whether the image you see is a benign or a malignant mass, and what the diagnosis is.) "The mass border is not complete." The program interrupts: "Speculating about whether the mass density has changed—I'll guess it has increased; like, for example, case 14 (a 46-year-old patient; the diagnosis was infiltrating ductal carcinoma), or case 20 (a 60-year-old; diagnosis was the same). Now, speculating about whether there is a comet—I'll guess yes."

These are not random interruptions and speculations. They indicate that this case has gotten off to a disturbing start. The high density of the mass and the incomplete mass border are not good. The system's speculations suggest that it's wandering towards a negative conclusion: This mass is probably malignant. It won't say so yet—that would be premature. But these speculations about increased density and the presence of a comet suggest malignancy.

You continue. "The mass border is lobulated. The border *is* defined..." The system puts in "I'm concluding at this point that there are no large calcifications, and no nipple inversion." Tending to suggest that, if the mass *is* malignant, the disease may not be far advanced.

"The mass density has not changed," you continue: a piece of historical data, which makes the situation look better. Maybe the mass is benign after all. The system says nothing. But then you zig back in the other direction. "There is no mass halo." "No? That's surprising," says the program. "But... consider cases 14 or 40. Both cases of infiltrating ductal carcinoma."

Things had started to look better. But then "no halo"—and this is interpreted as a bad sign. The program hasn't seen many cases with features generally like this one, *and also* no halo. It's a surprising and worrying development. There are a few instances with this combination of feature; the two it mentions are both malignant cases.

You add some more data; the system comments. Then you're done, and it's up to the program to guess: What's the diagnosis?

It presents a list of relevant precedents. It's a mixed and somewhat confusing list. Cases with malignant diagnoses occur, but this case strongly resembles some benign cases as well. The system takes a stab at a diagnosis. "Fibroadenoma?" A *benign* lesion. But then, thinking it over... The personal history of cancer that exists in this case is disturbing, in light of all the other ambiguous signs. It withdraws its guess. The bottom line: "I can't say what the diagnosis is..."

Right! The correct diagnosis was "plasmacytoma"—a rare lesion that the system has *never seen before.* No way to guess this correctly. The program does exactly the right thing, and passes.

But we don't leave things there. It now speculates: "I don't know the diagnosis, but what's the bottom line? Is this mass likely to be malignant or not?" It guesses *malignant.* This was a complex and confusing case, but the system has (unfortunately) drawn the right conclusion.

The program I'm discussing was built by Scott Fertig, a researcher in our group at Yale. He's had significant help from several people, notably Dr. Paul Fisher, a Yale radiologist.

§ Nice trick, but so what?

Fine, you say, very nice. Of course, we've seen programs do tricks like this before.

But the point is that this program *knows nothing.* *No information* about diagnosing x-rays *whatsoever* was ever handed to this program. What it's got to work with is a database, period; in fact, a pathetically small one in this instance, so small it barely qualifies as a database at all. This program was handed the description of around seventy x-rays, with their diagnoses. That's all. On the basis of these seventy cases, it ad libbed a reaction to a new case that wasn't flawless but was damned good, and clinically on the mark.

It *is* possible to turn "memories" into expertise. The process is fairly simple, but subtle.

The Raw Material

First I have to spell out more precisely what "cases" and the "database" are like.

We describe a "new case" to the program. It comments about the new case—muses, prognosticates, fills in the blanks, *directs our attention to a small number of relevant precedents*, chosen from among a vast intractable pile of cases-on-file—and it does all this *strictly* by comparing the "new case" to the cases in this database. The *new case* and the *cases in the database* are, structurally, exactly the same. They are *lists of features.* A *feature* is an *attribute* ("hair") plus a *value* ("blond"). A value may be more than one thing: attribute "pets," value "fido, ernestina, spot." In the sort of interaction I just

Figure 6.1: (Right.) The transcript, as produced by the program (excerpts). Data from the user appear in the left column, the program's comments on the right.

```
(ID 30)
(AGE 42)
(MASS_DENSITY HIGH)
(MASS_BORDER_COMPLETE? NO)
```

> *Speculating: MASS_DENSITY_CHANGED?...*
> *Guessing INCREASED - e.g.*
> *case ((id 14) (age 46) (diagnosis CA_INF_DUCTAL))*
> *case ((id 20) (age 60) (diagnosis CA_INF_DUCTAL))*
> *case ((id 50) (age 70) (diagnosis CA_INF_DUCTAL))*
>
> *Speculating: MASS_COMET?...*
> *Guessing YES - e.g.*
> *case 14*
> *case ((id 40) (age 69) (diagnosis CA_INF_DUCTAL))*

```
(MASS_TYPE_BORDER LOBULATED)
(MASS_BORDER_DEFINED? YES)
```

> *Concluding*
> *(LARGE_CALCIFICATIONS? NO)*
> *(NIPPLE_INVERSION? NO)*

```
(MASS_DENSITY_CHANGED? NO)
(MASS_HALO? NO)
```

> *NO is unusual in this context - see e.g.*
> *case 14*
> *case 40*

```
(BACKGROUND_DENSITY FATTY)
...
(FAMILY_HISTORY_CA NO)
(PERSONAL_HISTORY_CA MYELOMA)
```

> *!! Never seen this value before.*
>
> *Closest cases in DB:*
> *(4) (NO) (FIBROADENOMA)*
> *(6) (YES) (CA_COLLOID)*
> *...*
> *Speculating: DIAGNOSIS...*
> *Guessing FIBROADENOMA*
> *Checking expectations...*
> *...*
> *Withdrawing this guess.*
>
> *Speculating: MALIGNANT?...*
> *Guessing YES*
> *Checking expectations...*
> *...*
> *Accepting this guess.*

presented, the user describing an x-ray to the system, the user is
building up a new case feature-by-feature. At first, the new case has
only one feature; the system muses about that. Then the user tacks
on a second feature, and the program muses about this two-feature
case; then he tacks on another, and so on. Each time the case grows,
the system thinks it over.

(Here and throughout, if I say that the program is *musing* or
thinking or whatever, I'm obviously using these terms metaphorically.
My goal is to get the basic idea across with minimum fuss. I am not
suggesting that by *seeming* to think, the computer actually *is*, in the
human sense of the word. Some AI researchers are sensitive about
this point. They will go to any lengths to avoid this kind of usage, on
the theory that the typical reader is extremely gullible and to boot
rather dim. Such meticulous sensitivity is touching but absurd.)

So, in referring to "the new case," I mean the growing list of
features that a user presents to the system. In a Mirror World,
a "new case" will be a list of features describing whatever *current
situation* the user cares about. A committee in mid-deliberation
(who's present, what's being argued, when and where it is all taking
place, the political context); a hospital patient; a business plan; some
particular state of the machinery, and so on.

Sometimes it will be useful to refer to the database as the "memory pool," for obvious reasons. The cases in the database are a
software version, a *simulation,* of the *memories* of *particular cases
or experiences* that are stored inside a human expert's head. And
if a database sometimes acts (or tries to) like a memory pool, then
retrieving something from the database will often masquerade as *remembering.*

...And Its Implications

I will be turning repeatedly to the yawning gulf between some piece
of a *simulated* mind and the real thing. But this is no mere exercise in
computational humility, be assured. Perish the thought. The goal is
to establish not merely how far we have to go, but in which direction
we ought to be setting out.

First I need to establish (and believe me it will be no sweat to do
so) that our raw material, our "simulated memories," are lousy, third-

rate imitations of the real thing. Soon our little fleet of software tools for the manipulation of simulated memories—a dump-truck and a bull-dozer (let's say)—will emerge from their garages and go through their paces. The next question, the *real question*, will be: Okay, these tools are *useful*, but what are the implications?

The *implications* all ride on the fact that the tools are demonstrably *useful* when they have lousy material to work with. But suppose they had *good* material?

They *might* be amazingly powerful.

But what *is* good material? What's wrong with what we've got?

§ **Real vs. simulated memories**

The cases in the database are *simulations* of the *memories* of *particular cases or experiences* that are stored inside a human expert's head. Weak and feeble simulations: When an expert remembers a patient, he doesn't remember a mere list of words. He remembers an *experience*, a whole galaxy of related perceptions. No doubt he remembers *certain* words—perhaps a name, a diagnosis, maybe some others. But he also remembers what the patient looked like, sounded like; how the encounter made him *feel* (confident, confused?)... Clearly these unrecorded perceptions have tremendous information content. People can *revisit* their experiences, examine their stored perceptions in retrospect. In reducing a "memory" to mere words, and a quick-march parade step of *attribute, value, attribute, value* at that, we are giving up a great deal. We are reducing a vast mountaintop panorama to a grainy little black-and-white photograph.

There is, too, a huge distance between simulated *remembering*—pulling cases out of the database—and the real thing. To a human being, an *experience* means a set of coherent sensations, which are wrapped up and sent back to the storeroom for later recollection. Remembering is the reverse: A set of coherent sensations is trundled out of storage and replayed—those archived sensations are re-experienced. The experience is less vivid on tape (so to speak) than it was in person, and portions of the original may be smudged or completely missing, but nonetheless—the Rememberer gets, in essence, another dose of the original experience. For human beings, in other words, remembering isn't merely *retrieving*, it is *re-experiencing*.

And this fact is important, because it obviously impinges (probably in a large way) on how people *do* their remembering. Why do you "choose" to recall something? Well for one thing, certain memories *make you feel good.* The original experience included a "feeling good" sensation, and so the tape has "feel good" recorded on it, and when you recall the memory—you feel good. And likewise, one reason you choose (or unconsciously decide) *not* to recall certain memories is that they have "feel bad" recorded on them, and so remembering them makes you feel bad. (If you don't believe me check with Freud, who based the better part of a profoundly significant career on this observation, more or less.) It's obvious that the emotions recorded in a memory have at least *something* to do with steering your solitary rambles through Memory Woods.

§ Software: Fundamental Limits?

But obviously, the software version of remembering has no emotional compass. To some extent, that's good: Software won't suppress, repress or forget some illuminating case because (say) it made a complete fool of itself when the case was first presented. Objectivity is powerful.

On the other hand, we are brushing up here against a limitation that has a distinctly *fundamental* look. We want our Mirror Worlds to "remember" intelligently—to draw just the *right* precedent or two from a huge database. But *human beings* draw on reason *and* emotion when they perform an act of remembering. An emotion can be a concise, nuanced shorthand for a whole tangle of facts and perceptions that you never bothered to sort out. How did you feel on your first day at work or school, your child's second birthday, last year's first snowfall? Later you might remember that scene; you might be reminded merely by the fact that you now *feel* the same as you did then. *Why* do you feel the same? If you think carefully, perhaps you can trace down the objective similarities between the two experiences. But their *emotional* resemblance was your original clue. And it's quite plausible that "expertise" works this way also, at least occasionally: I'm reminded of a past case not because of any objective similarity, but rather because I now *feel* the same as I did then.

I'll return to this hugely important issue: Mind-stuff consists of *rational* and *emotional* strands *densely interwoven.* Your intellectual faculties depend on your emotions and not merely your "reason." And these are issues that AI rarely confronts. Understandably.

But we'll naturally be drawn to ask: Stored cases can *evolve towards* real experiences, can't they? Stored images and stored sounds might ultimately be integrated into a far more vivid and complete simulation of a "memory" that our mere lists of words. And emotional processes might be simulated, too, at least in principle. But it all sounds like a lot of work, and raises hard, unanswered questions. Is this a reasonable research direction?

The answer will emerge loud and clear: *Yes.*

Now, back to reality...

So what about "speculation"?

We'd like to squeeze knowledge out of our database: comments; relevant citations. Standard statistical techniques can be very helpful in doing so. But they run out of gas before we have arrived at our destination.

Let's say you have lots of cases in a database. Now a new case comes along, and I say "classify it." The stored cases are all tagged with some kind of classification label; you're trying to attach such a label to the new case. Each case and its label can be anything you want, more or less. The case might describe a patient and the label is the diagnosis. In a classic example that recurs as a benchmark or test case in the literature, each case describes an iris, and the label says what kind of iris.

Now, I've given you a new case; by applying some statistical analysis to the existing cases and their labels, plus the new case, you can guess the new case's label. The details are tricky, and there has been much discussion about the best and most accurate way to do it. But the basic idea is simple. No "simulated mind" or anything like that; just straight statistical analysis.

This problem is clearly related to the one in which we are interested. And the program we've built incorporates statistical analyses that are very similar to the classical straight-statistics approaches. But unfortunately, these techniques aren't good enough in the hard cases; and the hard cases are the *interesting* ones, after all.

Human experts have a useful characteristic: Even if they don't know what the answer is, they can tell you something interesting anyway. They can go out on limb. They can propose possibilities. They can *speculate*. That's the sort of behavior we must try to simulate.

§ Simulated Speculation: *Why?*

We've hypothesized that *real, important* information gets communicated when Joe Expert speculates. His speculative comments help reveal what is likely to be important and what isn't; what lines of attack are worth pursuing (they may not be ones you would have expected); what developments to monitor as the situation evolves.

Ideally, our expert backs up his musings with examples: It might be that the following is true... as it was in the case of Mrs. Fruitford. Remember her? (We scurry off to grab the Fruitford File, study it and, sure enough, there are thought-provoking similarities...) Clearly the process of speculation is related to the process of *remembering*. And if an expert tells you "this case reminds me of *x*, *y* and *z*," you've learned something important. You can look those cases up, study them and compare them to your current case.

This is what we'd like the Mirror World to do. When you describe some current situation and ask it for historical precedents, you will get precedents *and* speculations: the two are intimately related. You may also get conclusions, in those cases where they check out using conservative statistical methods. It's clear that this bill *will* pass (consider the following precedents), it's clear that the patient has *x* and not *y* and so forth.

§ Speculation: When and How?

How to simulate speculation? Some principle is at work when an expert decides that something is worth remarking on—is *remarkable* in other words—and there is the rub, precisely. *Remarkable* means "worthy of notice." Two observations follow. To *notice* something means to devote some attention to it, in some sense; to be *distracted* by it. (If your attention remains wholly focussed on *x*—say on "the large dirigible that is about to crash into my petunia bed"—you can't notice anything else. To the extent that you *do* notice something else, say the fact that it's a nice day, or that the dirigible seems to be leaking, you have temporarily stopped noticing whatever you *were* attending to. In the second case, you stopped thinking about the dirigible and the petunia bed in general, and concentrated instead on just one interesting facet of the situation.

Second: To be *worthy* of notice means to be "interesting," in some sense. So *to speculate* requires that you *be distracted* by *something interesting.* Hence we need to build a program that is capable of being distracted, and we need a working definition of "interesting."

§ What's interesting?

Interesting within the narrow, technical confines of listening to a new case description, of course. What makes a painting or a novel or a lady interesting is another matter. This is an important point.

Simulating expert behavior is a major goal of artificial intelligence. Expert behavior depends among other things on the ability to speculate. Speculation depends on some notion of what is interesting, and interesting-ness depends *ultimately* on *emotional and not merely intellectual* criteria. So here we are *again.* Mind-stuff consists of rational and emotional strands densely interwoven. Emotional processes are a fundamental part of intellectual ones.

Luckily we *can* achieve an unemotional definition of "being interesting" that's effective for our purposes...

We'll say that something is interesting if it is *an evocative possibility.*

§ What does "evocative" mean?

Intuitively, something is *evocative* to the extent that it brings other things to mind—sets a mental train in motion. For example, the phrase "cool bright Spring morning" might be fairly evocative for you and "galvanized steel roofing nail" might not be. *Might*: This is a strictly personal issue.

We need to be more precise for software purposes. Something is evocative *with respect to something else* if it brings something to mind *a propos.* "Headache" is not terribly evocative with respect to "diagnosis" because a headache could mean anything or nothing. It sets no clinical train of thought in motion. "Prominent auditory hallucinations" are more evocative: They *do* suggest possible diagnoses. "Blue eyes" are unevocative with respect to "diagnosis," but quite evocative with respect to "hair color." Note that being evocative doesn't mean *pointing definitely* to a conclusion, merely *suggesting* something or other.

(We borrowed this term "evocative" from a path-breaking AI program called "Internist," developed during the late seventies by Jack Meyers, Randy Miller and Harry Pople at the University of Pittsburgh. Internist did a remarkably good job of diagnosing highly complex diseases in the field of internal medicine. A striking thing about the program was the simplicity of its logic: no deep model of cognition, just a few simple moves that worked remarkably well. This should bring Brooks's insects to mind. Internist had nothing to do with a database of cases in our sense, and its idea of "evocativeness" isn't terribly much like ours. But ours does build on Internist's in a sense.)

Now, given a database, we can decide automatically what is evocative and what isn't. Let's say you're given a million person-descriptions: Each one describes a person, in terms of a list of attributes: hair blond; eyes blue; favorite planets Venus, Jupiter (an attribute can have several values associated with it), and so on. I can now establish automatically what is evocative with respect to what, simply by auditioning each possibility in turn. Question: Is blond hair evocative with respect to favorite pizza topping? I look at all my blonds: Do they show any *pattern* in their pizza-topping preferences? If they have pretty much the same pizza-topping attitudes as everyone else, I conclude that blondness is not evocative in this respect. But *if* eighty per-cent of my blonds go for anchovies, then blondness *is* evocative here. If I run a pizza take-out and a blonde saunters in, I often catch myself saying "anchovies—right?" Blondness sets a thought train in motion.

Something is interesting if it is *evocative* and *possible*. How can I tell whether something is possible?

Good question. It's time to launch our two Simple Mind Machines.

What's Possible?—The Basic Operations

We come now to the heart of the matter, the two basic tools that will assist us in turning data into simulated wisdom (or in other words, lead into gold): our two simple mind machines. I'll refer to the two as *plunge* and *squish*.

Imagine that someone is describing a new case to the program. Every time he mentions a new attribute of this case, the program "looks around" in its database. The question it asks is *what other cases are similar to this one?* A case is *similar* to the extent that its attributes match those of the new case. Attributes aren't all equally important, of course; the more *evocative* an attribute and its value, the more significance in matching it closely. If I'm looking for a diagnosis and I happen to learn your hair and eye color and your favorite pizza topping, some of my stored cases might show *exact matches* on all three. But so what?—that doesn't mean they are "close" to this case, because these three attributes are unevocative for diagnosis. The cases that *are* close to the new one are the cases that tend to match on evocative attributes.

This is *plunge*. Take a new case—one attribute or many attributes, doesn't matter—and plunge it into the memory pool. The plunged-in case attracts memories from all over: The "force fields" inside the system get warped in such a way that every stored memory (every case in the database) is re-oriented with respect to the plunged-in "bait." The *most relevant* memories approach closest; and the less-relevant ones recede into the distance.

Let's be slightly more precise. Your new case is a list of attributes: *hair blond, eyes blue...* I go through *my entire database* with this list of attributes in hand. So let's see: The *hair blond* cases in my database are closer to the new one than the *hair dirty blond* cases, which are closer than the *hair brown* cases... The *eyes blue* cases are closer than the *eyes hazel* cases, and so on. Every case in the database has a mess of separate closeness ratings. Some cases are obviously irrelevant (they don't have a single close match—or they might not even *include* the attributes that my new case includes). I can throw those out. What about the rest? I have to *integrate* all these separate closeness-scores, taking *evocativeness* into account— and also accounting for the fact that some of my memories may include attributes (shoe size?) that the new case simply doesn't have, or they may lack attributes that my new case does have, and so on. This "integration" process is tricky and finicky in detail. But the basic idea is simple: The tighter, more "relevant" your overlap with the new case, the closer you come.

So: We tell the system the "key question," what we're interested in (which could be more than one thing, by the way—diagnosis *and* favorite pizza topping); then we describe a new case. Each time we add a new piece of information, the program plunges the case into its database and attracts a collection of "close cases." We can say, if we choose, that the new case "reminds" the program of those close cases.

§ Squish

Squish means to look at the closest cases that are attracted by a *plunge*, and compact them together into a single "super case." We take all these nearby memories (in other words) and superimpose them.

Let's say we're squishing three memories. One reads *hair blond, eyes blue, lipstick red;* a second is *hair blond, eyes blue, lipstick pink;* the third is *hair blond, eyes hazel, no lipstick.* (These skimpy three-attribute memories are only by way of illustration. The average case in our radiology database has about twenty attributes. It's easy to imagine a database where most cases have hundreds or thousands or more.) When we squish them together, we get a single super-memory that reads *hair blond; eyes blue (2) or hazel (1); lipstick red, pink or none.* To understand a squish, *look* at it. Visualize it. Imagine that this squish describes a photograph. Hair color is clearly discernible: The "hair" attribute has a single value, it's in sharp focus. But when you try to figure out what's going on in the lipstick department, you see a blur. "Lipstick" values are all over the map in your squish, not *sharply focussed* on anything. The eyes *seem* to be blue; maybe hazel. But blue is a reasonable guess.

(If we were dealing with real memories—experiences and not mere words—then *squish* would produce a new memory that could be re-played, *experienced*, like any other.)

§ Possible? Definite? Surprising?

An attribute is *possible* in the context of some new case if you are reminded of a bunch of cases that have this attribute: in other words, if this attribute is well-defined in the squished-together results of a plunge. Let's say you haven't told me yet whether my new case has attribute x (either because I haven't gotten around to it or I don't know); but if I'm reminded of lots of cases that have x, then x is probably a reasonable guess in this case too.

In fact, it might not *merely* be possible; it might be virtually *definite*, in which case the program will treat it not as a *possibility* but as a conclusion. For example, you tell the program "I've got a young lady named Ingrid here; she's Icelandic; she's got blond hair, fair skin, and her eyes are..." "Blue," says the system (and yawns). Sure it *could* be wrong (cocky insouciance is generally the wrong attitude for software to adopt in any case)—but that doesn't make the conclusion unreasonable. It looks like a safe bet. Note that, whenever the program reaches this kind of conclusion, it can back it up with examples: I've concluded that x is so, as it is (for example) if the following cases—

I can also notice when something is *surprising*. Say I want to conclude something, because all my close cases have it—but I notice that you've already *told* me about that attribute, and I'm wrong. I *wanted* to conclude that you have blond hair, but in fact, you've already told me that it's black. So the program gets *surprised* and duly mentions the fact: "This *black hair* stuff is surprising; I was expecting blond."

We have now determined what an *evocative possibility* is. As you describe a case, the system is "reminded" of other cases. To the extent that many of those other cases have some particular attribute, that attribute is a *possible* feature of the new case too. Some of the possible features are boring, trivial or irrelevant. Sure Ingrid probably has straight hair, but if we are trying to guess which candidate she'll vote for in the upcoming election, that fact doesn't help much. But *some* possibilities will also be *evocative* with respect to the question we are trying to answer... and *that's* where we would like to see a bit of speculation. Say we have just been told that Ingrid is an enthusiastic fox hunter. Suppose that many fox-hunting enthusiasts are members of the Icelandic Rifle Association, and such people almost always vote for the Hrufyavid party candidate and virtually never for the Glugyadtyks. Our program ought to speculate—might Ingrid *in fact* be a member of the Association? *That* would be a datum worth knowing.

The Implications of *Plunge* and *Squish*

It's important to keep in mind that the new case we plunge into the memory pool might be a single attribute. We could plunge the phrase *diagnosis schizophrenia* into the memory pool, and every memory that includes this phrase will come swarming. The new case has only one attribute, so deciding on "closeness" is simple: The cases in the database that *include* this phrase are close, and the rest aren't. We are now in a position to figure out, by examining the squish of those cases, exactly what "schizophrenia" means. For our purposes, it means "what these cases have in common."

§ Now, suppose you had *real* memories,...

plus *plunge* and *squish*. A thought experiment: You allow our little bull-dozer and dump-truck to drive right into your brain and mess around with your memories. Or if you are the squeamish sort and simply *do not allow* heavy construction equipment into your brain, even on a thought-experimental basis (I guess I can understand this attitude), imagine that plunge and squish have genuinely *good* imitations of human memories to play with.

Suppose you plunge the phrase *color blue* (all by itself) into this realistic memory pool. A swarm of memories approaches. All these memories have the sensation of *seeing blue* embedded in them. And so, when you squish them all together, the sky memories and the swimming pool memories and the blue-crayon memories and the forget-me-not memories and the blueberry memories—the squish is blurry in every way *but* (nothing matches *except...*) for this sensation. The sensation of *seeing blue* emerges clearly when you replay the squish (just like blond hair or a definition of "schizophrenia" might emerge). And you thereby learn (if you happen to be a young child, and you hadn't known already) what "blue" means.

In fact, this squishing operation is the *one plausible mechanism*

for establishing a correspondence between a label (like the word
"blue") and an indescribable sensation (like *seeing* blue). All those
memories had the word "blue" pinned to their lapels (if you are a
young child, someone—we'll assume—described each one of them to
you as "blue"); and so they all came swarming when you *plunged*
the word "blue" into memory. And then when you *squished*, the
sensation of seeing blue popped out. The *one plausible* mechanism:
If you are a child, people are always telling you "what a nice blue
picture—we'll put on your blue sweater—let's play with your blue
ball" and so on. But what exactly is *blue* about these things? Their
shape, size, fuzziness, location, mood? The only way to find out is
to squish them together and see what they have in common.

(This is a learning process sometimes called "induction." "Many
lessons may be needed, so as to eliminate wrong generalizations based
on shape, material etc., rather than color... Like all conditioning,
or induction, the process will depend ultimately also on one's own
inborn propensity to find one stimulation qualitatively more akin to
a second stimulation than to a third..."[1])

§ Building abstract ideas out of concrete memories

Once you've figured out "blue" and some other colors, you can figure
out what an abstract word like "color" means, simply by squishing
together all those squishes. What do the blue squish, the purple
squish and all those other squishes labeled "color" have in common?
That's not a simple question to answer. But luckily you don't *have*
to answer it. You need only do the squish and *experience* it.

Or consider words like "wood," "metal" and so on; and then an
abstraction like "substance." How do you know what "irony" means?
The dictionary definition isn't a lot more useful than the definition of
"blue." A young child is told "those things are blue," "those things
are wood"; a slightly older child is told "those things are ironic."
When you squish them together, all those memories with "ironic"
pinned to their lapels, you figure out what the word designates.

In short, a child can figure out what purple and wood mean
strictly on the basis of comparing like-labelled experiences (purple

things, wood things). He can then proceed to figure out what *color* and *substance* mean, in exactly the same way. And in this fashion he can build a hierarchy of abstractions from the ground up.

Yes, and...? So what? Well...

§ Understanding language

has always been a holy grail of AI research. Plunge and squish are, potentially, a significant part of language understanding. Ultimately, the way you attach a *meaning* to a *label* (*blueness* to "blue", *substance-ness* to "substance") is by plunging and squishing. This is merely the flip side of the original problem we examined—attaching a *label* to a *"meaning"* (the label *malignant* to an image on a film, the label *Iris Setosa* to a particular plant...).

Put another way, our problem of "correct diagnosis based on experience," or the related problem of "finding the right precedent," is *the same problem*, in terms of what you need to do in order to solve it, as the problem of learning the meaning of a word like "blue." Learning correct diagnosis based on experience is, in one sense, merely *extending your grasp of the language*. In working on any one of these problems (say diagnosis) we *must*, at least in some sense, be working on the others (say, language understanding) too.

If we are ever to build software that understands language in a deep and convincing way, we will have to master plunging and squishing.

Stay tuned. Now, back to our existing software...

Achieving Distraction

We've discussed one way to define "an interesting possibility." Speculation requires "being distracted" by such a possibility. How does software get distracted?

We'll take a simple and obvious approach. The program temporarily puts aside the new case it is examining, and focuses instead on the interesting possibility. It treats this possibility as if *it* were the new case, the thing it is asked to comment on, the matter at hand—the fishbait to be lowered into the memory sea. If "membership in the Icelandic rifle association" is the interesting possibility, the program temporarily focuses on this possibility alone. It plunges the case "member Icelandic Rifle Association" into the memory pool and squishes the results.

Maybe we can't build a direct path from Ingrid to Association membership, but we *can* build a path from *being a member* to Ingrid. Let's say that Ingrid strongly recalls a few dozen people, and four or five are Rifle Association members. Not an overwhelming case in itself for Ingrid's being one. But now let's say I focus on *all Association members* by plunging "member Icelandic Rifle Association" into the memory pool. These cases might have dozens of attributes, but it *could be* that most of them are irrelevant. They might all disappear (*blur up, fuzz out*) when I do the squish—because there might be *no agreement* on them. There might be exactly *three attributes* (say) that virtually *all* Association Members have in common, and all the rest are a blur. Furthermore (say) when we run a check on these three—when we plunge all three together into the pool—the close cases are in fact mainly Members.

The point is to allow us to guess when a bunch of attributes are evocative *as a group*. We can't pre-compute the evocativeness of all possible groups in advance: There are simply too many of them. But we can now return to Ingrid and check her for the *bunch* of features that point collectively to Association membership. If she matches, we've got a case for believing that she might be a member too. If she's got some but not all of these features, we can speculate about the missing ones.

None of this is *certain* and the program won't claim that it is. It's merely speculation. But it's informed speculation and it *might well* be correct...

Putting It All Together: the Basic Cycle

We learn an attribute. We add the attribute to our new case. We plunge the case into our pool of memories, and attract a collection of "close cases." We squish the close cases together, and examine what they have in common. If we reach any conclusions, we add them to the new case. If we notice any evocative possibilities, we get distracted and speculate.

To speculate is (in essence) simply to repeat the cycle again.

We take the evocative possibility, plunge it into memory and attract
some close cases. We squish them together and see what they have in
common. We plunge the common elements and see if they point back
to the evocative possibility. At this point we stop being distracted,
remember the original case and compare it to what we've learned
about the evocative possibility—is there a decent match? Does the
evocative possibility remain merely *possible* or has it become proba-
ble? If it seems likely, we can add *it* (tentatively) to our new case as
well.

The new case may have grown: We might have added some conclusions and some speculative possibilities. So we can plunge the new
expanded case back into memory, and attract (possibly) a slightly
different set of cases, and squish *them* together, and so on... Until
we learn nothing more. Then we can go back to the user: Anything
else you want to tell me about this case? If so, I tack on the new
attributes, and start the cycle again.

Plunge and squish, plunge and squish.

Squishing and Its Consequences

If you squish the same pile of stuff together often enough, it may be
that the pile will *stay* squished.

Let's say that your program is designed to work as a Complexion
Counselor in a department store: Users describe themselves and the
program tells them what color lipstick to buy, or something like that.
It build its database by remembering each customer. To impress the
clientele, the software wants to makes guesses, cite precedents, reach
conclusions, speculate and so forth. Whenever a customer starts
by entering "my eyes are blue," the system performs a plunge-and-
squish and concludes that most likely her hair is blond and her skin
is fair. This happens many times a day.

Eventually the system notices that it is constantly called upon to
prognosticate about the implications of blue eyes; it can save itself
a bit of trouble by leaving all those shared segments, the segments
that say "hair blond, eyes blue, skin fair"—squished together. Now
of course the case of Customer Fruitford (say) amounts to a lot more
than merely blond hair and blue eyes; but *this particular segment* of
her dossier is shared with lots of other customers. As you scan down

it you see "hang-gliding enthusiast; three children; pet raccoon—and, a typical blue-eyed blond."

Maybe the system does this. It's not inevitable. It gains the system *nothing* in terms of accuracy (in fact it loses something, as I'll discuss). You obviously *can* cook up generalizations like this on the spot, whenever you need them. But "perma-squishing" is nonetheless an interesting possibility, for several reasons.

When we form a permanent squish, we are creating a *rule* or *principle* or *template* or *generalization*. We've taken leave of our particular memories, and substituted a general-purpose template instead. Another name for this kind of generalization is *forgetting*. I've forgotten the distinctions between a bunch of individuals. I've remembered only the similarities. It may be that Customer Fruitford had slightly lighter hair and darker eyes, and Customer Prunestein the reverse, and Customer Piffelini something else again, but these distinctions are gone. They've all turned into mere blue-eyed blondes, period.

Consider (moving over into humanware) the color blue. *Blueness* is the sort of concept that comes in handy. It's easy to believe that, during your struggles to learn the language, a bunch of blue memories soon become permanently squished. This leaves the blueness sensation and the *word* blue (the two clearly-focussed pieces of the squish) permanently chained together.

Back to software: This kind of forgetfulness will be extremely useful, because *it saves space*. Mirror Worlds accumulate massive archives. It's one thing to say *data storage is cheap* (it is), and that *we know how to use parallelism to search massive databases very fast* (true), but come off it, seriously speaking—there are limits. Ultimately we *must* have a strategy for controlling the monumental oceans of data that a Mirror World remembers. Forgetfulness is a promising one. Mirror World storage areas come equipped with "forgetting thresholds." If two cases are closer together than the threshold, they stay squished together. If the threshold is zero, we never forget anything: Every individual memory—every case, scene, machine-state, patient or whatever—remains distinct. As the threshold widens, the system starts to blur nice distinctions. As it widens further, we loose increasingly larger distinctions, and ultimately the system becomes "infinitely forgetful"—meaning *not* that it's got nothing upstairs, database empty—meaning rather that *ev-*

erything it's ever seen is squished together into a single opaque black-hole blob.

There should be some happy medium that allows us to preserve interesting distinctions, but to save lots of space by forgetting minor ones.

§ Time and forgetting

The *age* of a memory is one of its attributes. Suppose the system has two very similar memories—that is, two very similar elements in its archival database. Suppose that one dates from this morning and the other from two weeks ago. How close are these two memories? I need to measure closeness in terms of *every* attribute that the two share. "Age" is one attribute. How can I tell when two memories are close in age?

Let's say that age-closeness depends on a ratio of distances-from-right-now. Today, those two memories are far apart in age, because *two weeks* is a lot further than *this morning* from *right now*. So maybe these two memories do *not* slip under the forgetting threshold. They're similar in lots of ways, but far apart in age, and so they remain distinct.

Time passes. With each tick of the clock, those memories grow relatively *closer* in age. Three years into the future, those two memories are separated from *right now* by—relatively speaking—nearly *identical* amounts of time. From the standpoint of three years, two weeks doesn't matter much. And so it's very possible that, *eventually*, if I wait long enough, the two memories *will* slip under the forgetting threshold and get blended together.

In this way the Mirror World can simulate, if it chooses, the human tendency to let distinctions slip away as time passes.

In short: perma-squishing (this special form of *forgetfulness*) saves space.

It also accounts, one might easily suppose, for the entire epistemological universe: rules, principles and abstractions. If abstract principles exist, this is where they come from.

The Software Architecture

Our program is called the FGP Machine, after its three operations—the two biggies and a helper—called Fetch, Generalize and Project. "Fetch" is *plunge*. "Generalize" is *squish*. "Project" merely allows you to pick what you want out of a squish.

When you press the Mirror World's "experience" button, you are in effect presenting a new case to an FGP infomachine. The "case" is whatever you've indicated on your screen. You give the system some idea of what you're interested in, as a focus for computing evocativeness. What are you trying to "diagnose?"—the chance that this bill will pass? That the factory will meet some production quota? The best medication for this patient? The entire archival history of this Mirror World serves as our database. Most of the elements of the database are completely irrelevant. They share no attributes with the situation on your screen. We don't even need to look at them. But most likely there *are* some potentially relevant cases, and we look carefully at those.

The system *could* take the case you are interested in and plunge it into memory as a single object. Conclusions, speculations and particular precedents emerge. But it will often be useful for the Mirror World to run down the attributes of the new case one by one, as if they were being presented conversationally—as in the radiology example. The result is a kind of commentary on each attribute of the case, culminating in a "diagnosis" and a list of the closest, most interesting precedents.

How do we achieve decent performance if we need to manipulate (say) millions of individual cases while the user waits? Ensembles again, in the interest of speed: Throw lots of workers at the problem simultaneously. Any decent-sized Mirror Worlds will incorporate some large, shared information depots. These machines store lots of data, and provide lots of computers for looking at the data. They are large, "classical" parallel machines—many computers packed into a single box.

The FGP program I've described is still an *un*parallel program, a single infomachine. We are in the process of ensemblizing it right now. The techniques involved are pretty simple, much like the database search problem I described in chapter four.

I'll discuss three sets of implications. The first is an engineering matter. The second (having to do with language understanding) strikes close to the heart of AI, and the third hits the jackpot: What is thinking?

Implications I: The Ultimate Reference Room

The possibilities under this heading are close to obvious. Provide every book in your library with an abstract—likewise for every newspaper article, journal publication and so on. Dump all the abstracts into a world-wide database. When I'm interested in some topic, my interests become the fishbait for a plunge into the world library pool. I attract descriptions of relevant documents from all over the world and all over history.

Implications II: Understanding Language (?)

Getting software to understand human language has been a goal of AI research almost from the start. How do you do it? Answer: not easily. Pull up a chair.

Here is one important facet of the problem. It has long been noticed by the AI community, and also by everybody else (but only the AI community seems to take it personally), that human conversation is exceptionally elliptical. People are always *leaving things out* (dammit). They emit some utterance or other that simply *doesn't make any sense*, in and of itself; but other people understand it anyway. People are able to connect the dots—to fill in the blanks—automatically and nearly instantaneously.

How do they do this? Plunge-and-squish offers one approach to an explanation. (But it's not the standard or "conventional" approach, which I will also introduce, in passing...)

Consider the problem. Say Ingrid is visiting her relatives on Long Island. "Let's go to the beach. Is Ingrid coming? Then take the umbrella." In itself, this makes no sense whatever—what do you mean, *then* take...? This is *not* a self-contained logical proposition, any more than "It's Tuesday? Then how about a case of dill pickles?" We need to fill in the blanks: Ingrid is very fair. Such people sunburn easily. It's sunny at the beach. Umbrellas are a good way to keep out of the sun. You need to know *all* of these random facts in order to make sense of the pronouncement about Ingrid.

Unfortunately, you can't get a computer to understand a sentence simply by teaching it grammar and handing it a dictionary. There is a tremendous pile of odd rules and principles that you must have on hand (fair people sun-burn easily, beaches are sunny, *ad infinitum*) if you are to have any hope of understanding human language. Recognizing this state of affairs constitutes, in and of itself, one of the more significant achievements of language understanding research in recent years.

How do you know all this stuff? Are we really going to have to sit down and make a *list* of all these intellectual pearls? *Fair people sun-burn easily.* How many of these lapidary pre-cooked Wisdom Nuggets will our program need to ingest? Millions, according to current estimates.

But—how do *people* acquire this basic information? No-one ever served it to *you* as a pre-packaged ten-million-course TV dinner. No-one ever made up a list and taught you every item one-by-one (what people *have* proposed doing with software—what almost seems like the only available alternative, in dealing with software). They stuffed the raw material of experience into you like vegetables into a food processor, holding down the plunge-and-squish key full blast as they did so; and common-sense knowledge simply *developed.*

So I'll discuss, first, how you can build a mental food processor using plunge and squish. This handy machine converts particulars into *abstractions*—particular experiences into general wisdom. Not *our* plunge and squish; not the ones that are part of our current, operational FGP program. We'll need *far* heavier-duty versions, and building them will be intensely difficult—an enormous job involving lots of research. But *logically* these heavy-duty bruisers *are the same as what we already have.* A rocket engine is a rocket engine. Compare an early-fifties rocket plane to a late-sixties moon blaster: The difference represents a huge leap in engineering prowess. And yet *at base* they are two versions of the same thing.

Okay, but who cares how *you* came by your hard-won basic common-sense knowledge? It would be much easier *for the program* if it could skip this process, whatever it is. Why not simply distill all of Common Sense into a modest bottle and say *Drink up!—down the hatch...—congratulations!* you're smart...? You know enough to understand human language.

Unfortunately, there are reasons to doubt whether any such approach can possibly be successful in the end. People are *dynamic* information processors. Not in the sense that you spend a lifetime acquiring the basics of common sense: No doubt you *have* mastered the basics by age so-and-so, and if we could take a snapshot of your Inner Head at just that point—we've got what we need. The problem is more subtle but just as important. Namely: The process of *bringing knowledge to bear* on a problem appears to be logically identical to the process of *accumulating knowledge in the first place*. In order to *use* your knowledge you've got to have *plunge* and *squish* (or something comparable). In order to use *its* knowledge, the *program*, the *Simulated* Mind, will *also* need plunge and squish. However much it costs to build these things, we're going to have to pay up. We need them. TV dinner or no TV dinner.

§ Plunge, Squish and the Mental Food Processor

I've talked about *blue, color, irony*. Plunge-and-squish allow you (or a simulated *you*) to attach meanings to words like these.

Now consider the *rules* and *principles* on which language relies. Returning to our Ingrid pronouncement... You had to know, in order to understand it, that Ingrid is fair. How did you know this? Let's suppose you're *reading* this dialogue in a story, and have never seen Ingrid or been explicitly informed that she is fair. But *still* you understand what's going on. You executed a piece of reasoning: Scandinavian girls tend to be fair; Ingrid is a Scandinavian girl; hence... Where and *how* do you get the knowledge that enables you to do this?

Abstractions can be distilled from *particulars* via plunge and squish.

Scandinavian girls tend to be fair: How do you know? *Did* beloved Mrs. Piffel drill it into your head in the fifth grade that Scandinavian girls are fair? Or could it be that you've actually *seen* some Scandinavian girls (in person or pictures) and reached this conclusion on your own? Or rather, not *even* reached a conclusion; just squished a lot of pictures together in your mind until those pictures *turned into* a kind of fact? The result is a "visual syllogism"—the major premise is a mental *picture*. I have a picture in mind of a Scandinavian girl. (She is fair...among other things.) Ingrid is a Scandinavian girl. So Ingrid is probably fair.

Chances are that a tremendously large proportion of the general rules and principles you know are, in fact, compacted *particular experiences*. Yes, sometimes you do learn something in the abstract: Mongolians live in yurts. Fine. But these abstract facts are mailed to you in "experiential envelopes." You read this fact at such and such a time, or such-and-such a person told you, or whatever. It did not pop into your brain by order of the surgeon general. If you've been told often enough, or you've *used* this abstract fact (and thus *recalled* it) often enough, the fact may become completely dissociated from its various "learning experiences." But what's happened is just like blueness or Scandinavian girls: Individual experiences (the experience of *being told* or the experience of *recalling* what you have been told) were compounded into a general rule. The *basic stuff* out of which the rule is built is still the "particular experience."

Are the abstractions, rules, principles and common sense that language-understanding requires merely wine plunge-and-squished out of Experiential Grapes?

§ Time

What about abstractions having to do with processes or time? I need to understand these also. "He ran over a nail and got a flat. It wouldn't have bothered him too much, but it was raining hard..." You need to understand *what happens* when someone gets a flat. There's a procedure that involves getting out of the car; hence if it's raining, that's bad news. How do you know the procedure?

How do you learn what goes into changing a tire, doing long division, having lunch in a restaurant? We're no longer talking about *identifying* something ("it's blue," "it's schizophrenia"); we're now talking about a *process*, a sequence of events. But at base, it's all the same.

AI research has gotten considerable mileage out of an idea called "scripts", due to Roger Schank of Northwestern University. (These "scripts" are completely unrelated to the ones I discussed in Chapter 3, which tell your Infomachine Actor what to do.) How do you know what to expect when you go to a restaurant? Well, there's a thing called the "restaurant script" that captures the procedure in outline. First you sit down, then you look at the menu, then you order some food and so on. People operate (it is conjectured) using mental scripts like this to guide them; and you can also write down a script and hand it to a program. So the program now understands what happens in restaurants. It can understand stories in which people go to restaurants. It's a useful idea that AI programs have relied on extensively.

But of course *fundamentally* a "script" is the same as *blue*. It's the same as *wood*, "schizophrenia," Scandinavian girls. When you squish a lot of restaurant experiences together, you get a script. In this sort of squishing, we need to respect and preserve similarities in the arrangement of events in time. If ten memories show more or less the same sequence of events, those ten events must emerge sharply, *in the right order*, in the resulting squish. And of course, this blending-together has to work right despite the fact that some memories may have extra events, others may be missing events and so on.

So what else is new? How do you know what a *chair* is, after all? There's nothing special about a "script." To understand chairness, you extracted a certain arrangement of *objects in space* from a bunch of squished-together chair memories. The legs go there, the seat over here, the arms over there... Extracting such patterns from a bunch of related, particular experiences is all in a day's work for the *humanware* version of plunge and squish. It's a neat trick computationally—recognizing common patterns like this. But people do it, and software can try.

And then finally, how do you learn syntax? How do you learn what makes a sentence and what doesn't? How do you know what a verb or noun is, and where a verb or noun *goes*? By squishing lots of sentences together, and extracting patterns—what other choice is there? A *grammatical sentence* is a *chair* is a *"script."* It's a certain *structure*: down there are the legs, then the seat, then the back; you order food, then you eat, then you pay; first comes a noun, then comes a verb... People learn to understand these structures whether or not anyone ever explains them. And obviously they learn to do so—what other choice is there?—by squishing lots of examples. Which is *also* the way we come to understand *blue*, which is also how an expert clinician comes to understand *schizophrenia*, and how the FGP program fills in the blanks as it listens to the description of a case.

Make no mistake about it—this kind of pattern extraction, squishing together a million declarative sentences and winding up with a general structure—is largely unknown territory, in computational terms. It looks *extremely* hard. We don't know how to do it. But one thing is clear—

Whether we can build heavy-duty quasi-human versions, or we limp along with our current weak imitations, *plunge* and *squish* are important. We can account for a *huge* range of basic mental phenomena using these little devices.

§ Why bother?

Understanding language was the problem, right? So what *is* the plunge-and-squish approach to a solution?

Well, we might in principle attempt to build a simulated mind starting with nothing but *plunge, squish* and emptiness. We start feeding in "experiences"—pictures, stories, whatever; every time we feed in something new, the program does a plunge and a squish and tries to fill in the blanks. Tries to attach labels; tries to find "meanings." In the beginning, it fails every time. The database is empty. *Plunge* recalls nothing. *Squish* reveals nothing. But we plug on anyway. Add more "memories." And eventually, things start to develop.

The answer in short is: Feed lots of experiences into the mental food processor.

That's an answer?

This is, in a sense, the *hardest* way to approach the problem. Lots of work is involved: many plunges, many squishes; and mountains of raw material—raw memory stuff—to work on. And this effort (*no doubt about it...*) presupposes knowledge we don't yet have: how to represent and store database elements that are more like memories, less like sterile, stylized shorthand; how to beef up *plunge* and *squish* so that they can handle these richer cases—can extract temporal and spatial patterns, and so on. These problems are all solvable, most likely. But they are also *hard*. We need to do more research. See you in ten years.

Why bother? As I mentioned, a program might have all this knowledge simply *bestowed* on it. You might sit down at your desk, sharpen your pencil, open your notebook, flatten it down very carefully, and then compile a complete orderly list of the rules and principles that define basic human knowledge. *All of them.* Then you knock off for lunch. This effort requires the creation of a kind of "mind map" that charts out all necessary rules, principles and categories, and their interrelations. A complete chart of the Cognitive Heavens.

There *is* a formidable research group that is working on this problem.[2] The whole thing may sound silly, but it is in fact heroic. It's just the sort of enterprise people dismiss as impossible (if they don't merely laugh at it) until some intrepid band actually sets out to survey the stars, conduct a census or compile the Oxford English Dictionary.

If it works, great. Many good insights about the structure of knowledge have already emerged from this project. No complete mind map yet; in time, maybe. But unfortunately: Even if the whole thing works perfectly; even if that hugely nourishing ten-million-course TV dinner pops out at the end, in a handy tin-foil tray...you *still* need plunge and squish. Sorry. You simply cannot get along without them. Any workable simulated mind—any mind with any shot at *real* language understanding—*must* have plunge and squish.

Why? Because the process of *bringing knowledge to bear* on a problem appears to be logically identical to the process of *accumulating knowledge in the first place.*

In *your* mind *particulars* turn into *generalities* gradually, imperceptibly—like snow at the bottom of a drift turning into ice. If you don't *know* any general rules, if you've merely experienced something once, then that *once* will have to do. You may remember *one* example, *or* a collection of particular examples, *or* a general rule. These states blend together: When you've mastered the rule, you can still recall some individual experiences if you need to. Any respectable mind simulation must accommodate *all three states.* Any one of them might be the *final* state for some particular (perfectly respectable) mind. (Many people have been to Disneyland once, a fair number have been there a couple of times, and a few, no doubt, have been to Disneyland so often that the individual visits blend together into a single melted ice-cream puddle of a *visit to Disneyland rule* or *script* or *principle* or whatever. All three states are real.)

Plunge-and-squish adapts to whatever you have on hand. If there is a single relevant memory, *plunge* finds it. If there are several, *squish* constructs a modest generalization, one that captures the quirks of its particular elements. If there are many, *squish* constructs a sound, broad-based generalization. You may even wind up with a perma-squish abstraction, if this particular *squish* happens frequently enough and the elements blend smoothly together. It all happens automatically.

You need plunge and squish.

One more point: Whatever stack of memories *you* have on hand, you can cut the deck in a million ways. You can reshuffle it endlessly. You *can*, if you need to, synthesize a general rule at a moment's notice. You see an asphalt spreader on the next block. You develop an expectation: The next block will smell like [*the smell of fresh asphalt...*]. What happened—did you wrack your brain for that important general principle, squirreled away for just such an occasion—fact number three million twenty-one thousand and seven—*fresh asphalt usually smells like...?* Or did you *synthesize* this rule by doing a plunge-and-squish on the spot?

Clearly you *can* cobble together an abstraction, a category or an expectation at a moment's notice. You *can* create new categories to order whenever they are needed. (Unpleasant vacations? Objects that look like metal but aren't?...) Any realistic mind simulation must know how to do this.

Gotta have plunge; gotta have squish.

And so we arrive, finally, at two radically different pictures of the mind. In the mind-map view, there is a dense intertwined superstructure of categories, rules and generalizations, with the odd *specific, particular* fact hanging from the branches like the occasional bird-pecked apple. In the plunge-and-squish view, there are slowly-shifting, wandering and reforming snowdrifts instead, built *without* superstructure out of a billion crystal flakes—a billion *particular* experiences. New experiences sift constantly downwards onto the snowscape and old ones settle imperceptibly into ice-clear universals, and the whole scene is alive and constantly, subtly changing.

It's too soon to say which view is right. Both approaches need a lot more work. Both have produced interesting results. But if I had to guess... I mean, if you *forced* me to pick a winner...

Implications III: The Mind Spectrum

Suppose we were to equip our FGP program with a "concentration knob." We can dial up any concentration setting we want, from *max* down to 0. With concentration set at maximum, the program is incapable of being distracted (by *anything*, no matter how interesting and evocative). As we turn the level down, concentration lapses and the program becomes more distractable. At zero concentration, the program can't keep its simulated mind on anything.

Meaning? After each squish, the program must decide whether anything in the squish is worth speculating about—whether anything in there is distracting enough to justify a speculative excursion. How is the decision made? Although we haven't mentioned it explicitly, clearly there must be some threshold value stored in the program somewhere. *If* some attribute-value combination in the squish has an evocativeness higher than 17 SEU's (standard evocativeness units—I just made this unit up, don't bother consulting your dictionary)...*then* it is evocative enough to justify a speculative excursion.

Now: If we set this threshold to *max*, the cut-off value becomes infinitely large. Nothing is *ever* evocative enough to justify an excursion; the program never does *any* speculation. It plods along like a pack-mule. Nothing ever catches its attention. It never strays from the straight and narrow.

As I turn "concentration" down, there are three related effects, all tending to increase the program's distractability. The program gets lazy about squishing, the distraction threshold falls, and it develops a tendency to *continue* an excursion instead of returning immediately to home base.

Things still have to be "evocative" but (increasingly) I don't care with respect to what. If Ingrid brings Ingrid Bergman to mind, who brings to mind a movie which brings to mind a particular evening which brings to mind a notorious blimp accident on Piffel Boulevard...fine. Evocative with respect to *anything* is okay. Eventually, as "concentration" continues to fall, squishing laziness sets in. I do a plunge, and merely grab *any individual* memory that has an evocative overlap with the plunged-in memory. (Squishing is a kind of mental *work*. It requires concentration, of a sort.) *And* I develop a tendency to prolong my excursions.

In the FGP program, *getting distracted* means performing a plunge and squish, and then attempting to find a path back to the original topic. But in principle, having done a single plunge-and-squish, I might do another: I might allow myself to be distracted yet again by *another* interesting possibility.

For example: In dealing with Ingrid's likely political preferences, I may be distracted by the matter of her possible Rifle Association membership. I switch my focus to the rifle association, via plunge and squish. But let's say that, instead of returning immediately to Ingrid, I can't help but notice that a certain number of rifle association members seem to list Piffel's Extra-Heavy Lager as their favorite beverage. *Hmmmm*, I say, *that's interesting*—and I get distracted again; this time, I focus on Piffel's drinkers. I plunge-and-squish on *favorite-drink Piffel's*, and examine the resulting squish.

In principle this could go on indefinitely; but let's say I call a halt to the excursion at this point, and retrace my steps. Maybe I can build a path from Piffel's drinking back to rifle association membership? Suppose I establish that, while being an Association Member doesn't mean you drink Piffel's...being a *Piffel's drinker* means that you're very likely to be an Association Member. Fine. Now I try to build a path home to Ingrid: Doing so could be easier, given what I've learned about Piffel's. If she's a Piffel's drinker, I'm all set.

In short, straying outward into the mental countryside can be useful, occasionally. As *concentration* falls, the program's tendency to stray increases. The lower the setting, the further it's willing to wander before it decides to come home.

With concentration set at zero, it *never* comes home. It merely wanders from one evocative memory to another, completely ignoring the human user and everyone else.

In describing the FGP program and discussing the radiology example, we assumed implicitly that "concentration" was set fairly high. Only attribute-value pairs that were strongly evocative with respect to diagnosis could set off a speculative excursion; and such excursions could only venture a single leap away from home. But in fact, an FGP program can execute at *any* concentration level.

Which leads us to several conclusions. First, two styles of thinking which are almost always treated as *separate, unconnected points* are in fact merely the endpoints of a continuous spectrum. And the existence of this spectrum suggests that, once again, all useful thought depends on a highly significant dollop of *non-rational* thinking.

§ **Thought Styles**

The main business of a human mind is to string thoughts together. What are the rules that govern thought-stringing? Starting with some particular thought, how do you decide which thought should be next?

The FGP program suggests that thought-stringing is a spectrum whose two endpoints are *concentration max* and *concentration 0*. In the first case, there is a *starting point* and a *goal* and every mental act is designed to carry you one step further along the path that connects them. We grab every memory we can find in the attempt to get to the goal, but we *never* stray off the track by diverting attention from Ingrid to the Rifle Association, much less to Piffel's Drinkers. In the second case, each thought merely *overlaps* some previous thought. Two adjacent thoughts in the string have some common element, or they are expressed in similar words, or similar sounds, or in terms of similar images; or they may evoke the same emotion. The points of overlap—the words or sensations or images that serve as pivots between two thoughts—aren't randomly chosen; they tend to be the most *evocative* elements of any particular thought. You tell me "I'd like to know who the following person is apt to vote for in the up-coming election," and you describe Ingrid. I think "Ingrid—Ingrid Bergman—Casablanca— DC-3's—Cape Cod—*whatever.*"

The observation that two different thought-stringing methods exist has been traced back to Hobbes[3]; thoughts may be laid down like stepping stones leading to a goal, or they may ramble without apparent direction. Psychologists usually refer to the first as "problem-solving" or "reasoning"; the second is more of a puzzle. In purest form, it's usually called free-association. Slightly diluted, it's related to what Freud called "primary process thinking," and to what is sometimes called "divergent thinking" by cognitive psychologists.[4] Experimental psychologists who study daydreaming are examining another closely related topic.

Everyone understands what "reasoning" is for, but there's very little agreement on what purpose "free association" serves. At first blush, it seems like a waste of time. Freud believed that the "primary process thinking" of dreams and waking fantasies represents a pursuit of wish fulfillment. Modern experimentalists propose that day-dreaming helps us anticipate contingencies, and gives us something interesting to do in the absence of anything better.[5] (Amazing stuff, no?)

But no one seems to doubt that you are either *reasoning* or you are—dreaming, day-dreaming, fantasizing or whatever. The two alternatives are mutually exclusive. And *reasoning* is what serious thought *is*. Granted, it's hard to find any kind of standard definition of "thinking." But Robert Sternberg, a leading cognitive psychologist, is trying to tell us something when he writes that "Reasoning, problem solving, and intelligence are so closely interrelated that it is often difficult to tell them apart." Cognitive psychologists often equate *intelligence* and *thinking*—thus, for example, the emphasis on "thinking skills" in their attempts to define intelligence. *Reasoning* and *intelligence*—hence *reasoning* and *thought itself*—are more or less the same thing.

According to the FGP program, this is all wrong.

These two thinking styles are *not* mutually exclusive: A continuous spectrum connects them. At any point *along* the spectrum, my thinking is *partly* straight-arrow reasoning and *partly* free-association, in the sense that *gray* represents some black and some white mixed together. "Thinking" is not the same as "reasoning." Reasoning is merely *one endpoint* of the thought-spectrum. Speculative excursions are *fundamental* to useful thinking, and *speculation* is merely, precisely and entirely a low-key, well-mannered version of free association. Turn up the heat, and speculation boils off into pure *mental rambling* through the cognitive countryside. Turn the heat off entirely, and you have "reasoning"—pure, "goal-directed" (a favorite AI term) problem solving; boring, and in many cases futile.

You need *both* these thought styles to make a mind. *Intelligence* requires both.

The implications over-slosh the boundaries of this book alto-
gether. (Some of them are discussed in greater detail elsewhere.[6])
But the moral of the story for *software* is, again: Forget "rational."
There is more to human thought processes, hence there must be more
to any really *good* simulation, than focussed unemotional reasoning.
Much more.

Conclusions

All this to make a single key work. But now we can go ahead and
put our Mirror World together.

Chapter 7

Building Mirror Worlds

We've laid the foundations. Now we'll build the building. But first, let's take stock.

Facts vs. Forecasts

A large bunch of software ideas have paraded gamely past the reviewing stand one-by-one, trumpets blaring; and by this point, it may no longer be easy to keep them all straight. So here is a quick summary.

Garden-variety infomachines are (of course) a fact of life. *Ensembles* are also a fact: Programmers build and run them every day. Linda is a fact; its presence continues (at least for now) to expand, as a research topic and as a practical tool. The roping together of networked computers into a single "hypercomputer" is a *new* fact—esoteric stuff; but it's such an obvious and compelling idea, and it's working so well in practice, that it continues to come on strong.

The World Tuplesphere is of course a non-fact. It's a mere forecast. But—*some* sort of integrated worldwide communication scheme, based on persistent information objects, will eventually exist. That's a forecast that is almost inevitable.

The Trellis as a working ensemble is a fact. Substantial prototypes are up and running; they perform as advertised. The Trellis as a daily tool is a mere forecast. The Trellis is still a creature of the research lab; but it's packed and ready to leave home.

The FGP infomachine is a fact, too: Real prototypes are up and

179

running. Like the Trellis, it's still a laboratory creature. Like the Trellis, it will be ready to leave home soon. But the FGP infomachine that leaves home first will be a simple, in some ways primitive version of the system that further research will *eventually* produce. An FGP machine that can cope with "emotion," with full-fledged pseudo-memories or with human language is a mere forecast. Of course, we don't need all this fancy stuff for a Mirror World. The FGP software that exists today isn't far from meeting all of our immediate Mirror World needs.

These are the Mirror World's ingredients—Trellises and FGP machines; above all, ensembles, and the software technology to build them cleanly and support them efficiently. The raw materials are in place. Could we build a full-fledged, industrial-strength Mirror World tomorrow? No; more research is needed to fill some significant gaps and smooth some rough edges. Are Mirror Worlds technologically plausible, right now?

Yes, they are.

If we had the luxury of devoting ourselves to full-time Mirror Worlding, we'd have a complete prototype in a year or two. One way or another, we or some other research group will almost certainly have produced a full-fledged, large-scale Mirror World by the end of the decade. Not a top-of-the-line model, necessarily; maybe *not* decked out in multiple video feeds, near-instant total recall and a few other nice features. These depend on further progress in the world communications infrastructure, in computer design and in the widespread dissemination of cheap parallel machines. All inevitable; but it's hard to say exactly when. So the Mirror World you get at the end of the decade may not the Ultimate Mirror World. But it will be a solid little performer.

End of the decade... or maybe sooner. But let's be conservative, okay? Aren't we always?

One final step before we start. The Mirror World's roots aren't exclusively technological. They reach just as deeply (or more so) into the cluttered, compelling history of miniature worlds.

The Urge...

to build microcosms is a fixture of cultural history. It's so obvious and so basic that you rarely hear it discussed. But let's: This is a necessary prelude to the building of Mirror Worlds. Microcosms are like ensembles, so pervasive and varied and strongly colored, dressed up in some many radically different ways, that you wonder (naturally) how important the shared essence under the wrappings could really be. So much of what people do falls into this category; but let's stop anyway, at a few interesting points.

Let's start outside in the garden.

The Zen garden ideal is "reducing thirty thousand miles to the distance of a single foot,"[1] and many Japanese gardens present abstract, graceful sketches of vast scenes on little plots. A "box garden" (near relative of the *bonsai*) is a whole landscape in a small container. The Islamic Paradise Garden, more ambitious, compresses "within itself a total reflection of the cosmos,"[2] and the four watercourses emanating from its central fountain are stand-ins for the outward-flowing rivers of the Garden of Eden. Advice to the builders of nineteenth-century French wintergardens: "A small brook should wind through a carefully-chosen glade, alive with tropical fish, then rush cascading between rocks, to spread out finally in a wide calm basin surrounded by sand and gravel..."[3] Europe has explored the abstract microcosm too, of course—the Gothic cathedral "is perhaps best understood as a 'model' of the mediaeval universe."[4]

Museums, exhibitions, toys: The King invited the populace to the British Empire Exhibition at Wembley, which "reveals to us the whole Empire in little..."[5] The Perisphere was a huge concrete ball at dead center of the 1939 New York World's Fair. Visitors entered at balcony level, and below them "Democracity," a scale-model Utopia, "symbol of a perfectly integrated futuristic metropolis pulsing with life and rhythm and music,"[6] stretched out twinkling in the dark. The history of toys is a history of microcosms: puppet theaters and dollhouses and snowdomes, model railroads and toy soldiers, music-boxes with dancing figurines and goldfish bowls with tiny divers on blue-gravel floors. The capital of this world is The Hague, where a park called Madurodam reproduces a whole city in loving detail on a one-acre plot. No child who sees it ever forgets it.

All this is peripheral to the main locus of microcosmic creativity through the ages, painted and sculpted art. The intriguing sensation of viewing a small world depends mainly, I think, not on the *size* of the scene before you but on its self-containment. The world of Keats's Grecian Urn, the miniatures of life from season to season in the opening calendar of a medieval Book of Hours, Vermeer's view of Delft or (for that matter) of any specimen of domestic silence—all these are microcosms in the broader sense. And there are plenty of *literal* microcosms, too: I'll stop briefly at three of my favorite spots, three outlying points that are fascinating for their microcosmic fanaticism...

The painterly curiosity called a peep box is "apparently a Dutch invention."[7] (The microcosmic Dutch again.) A box with peepholes, painted on the inside, designed to create the illusion when peeped-into of a miniature three-dimensional space. "A peek through either hole of the box presents a delightful surprise: we experience an almost perfect illusion of standing within a seventeenth-century interior."[8] That weird production of Marcel Duchamp usually called the *Étant Données* is a beat-up old door with (again) two peep holes. A visitor who peers in "will see a scene he is not likely to forget...a wide open space, luminous and seemingly bewitched"[9]—a sprawling nude holding a small gaslamp; a waterfall. And Joseph Cornell's famous, haunting boxes. Productions mainly of the 1940's and 1950's, they are miniature dreamscapes in small wooden containers, the moodiest, most brooding-evocative art of the twentieth century.

And finally there is that purest, simplest microcosm of all: the Golden Orb, symbol of kingship.

What do we learn from this whirlwind tour? Merely that this "microcosm" category includes some of mankind's most compelling artifacts. And *this* is the stage onto which the Mirror World is diffidently preparing (as it waits nervously in its dressing room...) to step. In claiming to be, in one sense, the ultimate microcosm, it knows that it is bound to be judged not only as technology but as art.

But one more question, a crucial one: *Why* are microcosms so compelling?

Why?

Why are people drawn to microcosms? After all it *could* have been otherwise. In some other universe somewhere, people might *not* be drawn from childhood to create worlds in miniature. But in our universe they *are* so drawn. Why?

Two reasons, one small and one larger—

Small: In the act of recreating a large scene on a small scale, I heighten its intensity, in the sense of focusing a beam of light. I experience it more vividly. And human beings seem to enjoy vivid experiences. As you may have noticed.

Can you imagine a Vermeer at the scale of Rubens? His sharp concentrated quiet—the whole room draws in breath and pauses— couldn't exist on a larger scale. I must be able to see and comprehend the whole thing in detail at once; it must be focused onto one narrow patch of space. Indeed the world's few (relatively) large-scale Vermeers are mainly failures. Vermeer's fascination with the *camera obscura* is perfectly in keeping with an urge to concentrate and intensify. This microcosmic Intensification Urge is something that you can hear, too—in late Beethoven, for example. Not merely in the proliferation of intense short movements, but in the searing point-focus of the musical thinking *itself* onto a single line. When I twirl the focus setting to maximum-sharp, the harmony is absorbed and disappears: consider the opening movements of the last piano sonata, or the last symphony, the *Credo* of the *Missa Solemnis*; the burgeoning of fugue themes everywhere.

But there's also a larger, more inclusive answer. *People build microcosms to find topsight.*

Topsight is an elusive goal. The simplest way to get it—the immediate, obvious, child-like way—is to *recreate* a big scene in little. Then I can soar above it—tower over it; literally *see* the big picture. Naive, childlike, *effective.* Microcosms are satisfying because they give you the sense of comprehending *the whole thing*, of understanding how the parts fit together and what it all means.

Don't mistake this topsight search for a mere *intellectual* drive. It's an emotional quest too. Now, towards the end, it's time to come clean about this phenomenon. When you've achieved topsight you are, yes, looking *down* at something. You hold it in the palm of your hand. It will come as no shock if I assert that people take satisfaction in the sense of mastery. The barely visible sliver of *double entendre* winking out from underneath this word *mastery*—of the piano? of your enemies?—makes it clear how largely our grandest accomplishments reflect the innate urge to dominate. This is sobering. What's reassuring is to reflect that, after all, the ugly inclination that is responsible for fistfights and world wars also accounts, ultimately, for Newtonian mechanics. The pursuit of topsight is intellectually compelling because it is *emotionally* compelling.

I've claimed that Mirror Worlds are a development of large potential importance. This is why. True, they have appeal of a purely technical kind: They'll make the world run better and smoother. Operating your world without them will seem, in retrospect, as appealing as running your car without oil. But what lends them a uniquely *potent* potential is the submerged iceberg mass of their emotional appeal. This sort of phenomenon is hard to picture before the fact. But my guess is that, by offering topsight to the millions (not merely to the visionaries who have monopolized it in the past), they speak directly to the large, perpetually unsatisfied human craving to understand *what's going on*, to see things whole. For "reasons" that transcend the rational, they will be hard to resist.

They scotch that great primal modern fear, to be entangled by the sucker-arms of the modern institutional state, and all those private mini-states within which (live insects in congealing amber?) we hang embedded. They offer penetrating vision; they repair the shattered whole. Fittingly: The ultimate Kafka Killer is the last word in engineering, a really nice piece from the workshop of Technological Man.

The Basic Design: One More Software Architecture

In principle there are lots of ways to build a Mirror World. I will describe just one—the one we're using (at least for the time being).

This architecture is a bit subtle, because it emerges when two separate designs are superimposed. Imagine a stock-exchange trading floor surrounded by a balcony. Or a legislature, with a gallery. The action takes place down there, and you watch from up here. A

Mirror World works this way. The action takes place in the so-called Agent Space. The onlookers crowd around on the balcony.

But they don't merely hang over the railing, taking it all in. The "balcony" holds several odd little structures, and each onlooker is *inside* of one. An Agent Space is complicated. The stuff going on down there has to be organized, or it won't make any sense. The structures on the balcony exist to impose organization. Each one creates a different sort of organization—a different *viewpoint*. One Mirror World might give you a geographic viewpoint, a personnel viewpoint, a financial viewpoint and whatever; for each one, there's a corresponding structure on the balcony.

The shape of each structure (each "recursive free-form doll-house") captures the shape of one viewpoint.

I need to explain, in short, *Agent Spaces, recursive free-form doll-houses*, and their cross-relationships.

The Agent Space

Agents are the players on the Mirror World stage. They make everything happen. They react to information and synthesize it, display it, study it, investigate it, double-check, analyze and digest it. Agents snoop for you; other Agents guide you through the Mirror World; other Agents do the main, impersonal business—looking at information, answering questions, setting off alarms, painting the big picture.

An Agent is merely an infomachine, of a special kind. (Unlike a Trellis element, Agents *are* infomachines in the direct and simple sense.) The set of all Agents is a dynamic ensemble. *Dynamic* because new Agents are created and old ones disappear all the time.

A decent-sized Mirror World is likely to have thousands or tens of thousands of Agents in play around the clock. Inside a vast "Agent Space" they hang suspended between two information worlds, the Chronicle Streams overhead and the Data Fields beneath. Data generated in the outside world course through the subterranean Data Fields. The Agents themselves build the Chronicle Streams in response. Up above, an endless rush of notes, files, records and inter-Agent chatter recedes into the past, stretching backward to the very beginning of this Mirror World, fermenting into archives as it goes, grist for an experience-extracting battery of FGP machines. Down beneath, a forest of Trellis machines (like a field of oilpumps) moves data upward from subterranean reaches into the Agent Space. Agents consume data, drawing it upward through the Trellis fields; they generate new information and release it high overhead into the chronicle streams, whence it flows backwards into history (or actually stands still, while the Mirror World voyages forward through time).

Agents may extend their tentacles downwards or upwards or both. Or their *dendrites* if you prefer, on analogy with the information-gathering offshoots of neurons. These dendrite-tentacles are the information channels that connect an Agent to the Mirror World, and indirectly to the world beyond. Downward-reaching tentacles suck up information. An upward-reaching tentacle may read data from a chronicle stream, or release new data. Some Agents reach downward only, some upward, some both. We can use this fact to impose a loose hierarchy on the Agent Space. In the bottom level are downward-only Agents, in the top level upward-only ones; the others float in the middle space.

The Agent hierarchy isn't like a Trellis hierarchy, though. Unlike the elements of the Trellis, Agents never talk to each other directly. Every dendrite stretches downward into the Data Field, or all the way upward to a chronicle stream. Thus the Agent Space is really only one Agent thick. And it starts to look (ever so slightly) like the retina—like that one-cell-thick middle layer of neurons that hang between the outer data-grabbing light-catchers and the inner ganglion cells, gateways to the brain. Like Agents, their mission is to pass information judiciously from the outer world to the inner. Like Agents they form an ensemble, all work in parallel; like Agents they talk only to the alien layers above and below them, never to each other.

But—the resemblance is mainly pictorial. You might say it's merely anatomic, not physiological. And truth be told, it's not all that close anyway. But why not grab *any* image that can help illuminate our structures and our thinking?

§ The Trellis Fields

Listless data trickles, placid data brooks and fast-pounding data rivers flow beneath the Mirror World's surface. A forest of Trellis machines taps into this data world. *But*: A full-blown Trellis is a

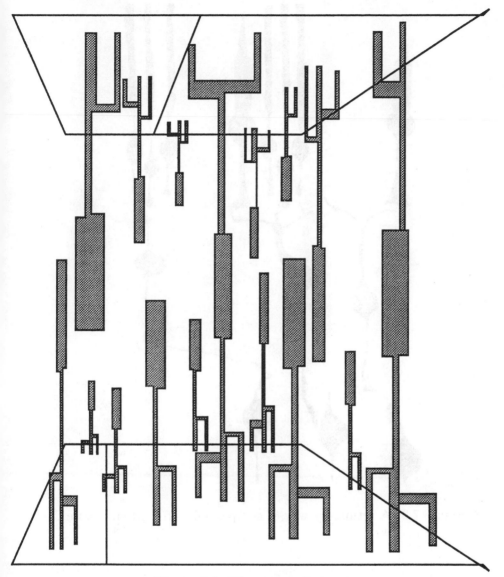

Figure 7.1: The Agent Space.

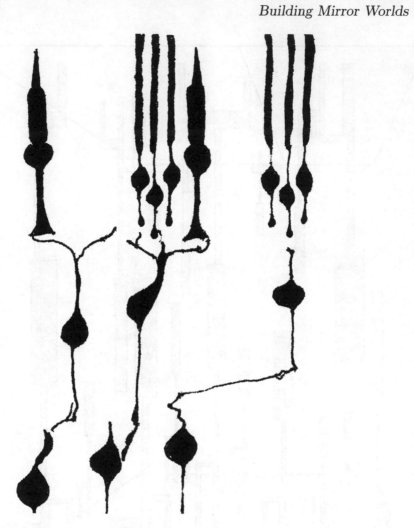

Figure 7.2: A retina, by way of comparison: after Mountcastle.[10]

highly specialized piece of equipment. When you're dealing with a bunch of related, fast-flowing streams, a fancy Trellis is just the thing. But Navies need cruisers, not just battleships. In fact they need a lot *more* cruisers. Lots of important data arrive in sluggish trickles. *Any* data source that depends on human data-entry is a sluggish trickle. An occasional Mirror World may depend *only* on such sources. Most Mirror Worlds will depend on them to some extent, at least.

Every data pump is a Trellis, nonetheless. Of course, a Trellis might consist of a small handful of elements or (in the degenerate case) exactly one.

For example: In a hospital Mirror World, the initial data-entry session that accompanies every patient admission is a vital data resource. But obviously, we don't need an elaborate Trellis to handle it. One element might deal directly with the receptionist at her computer terminal; a lone "high-level" element might convert the stuff she types into standard Mirror World format. That's it: a two-element Trellis. Humans typing in their characteristic (from a software perspective) frozen-in-time fashion are ubiquitous, and simple one- or two-element Trellises will be likewise.

Of course, a hospital that has lots of slowly-typing humans is likely to have plenty of sensors and data-gathering monitors as well. You need big Trellises to handle these.

Why call the little ones Trellises at all? *Obviously*, in the interests of imposed uniformity—*espalier*. Agents can deal with every data source in the same way. It may be a single trickle or a hundred raging rivers side-by-side, but *whatever*, it will be managed by a Trellis whose elements respond to the same commands in the same ways all the time.

§ Dealing with Data

A downward-curling dendrite is precisely a read probe. Agents stretch read probes downward onto whatever Trellis-field elements they care about. A state-government Mirror World may have a transportation network Trellis. A visitor might feel the urge to project this morning's traffic-congestion information onto a street map of whatever corridor he travels. His Agent sends a read probe downward to the appropriate Trellis element, sucks up data and projects it onto the specified map. A financial-markets Mirror World has a Trellis field with lots of current-prices information; you might want to know when a certain bunch of prices moves in a certain way. Your Agent sends probes downward to the appropriate Trellis field elements. And so on.

In these and similar cases *ad infinitum*, Agents you install are acting exactly like *ad hoc* Trellis elements. That's fine. We'd like to get as much mileage as possible out of every structure and concept in the system (so that we can keep our library of basic, underlying structures small); and in fact, the Trellis field blends smoothly (almost imperceptibly) into the lower reaches of Agent Space. But Agents, even this kind, aren't exactly like Trellis elements. For one, they don't speak Trellis-lingo. They don't need to respond in the agreed fashion to upward-percolating data and downward-flowing queries. For another, the Trellis fields are public and some Agents are private. A Mirror World's designers supply a set of data sources for public use. They also provide a basic (and probably large) set of Agents; but users install private Agents to suit themselves as well. So they must be allowed to alter the Agent Space—to set up new Agents and remove old ones—but not the Trellis fields; the fields are a quasi-permanent resource that any user must be able to count on.

The Chronicles

Communication within the Mirror World flows through the chronicle streams. To explain how they're used, it's helpful to define a term: To *hang* on a stream means to sit around waiting for a new element to be attached to that stream. When a new element is attached, you wake up and take a look at the new element.

Agents may hang on a group of chronicle streams (like a spider with a group of web-strands underfoot). Whenever something shows up on *any* of those streams, the Agent wakes up and checks it out.

This "hanging on" procedure is in concept *exactly* the same as a Trellis element's relationship to its inferiors. A Trellis element waits until *any one* of its inferiors has produced something new; then it wakes up and recalibrates its own view of things. We've merely translated this Trellis idea into a different setting. Here, Agents are hanging on passive (though constantly growing) streams of stuff—

Everything that's interesting, everything you might want to have

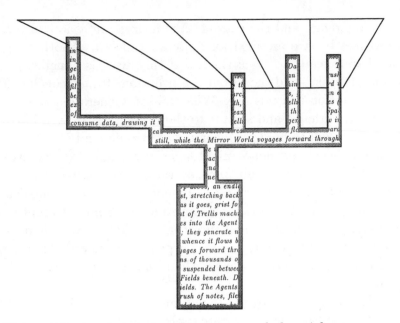

Figure 7.3: An Agent, hanging on several chronicle streams.

a *record* of, ever category of inter-Agent chatter has its own chronicle stream.

The hospital Mirror World (for example) has a chronicle stream for every patient in the building. In fact, it has a stream for every patient who's ever *been* in the building. A patient's complete history (so far as this hospital is concerned) appears in his chronicle stream. Whenever "something happens" to this patient, a new entry appears on the stream, deposited there by the appropriate Agent.

Whenever an Agent notices something that some other Agent might be interested in, it drops a note in a stream. Someone decides (let's say) to prescribe Propiffelin 250mg for patient Fruitford; the prescribing clinician makes a routine note on a computer terminal. Fruitford's chronicle stream is updated automatically. Let's say that Fruitford is a cardiac patient. The Agent who routinely follows the status of all cardiac patients wakes up and takes a look at the Fruitford chronicle. This Agent may have been notified that Propiffelin is an "interesting" drug because, let's say, some clinicians believe it to be obsolete—strictly less effective than some other, newer drug. Because Propiffelin is "interesting," there is a Propiffelin chronicle stream, and the Cardiac Agent drops in a note: Propiffe-lin has just been prescribed for patient Fruitford. Another Agent, created specifically to track the use of this drug, is hanging on this stream. It awakes and checks out the situation. It may conclude that this prescription is a mistake. What to do? Generate a message to that effect, perhaps, and send it to the resident on duty. (There's a chronicle stream to hold his incoming electronic mail.)

Lots of Agents (or none) might hang on a single chronicle stream. If Fruitford's problems fall into several categories, several Agents might routinely check every development in his case. A medication stream might be of interest to many Agents. Some of them might have particular opinions about the drug's applicability. Others might be passively monitoring its use, for purposes of a survey of some kind, or reordering. Likewise for tens of thousands of other streams in the system.

A chronicle stream, by the way, is merely a bunch of tuples. Each element in the stream is a separate tuple. These streams are built and maintained in exactly the same way as any other sort of information structure in tuple space.

§ Forgetfulness

Each chronicle stream has a forgetfulness threshold.

Forgetfulness allows the system to blur an older stream entry into a newer one, once the distinction between the two is no longer important enough to maintain. Each stream entry is marked with its time-of-creation, and so *age* can figure in the forgetting process. As of today, I might wish to remember that Fruitford got aspirin at exactly twelve, four and eight o'clock yesterday. Five years from now, it might be enough to remember that within a given two-week period, aspirin was prescribed frequently. (No? You want to remember *each* aspirin prescription *forever*? Fine, no problem: Determining the forgetfulness threshold is up to you. "You" meaning "whoever is responsible, ultimately, for creating this stream." Of course, the Mirror World Management reserves the right to level surcharges on users who create "abnormally many" total-recall streams...)

In the limiting case, I have no long term memory at all. I may be interested in a stream's most recent entry only. So I dial in *total forgetfulness*, and every time I drop a new entry into the stream, the previous one evaporates into a blur. Strictly speaking, the stream has two entries at all times: the most recent entry, plus all previous ones mushed together.

Now, up on the balcony...

The Recursive Free-Form Dollhouse

Imagine a structure that you can wander through, but also "deep into" and back out of. The RFF dollhouse consists of a collection of floating rooms. You can wander from one room to the next. But rooms may have other rooms not merely *adjacent to* but *inside* them. I can walk through a succession of rooms, business as usual. Or I can enter one room, dive into one of its sub-rooms, and then one of *its* sub-rooms and so on. In the second case, I'm not progressing *through* the structure. I'm journeying deeper and deeper *into* it.

Each room at the top level represents a major piece of the Mirror World. A piece may be geographical or conceptual. (A building; a state; the budget; the staff.) Inside a major piece there are less-major pieces, in the form of nested rooms.

It makes sense to think of a recursive dollhouse in concrete terms, as a structure in (imaginary) space. But it's *not* the kind of structure that can be captured in a blueprint or map or any physical model. It's an "impossible structure." It's built up out of spaces-within-spaces—but no matter how deeply I penetrate, everything is the same size and scale. And I can dive to the deepest room and, no matter how far into the structure I may have traveled, I can always create a new room right there; and dive deeper still.

A recursive free-form dollhouse is the Mirror World's stage set. Its layout captures some viewpoint on the action. When you shift viewpoints, you shift from one dollhouse to another.

§ Dollhouse Furniture

Dollhouse rooms are furnished with "televiewers" (or whatever you want to call them). Each televiewer is wired to some chronicle stream—it displays the stream's most-recently-added element. You

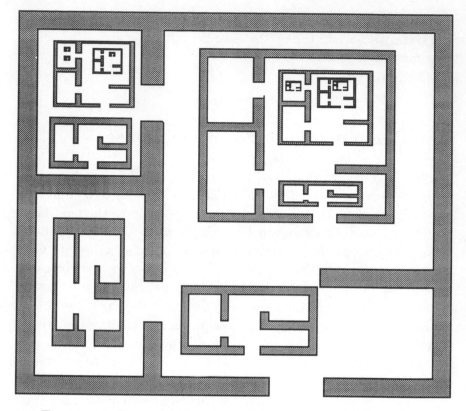

Figure 7.4: Recursive free-form dollhouse: partial floorplan.

can wire as many televiewers as you like to a single stream. And so the same piece of stream may appear in many separate roles, within many separate viewpoints, simultaneously.

§ Viewpoints

Consider our hospital Mirror World, for example: A *personnel* viewpoint might be the most logical and important perspective. The front lobby (the dollhouse room you enter first, off the street) contains one sub-room for each major group of people: say patients and staff. Inside the "patients" sub-room, there are sub-rooms corresponding to each major category: maternity patients, orthopedics patients, psychiatric patients and so forth. Inside "maternity patients" is one "room" for every individual. The room has a televiewer focussed on this patient's stream.

In a city Mirror World, *geography* is a natural viewpoint. The entrance-hall is pretty crowded, most likely. It might contain a separate sub-room for every building, road, bridge—every separate "object" in a comprehensive map. (The subdivision is arbitrary in some of its details—one room per street, one room per block? It's up to the "viewpoint designer" to make these decisions.) Most of those rooms probably contain no sub-rooms, and only a single televiewer focussed on this object's stream. Most such streams will be pretty slow and sparse. (They might acquire a new fire-inspection certificate once a year, a new set of allowable rent-increases every now and then... not much.) But *some* objects are full of sub-rooms. In a large public building, we might track the history of many rooms separately. Some buildings—hospitals, for example—contain *entire sub-worlds*. Such rooms are equipped with "walk-through televiewers"—look at the screen, and you enter an entire separate Mirror World.

§ Public vs. Private

The dollhouses are public space. Customers may occasionally design their own viewpoints from scratch, but there's no point in building more than one detailed geographic dollhouse, personnel dollhouse and so on. But many *Agents*, and the chronicle streams they write, are private. The typical dollhouse room may hold some televiewers that are focussed on *private* streams. For example, you're looking at the trading floor in a market of some kind, and public Agents are reporting on current prices, trends and so on. But private investors may have set up their own Agents as well, designed to run proprietary analyses over the market data. The convenient place for those private Agents to report is right here, in the trading room. How do we make sure that private Agents stay private? That visitors see only what they're entitled to see?

For that matter, how do we make sure that visitors see *anything?*

§ The Roving Camera Crews, and Keeping Secrets

When you enter a Mirror World, you enter with your cameraman by your side.

Your cameraman is a highly-trained professional, as infomachines go. He is the London cabdriver or Venetian gondolier of information machinery. He (all right, *it*) produces the image that you will see on your screen. When you enter the system, you enter with a single cameraman. But you might well occupy several rooms at once (that is, display *many* parts of a Mirror World on your screen at the same time). Wherever you go, you'll want to retain some *context*—some view of the surrounding countryside, so you don't get disoriented or lost. Luckily, your cameraman can reproduce himself instantaneously. (I've discussed how infomachines can create new infomachines). You start out with an individual, but you may quickly amass a whole crew. When you leave, your cameramen disappear, except for the main guy, the one you started with; he stays around, ready for your next foray.

This Chief Cameraman is a crucial figure in the Mirror World landscape. He knows all the technical details about the particular computers through which you customarily enter this Mirror World. He knows how their displays work; he knows which machine you're using at the moment, so he can make the picture come out right. Far more important, he knows who you are. He knows precisely which televiewers belong to you; which are public; which are private, but you're allowed to see; and which you are *not* allowed to have anything to do with.

A cameraman is (in short) nothing less than a respected Agent of the State. A civil servant. He looks out for your interests devotedly. But he protects the public interest as well.

So, what if you lose this state lackey—throw out your standard-issue cameraman and build your own? Forget it. It won't work. A major part of the Mirror World's security apparatus is concentrated right here. You can't "copy" a cameraman or change its script; you can't forge a cameraman's license. And only a cameraman with a valid license can show you information from a Mirror World. Techniques are available that allow you to build this kind of highly protected infomachine. They need further development in some respects; but the basic methods are in hand.

Many Mirror Worlds will contain a good deal of confidential information. Professional thieves will certainly be attracted. So will the typical undergraduate computer science major, and high school students who have successfully combined good technical skills with outstanding personal obnoxiousness. Evidently there are quite a few of them. Lucky us. Anyway: Can we guarantee absolutely that any attempted info-theft or vandalism will fail? Unfortunately, no. We can't make such guarantees about *any* information-storage system. Not even those top-secret files handwritten by ultra-trusted secretaries (since quietly executed) stored by the CIA within lead-and-kryptonite vaults *sealed with Crazy Glue* and deposited at the bottom of the Marianas Trench are *absolutely* safe, unfortunately. Can we guarantee, though, that if the issue is taken as seriously as it deserves to be—not sloughed off or saved for last, when implementation time approaches; that if time, money and effort are invested in protecting the security of information within a Mirror World—that such information will be just as safe as it would be anywhere else? Just as safe as it would be (for example) on paper, locked inside a file cabinet somewhere? Yes, I think we *can* guarantee that much.

§ So: What do the cameramen *do?*

They show you pictures.

But this is no easy to task. The televiewers don't have anything *like* pictures on them. Televiewers show you merely data from which you can *generate* pictures, if you choose. Rooms are equipped with blackboards that explain how each televiewer's display might be turned into some part of a big picture. In a City Mirror World, for example, the front lobby of the Geography Viewpoint has loads of televiewers, and blackboards spelling out the shape of a city-wide map, and other blackboards that explain how each televiewer's data might be integrated into the big map. That's all—*raw material* for a picture. The cameraman comes up with the *actual* picture.

This work gets done, by the way, on you own private computer. Most parts of a Mirror World live somewhere else, on public computers that you reach via network. Picture-generation, though, is the responsibility of your own desktop machine.

§ Building Dollhouses

A dollhouse is a nest of tuple spaces. The front lobby is the outer tuple space; the rooms it contains are also tuple spaces, nested inside the outer one, and so on. Each televiewer is an infomachine plus a tuple. (The tuple is the "screen" and the infomachine is the stuff inside the TV set, so to speak: The infomachine keeps the tuple up-to-date.) The blackboards floating around inside each room are tuples.

A tuple space, notice, has exactly the right characteristics for dollhouse purposes. It is an endlessly stretchable envelope: We can toss in new objects or remove old ones whenever we like. This is vital. Cameramen cruise from room to room, swelling one room's population and diminishing another's as they go. When visitors create new Agents and toss them into the thick of things, new televiewers are created too, and a room's population changes. Sometimes Agents die (they're created to monitor a set of stock prices until you make some decision, say). Their televiewers disappear—and for that matter, whole rooms may vanish. Stretchability is essential.

Tuple spaces have another attribute that is crucial for dollhouse building. Many infomachines may safely mess around with one tuple space simultaneously. One infomachine might be tossing something in, another might be hauling something out, several dozen might be reading tuples and a few more might be *modifying* tuples (by withdrawing and then re-creating them); and it all works out okay.

For Example

Consider a Mirror World that captures a fair-sized city. A particularly huge and complex example; obviously I'll merely sketch some possibilities here. There are smaller, better behaved examples (lots). But let's not edit out the sheer vast complexity of the kind of project we're discussing.

A City Mirror World is a an ensemble in its own right, but it can (and *should*) serve as an organizing framework for many other Mirror Worlds as well. Large institutions like hospitals, universities or stock exchanges are prime candidates for Mirror Worlding. But if they are located physically in Greater Metropolitan Piffelbourg, I'd like to be able to *reach* those Mirror Worlds via the Piffelbourg Mirror World.

§ What do I see...

when I enter this Mirror World?

The "geography" viewpoint is my logical starting point, and no doubt the most heavily-used city viewpoint by far. So let's assume that we have entered the Geography Dollhouse. When I tune in, I see an intricate picture: a map of sorts, showing the whole city. "Of sorts" because I'd rather *not* see a conventional flat map. An axonometric drawing showing the general shape of every building would be nice. But of course we don't want a fixed, static display: We should be able to swivel and rotate the image, to get a better look at regions that might be obscured in the initial perspective. And we probably won't be able to fit the whole map onto the screen at an adequate level of detail; it should be easy to roll the picture back and forth, and to zoom in and out.

Now, how much information can we superimpose on this map? *Plenty.* We accept the fact that the resulting image will be dense and complicated. But if we design things decently, it won't be confusing. (Actually we may be *pleased* with the fact that it's dense and complicated. Edward Tufte claims that "we thrive in information-thick worlds..." Images that are dense with information "are an appropriate and proper complement to human capabilities." "High-density designs also allow viewers to select, to narrate, to recast and personalize data for their own uses..."[11])

To start, we'll choose a goodness-badness color scheme. The colors themselves aren't terribly important (though not irrelevant either); but the existence of the scheme itself *is* important. The top-level, front lobby display will attempt to show you the relative goodness of all sorts of things. In compacting the "goodness" of a complex system into a single gross estimate, all sorts of data are thrown away. But at the top-level, we don't care. Our goal at the top level is *overview. Quick sketch.*

So, let's say that blue is good, red is bad. These are reasonable choices because they give you a nice, intermediate range of blended-together purples. We'll use our color scheme in the obvious way to convey traffic information on the map. Empty streets are colored blue. They turn red as they get crowded.

We can annotate the map with other kinds of simple, geography-based information. If there are fires, water-main breaks, demonstrations, snowy or icy or flooded roads or presidential motorcades underway, the map shows their whereabouts.

Many parts of the map have "performance meters," using the blue-red color scheme, or superimposed notes (in the style of names or labels on a conventional map). In the simplest case, a single blue square means "doing okay." Often three little squares (stacked vertically, like a traffic light) will be useful. The top square is "performance right now," the medium square is a rolling performance-average over the last few minutes, hours or whatever seems appropriate; and the bottom square is a longer-term trend.

"Performance"—meaning? It depends. These meters measure radically different things in different contexts. They are designed to capture some (Agent's) quick, *intuitive* notion of "How well is it going?" The stock exchange has a three-square meter: Good means "prices up." The medium and bottom squares give trends for the last few hours and few days. The airport's three squares measure average departure delays right now, over the last hour (middle) and the last week (bottom). Every school has a performance meter. We dispense with the top square and rely on the bottom two: "Goodness" is defined (say) as "average reading levels at this school, versus the national average." The middle square tells you about this year, the bottom square measures the last five years. *Pretty reductivist, isn't it?* To reduce a school's performance to a couple of little blobs? Yes, it certainly is. If you don't like it—avert your eyes. But the public is entitled to this kind of information.

In many cases, we'd like a little array of squares instead of a single column. Each station on each bus line or subway (or monorail or whatever you've got) might have two columns, three squares each. The first measures on-timeness (over the last half hour, half day, this week...); the second measures crime at this station (if you should happen to have any crime in your city). Parks have two-column meters, measuring cleanliness and crime. We can reduce all sorts of city agencies to little two-column displays. Column one: Are you (at least) keeping up with the job? (How long are the lines at the motor vehicles bureau?) Column two: Is your spending within budget? Bridges and tunnels have two-column displays, for traffic load and physical condition. And so on.

In every case, these color blobs are mere "executive summaries," quick sketches—blatantly incomplete. You are welcome to dive deeper. But there *is* value in a well-executed quick sketch.

For every performance meter, there's an Agent whose job is to maintain it. Performance-meter settings (goodness or badness) are written to chronicle streams. TV's in the RFF dollhouse are tuned to the streams. (If I don't like some performance meter's behavior, by the way, I can always build my own Agent instead.)

Little blobs of color can't be the whole story, of course. City Hall has a small superimposed billboard (Snoutbrook hearings, 3:00 this afternoon). Other government buildings likewise. (Police commissioner press conference, in progress.) Museums and theaters can advertise their current shows in a word or two.

(What about shops and department stores? Can they advertise their current Spectacular Discount Events? Like hell, not while *I'm* Piffelbourg Mirror World Commissioner. *You* do whatever you want. But I'm not anti-commerce —how's this? For a modest fee, we'll label a store's image with its name. Then, if Macy's wants to provide its own Mirror World, fine: We'll be happy to let customers step directly from public Mirror Worlds into private ones.)

The map is ringed with smaller windows that summarize general information. There's a weather window, and a crowds window: About how many people, how many cars, how many delivery trucks are in town today? How many browsers are roaming through this Mirror World? We use the red-blue scale on the window borders as a quick shorthand. (Is the weather forecast bad or good?) There's a travel guide and a commercial infoservices window (see below). If I've installed personal Agents at the top level, they'll report in their own windows: Perhaps they'll show me some stock market numbers, current heating-oil prices, estimated travel time as of right now from here to somewhere else, the level of criminal activity in my neighborhood. And if I'm a sufficiently public-spirited fellow, I may set up my City Watch Agents right here, in the front lobby. My City Finances window, my School System window, my Local Economy window...

Wherever you can dive deeper (into city hall, a hospital, an airport, a bank or university or museum or courthouse), the map has some indication, say a little green X. When I move my cursor to the X and grab the altitude control, I dive into a new sub-realm.

§ The Public Infomarket

The front lobby's role is to show you a high-level picture of the whole thing. It plays another, related role as well: It's a natural trading floor for a vast range of infoservices.

There are several different kinds, and they blend smoothly together.

There are public information sources: Agents designed to answer my questions; also, real people.

I might need personal, custom-tailored information services as well. I can build my own Agents, using the Mirror World's Agent-building menu. Or I can buy an Agent from an infoservice company. And again, there are those "real people" hanging around on the sidelines. Using a Mirror World, I can find and connect to a private info-supplier so fast and so painlessly that a whole new breed of short-order consultants might easily leap into being.

Information about train schedules? I mouse over to the train station and dive in. Inside I'll find a "schedules" corner. I can also find out whether trains are running late, the fare, typical crowd levels—will I get a seat? But I may need to ask a specific question; I mouse over to the information kiosk and type out the question, using my ordinary computer keyboard. Somewhere or other, there's a *real person* manning this (imaginary) kiosk. My question appears on his computer screen. He types a response. The response pops up on my screen. If I insist, I can even place a call to this fellow, by mousing over to the appropriate little box.

If I need information on library hours, car registrations, school schedules, whatever, I use the Mirror World to find the source and

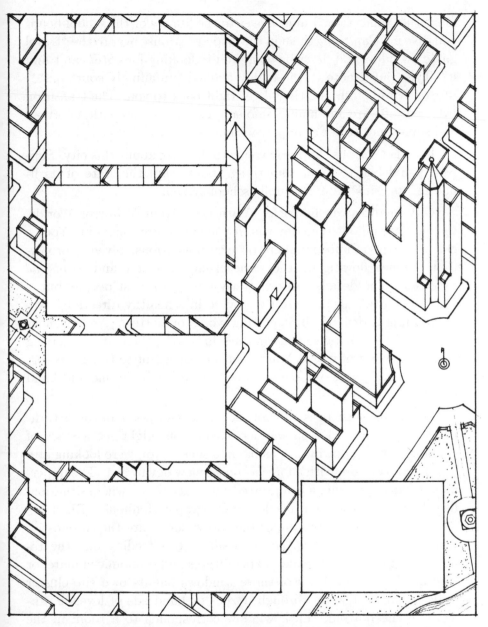

Figure 7.5: Piffelbourg Mirror World: front lobby, geography viewpoint. An abstract sketch, merely the general idea. This is a fairly
close-up, zoomed-in view. When you zoom out you lose some detail,
but you see a greater portion of the city. Zoom *all* the way out and
you see the whole thing.

make the connection. I mouse over to the library or the school board and dive in. Can't *find* them in the display? Mouse over to the "travel guide" window and describe what you're looking for. *Still* can't find it? Type out a note to the highly-trained (unfailingly courteous...) Mirror World staff, and they'll get right back to you. The transition between software and human info-suppliers will be smooth, effortless and sometimes (*often?*) imperceptible.

Let's get serious. Suppose you actually *care* about this city. Suppose you'd like to know something about (say) the state of its finances, its crime rate, its public school system.

City finances can be tricky. With the advent of Mirror Worlds, the data are all out there for you, if you can figure them out. You've got up-to-the-minute numbers on city obligations, revenue projections, money flowing in, the value of city property and so on, *ad infinitum*. The details will be utterly boring to most people, but— what does it all mean? Are we moving in a healthy direction? Are we running a deficit? Is it getting worse or better? Are revenues and spending moving roughly in tandem? No?—then, are we getting more or less out of wack? You might buy an Agent to track this sort of thing, or a public-service organization might build one and hand it out free.

(Most likely there is a whole separate viewpoint devoted to finances, of course. If you wander inside, you might see a stack of windows ranging downward, as if—in a sense—you were looking at a Trellis from on top, with a foreshortened view downward. The uppermost window presents a compressed summary of the whole situation, like the Finances window inside the Geography dollhouse. Right beneath, peaking out from under the top window, are the second-tier windows that summarize the main sub-factors feeding into the Financial big picture: revenues, expenditures and economic climate, or whatever they are. Each of those windows has its own sub-cluster underneath, and so on through dozens or hundreds of levels downward to the bottom. Each window corresponds to a room in the Finances RFF dollhouse—you're peering into each one through its glass ceiling, so to speak.)

Similarly for crime trends, or the school system, and lots of others. The Mirror World makes oceans of data available live and online. You wire your own Agents directly into the circuit.

Figure 7.6: The structure of a City Finances viewpoint.

Finally, all those "real people" info-suppliers.

Let's say you're interested in running for a seat on the local school board. You're not part of the political establishment, and you don't know how. So you hire an info-supplier consultant to give you advice. The whole transaction is handled *inside* the Mirror World. In principle, you could do exactly the same thing in the real world; but the Mirror World cuts the cost of performing this kind of service so drastically that more-or-less anybody who wants it can afford it.

You shop for a consultant in the "commercial services" window. You converse with your consultant electronically, inside the Mirror World: You type messages and (when he gets around to it) he types responses. No phone and no mail bills. No phone *disruptions*: save on secretaries.

When the time comes to make contact with potential supporters, election officials or the press, your consultant sets the whole thing up *inside* the Mirror World. To attend one of these meetings, you visit the consultant's electronic "conference room"—inside a private RFF dollhouse that you dive into from the Mirror World's front lobby. Each participant is represented by an on-screen blip, and you can open an electronic inter-blip conversation by typing the appropriate commands. Or, use the telephone (conference-call style: just type "phone call," and the phone rings on every blip's desk); or—*if* everyone has gotten around to installing a video camera and a digital interface at his site—set up a live video feed. Your consultant can attend the meeting if he chooses, easily enough. For that matter, he can attend ten meetings simultaneously.

When you need to advertise, your consultant dives into the local public school Mirror Worlds and posts your messages on the Issues bulletin boards. (A bulletin board is a TV focussed on a chronicle stream, into which all posted messages are dropped by the Agent on duty.) Or, of course, you can post your pronouncements yourself. You'll probably want to spend some time hanging around in local school Mirror Worlds in any case, chatting (electronically) with passers-by.

Yes of course, you'll want to meet people *for real* ("in person") occasionally. But those occasions can be *arranged* inside the Mirror World, they can be discussed afterwards inside the Mirror World— they might even be "broadcast" inside the Mirror World. (Say you debate the other candidates in an auditorium that's equipped with a Mirror World video feed. Browsers can tap into the feed and watch the debate. The debate hangs around in a chronicle stream, of course; voters can watch it during the event or long afterward.)

In short: The Mirror World relieves the whole enterprise of such a tremendous load of sheer organizational deadweight that virtually *anyone* can take a shot at it. You accomplish the greater part of your campaign by sitting in front of your computer and thinking.

One more example. Say you're glancing over the performance meters on the local bridges, and you happen to notice that, for the first time you can recall, virtually all the "physical condition" blobs are bright red. You wonder: When was the last time this happened? You press the "experience" key, circle the relevant parts of the display (the bright red performance blobs)—and, as it turns out, things have *never* been this bad before. So you look for a civil engineering infoservice and pose a question: What does this mean, exactly? The connection between you and the expert is so cheap, easy and quick to establish that this kind of occasional give-and-take—the experts talk to the public—could even become commonplace.

§ **Private Feeds**

The City Mirror World is a public infomachine. But it's a framework for private software as well. Private hospitals, banks, markets, stores or any sort of open-to-the-public institution may have private Mirror Worlds into which the public is invited, up to a point: Enter through the City Mirror World front lobby.

It would be nice if architects or the local historical association would donate computer models of interesting buildings. When I zoom in, I see perspective drawings, plans, interior views... For example: a coalition of architectural and engineering firms is now at work on the renovation of New York City's Grand Central Station. They have prepared a massive archive of computer drawings showing all aspects of the famous station at every stage of its history.[12] This fascinating and invaluable document is exactly the sort of thing that ought (ultimately) to be donated to a municipal Mirror World. Libraries and museums are fitting repositories for the community's physical valuables. A Mirror World is the proper home for its most significant and beautiful disembodied objects.

When I dive into a theater, I might find (privately-supplied) video feeds of current shows or coming attractions. Department stores might show me promotional stuff. Museums might have large collections of images and video feeds on file. Concert halls can sell me tickets. Banks or investment houses might offer private news feeds. Corporations might "broadcast" demos, sales pitches and so forth. The list goes on.

§ Diving In

You can dive into City Hall, a local school or public hospital, a courthouse, airport, whatever. Maybe you step into an entire, autonomous Mirror World; maybe you merely discover rooms within rooms. Dollhouse nesting can go as deep as you'd like. These "interior," more-detailed spaces are where you're likely to bump into other browsers, review past experiences, set up special-purpose Agents.

Dive into a public school, for example. What are the important issues in here? What are teachers actually thinking and saying? What are their current assumptions and favorite jargon terms? What's the general mood and worldview? In here, you can glance at the televiewers set up by the teachers themselves to keep track of system-wide issues. You can buttonhole a teacher and have a genuine, honest-to-god discussion. After classes, you can count on finding at least a handful of teachers browsing the school Mirror World, catching up on news. Each browser is represented on your screen. (We didn't bother doing this in the front lobby, because there are simply too many browsers. Down here, in the sub-room representing a particular public school, we don't expect to find more than a couple of dozen people at most—a lot fewer, usually; and so we can add a little blip to the display for each one.) By mousing over to a blip, you can (attempt to) start a conversation. You type some comments, and the other guy types responses. People who would never dream of buttonholing a teacher in real life can have nice long chats with teachers who'd never dream of being buttonholed.

Dive into a police station or the highway department or City Hall, and check them out, too.

Many people are curious to *some* extent at least about what the hell is going on out there, what people are doing and how, what they're thinking; how people in foreign walks of life are getting on;

but they lack the time or brashness to venture into the city and find out. The Mirror World is a device for converting *abstract* into *real* curiosity. For translating the casual *willingness* to be enlightened into a measure of real enlightenment.

I can't *know* the people who run my local world any longer. I can't be personal friends with the teacher and the grocer and the mayor and the town constable. But maybe via Mirror World we can be *impersonal* friends. Understanding the *feel* of those many closed sub-worlds that make up a city is impossible for most of us, for now. Dipping into these worlds, making contact—and then withdrawing to survey the whole picture, to fit the pieces together: one of the most tantalizing of Mirror World possibilities.

§ The Big Picture

What I've presented is the barest sketch of the City Mirror World. A thorough discussion would fill a much larger book than this. And it would be a book not merely about the future of technology, but the future of government.

Is this Mirror World messy? Crowded? Complicated? *Damned right.* And so is the city itself. But sometimes it's nice to step back for the long view, in search of topsight. The City Mirror World is convenient and intriguing and entertaining and all that, but it's more.

Grab your diving mouse and zoom out instead of in, up into the endless pseudo-space above the image. The map collapses gradually into a few square inches at the center of the screen, and you hover miles above it, looking down at a small patch of tiny red, blue and purple dots shimmering together. Turn off all your side-windows and just watch this little patch for a few minutes. That's the whole city. Any place you want to go down there, you can go. Anything you want to find out—if you have a right to know it, you *will* know it. It's yours. It's the collective property of *all* its inhabitants. Now close the cover of your laptop, heft the little machine: and there it is. You are holding it. The New Orb.

In Sum

Why stop at the city line?

The first Mirror Worlds will be much smaller (though still enormous in software terms): they will capture a hospital or university or private company, or a government institution—a court system, transportation network, school system. There is lots to do before a City Mirror World becomes practical.

But then, afterwards: why not capture an entire country?

How do you display the image of an entire country? The geography viewpoint is too broad for most purposes. But a display along the lines of the City Finances viewpoint might be right—a bottomless cascade tracing the state of the government, the economy, the polity downwards level by level from the big trends on top to a billion details far below.

When you wander backwards through time in this Mirror World, you have raw history, the past complete and unedited in your grasp.

Do people impart something of their personalities to their software Agents? Do their Agents outlive them? Do you encounter the software shadows of past lives as you wander backward?

Why stop at the borders? From the Mirror City to the Mirror Nation, to the Mirror *World* itself...

Where technology is concerned, it's easy, after a point, to predict what will happen. What's hard is to say what it will all mean. When the prediction of *grand implications* is the game, your only choice (pretty much) is to be wrong. About the details, at the very least.

Mirror Worlds will happen.

What will they mean?

It's easy to get carried away...

Television was new in the early 1940's. Commercially it was unborn. In 1942, one critic predicted that commercial television would reinvigorate family ties, cause an exodus from large cities and lead eventually to the demolition of all those ridiculous urban skyscrapers.[13] (The skyscrapers themselves were pretty new...) Yes, well; he was wrong.

But who was closer? This guy or the typical befuddled observer of that period, who was quite unconvinced that Mr. and Mrs. Joe

Average would *ever* swap their favorite radio programs for a stupid little low-grade picture that, because you actually had to *watch* it, made it quite impossible to carry on with your regular household chores? A royal nuisance. "Such fears about the rigors of watching television persisted in industry debates into the 1940s." [14]

Predicting *implications* is hard. But, my guess:

Mirror Worlds mark a new era in mankind's relationship to the man-made world. They change that relationship; for *good.*

Epilogue

One afternoon in late Fall two profs, Ed Florestan and John Eusebius (yes all right, these are not their real names) walked up Whitney Avenue toward the edge of town.

"I'll admit they're inevitable," Ed says, "and I find the general Mirror World idea intriguing. But I have some problems. Deep ones, so far as I'm concerned. But here is a warm-up problem just for starters. I hate computers, a lot."

A half hour's walk north of campus, there is a wide shallow waterfall that feeds a stream. A covered bridge crosses the stream. Near the bridge is a low brick factory that has been turned into a museum. The two of them have been visiting this waterfall together for years.

"You've got a Mac on your desk, right?" says John.

Ed is a composer and historian who teaches in the music school, and John is an electrical engineer.

"I'm not saying I don't use them. Of course I do. I'm not a fool. They're very useful. But the problem is—"

"Why bother hating an inanimate object? Waste of time."

"All right, I don't hate the object. I merely hate *having anything to do with* the object. Better?" "Is Object Hatred a big problem for you, in general?" "Drop dead." "All right tell me: Why do you hate computers? You've never said so before—" "Here's why. Speaking, understand, as a confirmed hard-core user... Let me see. How do I formulate this." They walk on in silence.

It's a week after Thanksgiving and the maples along this street are flat yellow—still bright, but no sparkle; the pin oaks are rust brown or a dry papery tan. Bright sky, fast-moving clouds.

"The problem is..." Ed the musician laces his hands behind his head, tenses them and frowns. "They impose on my time: I hate

213

reading owner's manuals. I'm just not interested. I don't *care* how my possessions work." He talks faster than Florestan and seems (as usual) slightly edgy and preoccupied. "The damned manuals do not interest me: It's as simple as that. This procedure, you pay money and acquire something and then you enter a prolonged period of study and contemplation in order to figure out how to use it, is perverse if not positively *depraved*, because it puts the ink and the pen on the same plane as the symphony, so to speak. It makes the mere body as important as the unbodied machine—or idea in this case—to use the book's terms. The *tools* are interchangeable. I don't care about them, and I don't want to waste time on them. I realize this is a *dangerously* bad attitude and I try to suppress it and I *do use* the damned thing, I can't afford not to. And it's great, once I've figured something out and it works. But when I look at a computer or a box of software I see *boring complexity*. Sorry. I see—*Form 1040! Your 1990 Federal Income Tax Return!* I *hate* boring complexity that imposes on my time."

"To the extent software is complicated, it's no good. Well-designed software is simple. Don't confuse the idea with a particular instance you don't like."

"Well okay, sure, but—"

They walk over a trampled-flat pile of yellow maple leaves.

"It's the nature of the beast, to some extent, isn't it?" Ed continues. "It's a machine, and you're *never* going to be able to tell it 'just figure out what I want and do it,' right?" "Right." "So it's always going to require a series of excursions downward from the *stuff-you're-thinking-about* level to the *working-this-fancy-machine* level and back up again. Which bothers me. It's damaging *precisely* to— like the book says—my *search for topsight*. All right, it's not such a big deal for now..."

John bends over and snatches a leaf off the sidewalk; twirls it stemwise between his fingers as Ed continues—

"But I wonder: Is the time approaching when, using only five percent of the time I use now, I'm ten billion times more productive... but the deal is, I have to spend ninety-five percent of my time worrying about computers? Because I'm not sure I like that deal."

They stop at a light. Whitney is a busy road all the way out to the waterfall.

"Granted," Ed continues, "it's not only computers. They're merely the vanguard. Today every damned thing comes with a user's manual. Tomorrow, shirts—rubber bands—hamburgers—each individual french fry... 'Congratulations! You have just purchased a genuine Hatsubatsu TM French Fry! Read all instructions carefully before consuming your new Hatsubatsu TM French Fry! First, set the digital clock-timer on your new French Fry! Find the small white 'time set' button and push five times while dialing the 'feature function' knob to seventeen! Now press...' But I'm serious. Somewhat."

"I understand what you're saying. But you still have a Mac on your desk."

Ed shrugs.

"All right," says John, "society is on a certain trajectory, and you don't like it. Because you don't like worrying about computers, but computers are too useful to ignore. And you think they'll become even *more* useful, and so you'll have to spend even *more* time worrying them. So; well." He drops the leaf. "You're probably right."

"Suppose the surgeon general determines that the absolutely infallible route to perfect health is a cauliflower a day. So I eat my cauliflower. But I'm not thrilled about it." "So *don't* eat it." "Granted, I make a choice. But not much of one."

"Sure... My own tendency is to say lighten up, these things are *fun*. Why get worked up about it? Y'know it's interesting..." He is walking now with his hands stuck in the pockets of his slightly raggy sportscoat. "The most talented programmers I know, the best hackers, are people who *appear* to the naked eye, to the untrained observer, like me, to *love* wasting time—"

The stop at another light (where a school bus pulls up with a hiss, and a squealing gear-grinding dump truck right behind it)—

"You ask them—what are you doing, you've been trying to fix that little routine for hours, and y'know it really *doesn't matter*, who needs it? And they look up at you in that miffed two-year-old way, and then ignore you. Which is *why* they're so good. Because of the knowledge they accumulate in their perpetually engrossed, bedazzled two-year-old approach to computers. I can't claim to be in that category of course, but even if you can't lose yourself in it completely—except maybe every now and then—it's still *fun*—just a *little?*—isn't it?..." He looks over at Ed. "All right. It isn't."

"*Fun* is maybe subjective? But none of this matters, much. Let me tell you what really bothers me about Mirror Worlds. Still accepting, of course, that they're interesting and at any rate, inevitable."

The late afternoon light hits the brick facades on the east side of the street full-face, and they drink it in like sun-bathers and glow. The yellow maples to the west are lit up from behind like stained glass.

"The stirrup," says Ed. "It arrived in western Europe in the eighth century, evidently. A nice, simple piece of technology." He pauses as they walk on, then continues: "What do you think the consequences were?"

"Can't rightly recall..."

"Serfdom." John frowns and Ed continues— "The stirrup made possible mounted shock combat: You hold a lance and ram it into the other guy. Weapons and armor changed—they got much heavier; and cavalry became decisive. The new weapons and the horses were expensive. There's a classic study by White on Medieval Technology and Social Change—and all of a sudden, you can't just join the army; you've got to be *equipped.* Now, when any old slob could join the army, certain basic rights were distributed fairly widely. But when it came about that you had to be rich to join the army, the trouble started. *If* the wide-scale semi-enslavement of the population counts as trouble. Now let me tell you what the point is..." "Yeah, this is kind of hacking with a pretty broad sword, isn't it?"

"Here is the point." They pass a jogger going the other direction. "First, new technology can have strange consequences. Obviously. But more important. A technology arises that, one, is terribly important, not merely superficially but fundamentally: I mean mounted shock combat. Two, for whatever reason, only a few people can really master it. The result is feudalism, actual or intellectual..."

It's getting breezier: The wind makes a whirlpool of leaves a few paces in front of them. Then the whirlpool unkinks and the leaves go pattering off down the sidewalk.

"Mirror Worlds come in, and related technologies—all this information handling stuff, communication stuff, Trellis stuff—computers are *no longer* pots and pans—important-but-trivial. I can *in fact believe* that a Mirror World would suck life from the *thing it's modeling* into itself, like a roaring fire sucking up oxygen. The external reality becomes just a little bit...not superfluous; second-hand. Not quite Center Court. Not *quite* where the action is. Couldn't it happen that, instead of the Mirror World tracking the real world, a subtle shift takes place and the real world starts tracking the Mirror World instead?"

"A simple question deserves a simple answer. And the answer is no." "Why not?" "Because these programs are creatures of their programmers. This semi-mystical Frankenstein view of software is just—no offense—stupid. *Stupid.* It cannot be. If you don't like what's happening, you *pull the fricking plug.* Right?" "Okay, but that's just the point. They're creatures of their programmers. *Important* creatures. And as a result, a dependency develops. The *programmers...*" "Do you know how a steam engine works?" "Roughly." "Okay, sure, but could you repair one? I couldn't. Steam power was important, but it didn't create feudalism or anything conceivably like it." "But there's a difference. Let me see. How do I..." He trails off, and they walk on.

"You see: You're not talking about steam engines," Ed continues. "You're talking about something more like eyeglasses, in an abstract sense. These things color your view of reality. They present the world to you. In a compelling way. More real than real. Steam engineers hardly made up a knightly order at the pinnacle of society. Granted. But the people who control these Mirror Worlds are more like TV people, sort of. Isn't that a priesthood? But we're talking about something far more significant to your daily life than TV is. We need these Mirror Worlds, they're great, they are *the* window on reality—when you shut one off, we get all lost-feeling and let down...and anxious...what's *going on??* I don't know *what's going on. What's wrong with my Mirror World??*"

The breeze sends another flock of leaves scuttling away down the sidewalk.

"And it's not that I *distrust* the software guys who design and build them. You see, that's just the point: I don't think they're going to screw me up. I think they'll be responsible, professional guys. They'll take good care of us. And that's *just* the problem. Serfdom means, above all, not slavery—slavery is slavery; serfdom is merely utter *dependency*—I don't understand these things but I rely on them, not just for *convenience* but in order to carry out my *thinking!* And—"

"Gimme a break. *C'mon.* These are just guileless programmers, *engineers*, not *prima donnas...*"

"Let me finish." "But you're just a *peon*, a humanities *serf*, I don't have to. Right? Oh all right. I realize you're serious. I just don't think you *ought* to be."

A bike rider in a sweatsuit pedals slowly towards them, making a wobbly long shadow. "Hey Walt!" Ed calls out. "You guys at it..." the rider shouts as he passes. The rest of the question gets lost.

"If you shut off your TV, who cares?" Ed says. "Who steals my Tube steals trash. But if you shut off your *Mirror World* in a fit of pique, you really *are* less well-informed than the other guy. There's really *no way* you can know as much about a Mirror Worlded reality if you don't watch the Mirror World. And that's a recipe for *real* dependence. The guys who run these operations are *like* TV people and they're not: because they don't just control entertainment. They control *reality*. Do you smell a fault? And it's far more than that. This evening, let's say, you mess with your computer and I play the piano. We're both just amusing ourselves, right? We're just playing. Neither activity is divinely blessed. We do what we like. Ten years from now, you've got Mirror Worlds, and the same thing happens, and suddenly—you are flying and I am walking. You simply know *so much more* about the city or the university or the state or what-ever Mirror Worlded thing you're looking at than I do, that I'm a damned near second class citizen. Yes I know *I can use the Mirror World, too,* whenever I want, sure, great. But let's be *honest,* okay? These things don't work by magic. They don't operate themselves. You've got to *know* something in order to squeeze all this knowledge out of a Mirror World. High school hackers are going to be a lot better at it than the chairman of the Political Science Department. *Relatively* speaking, while you soar to new heights of topsight, I sink into pig-ignorance. Modern technology is a centrifuge, isn't it, de-signed to stratify society based strictly on a person's fondness for playing games with machines? But forget about me, you're right, I don't mind computers that much and I understand them to some extent and I *would* play with a Mirror World because I *do* find the idea intriguing. At least I read books like this. I'll do okay. Many people—*most* people—won't."

"Okay. Here is your point. It is an *important* point. Enormously important. It's just that you are utterly, entirely, completely and absolutely wrong..."

"But not totally, or transgalactically?"

"Look. This technology *will have* a special, basic, *intellectual* importance. You're right. If people have no real idea how it works, but they rely on it anyway, uncritically, that is a *crisis.* A recipe for disaster. Or: If most people don't learn how to use it but a few do, or if most people learn in a half-assed way—if they won't bother to activate their brains long enough to figure out what the score really is—and you're right, they're *going to have to understand* the technology, not just use it blindly—you're right, they are really going to have to *understand* something about computers if they are *in fact* going to rely on them in this new, transcendental way—and if they *don't,* that is a genuine disaster. You're right. *But.* They *will* understand! *They will learn! Bingo.* Q.E.D." He punches a privet.

"Oh yeah? Do they understand now?" "Look. I think..." He thinks.

(His hair is cut rather short and it's not immaculately combed, and when you add the raggy sportscoat the whole impression is somewhat disreputable. Ed on the other hand is wearing a gray raincoat and looks like a businessman, but talks faster, and has piercing eyes that ignore you and focus on some abstract point ten feet away when he is fidgeting with an idea—which is usually.)

"Go back to the beginning of the book," John continues. "The water level is rising. True. Do people drown in droves, or do they learn to swim? As soon as you state this question, you answer it. *Obviously,* they learn to swim. In fact, that's the best thing *about* Mirror Worlds: Ultimately they *force* people to learn how to swim. They force people to come to grips with technology."

"It hasn't happened yet, with *any* technology. You asked me about steam power—how long has electricity been important? How many people know what it is? Can the average guy tell an amp from a volt?"

"Maybe—I don't know—look, people are lazy. I'm happy to concede the point. In recent decades your typical *intellectual,* so called— let alone your typical 'guy'—generally has not condescended to learn

anything whatsoever about science or engineering. *That will change.*
To avoid drowning, you wise up. Simple as that. Effective. And *great
news.* Today, when the science professors show up at—y'know—the
Great Cocktail Party of modern undergraduate education—sit-down
dinners where you get an honest meal being simply *too* boring—when
a prof shows up in his formal cocktail waiter's uniform bearing a tray
of scientific *hors d'oeuvres*, the neophyte intellectual waves it away
as if it were spam-on-toast. The typical attitude is, why should I
bother myself with *science*, that's what we have *scientists* for—just
like, why should I bother myself with driving? That's why we have
chauffeurs. That's why we have *Taiwanese graduate students!*" And
he veers off into a pile of brown leaves to the right, slosh-rustling
through them. "I'm not supposed to do that." He stops and turns
back. "I didn't really mess it up. Too much...?"

"I think you're overestimating the average student's *ability* to
learn this—" "No that's bull, you see, no offense, I'm not saying our
average undergrad is a potential Nobel physicist," they are striding
forward again, "but if he can't learn *basic* science *and engineering,*
what the hell is he doing in college? But in fact he *can.* No, the
problem is—'Physics this term? Sorry Dearie,' "—he has switched
unaccountably into falsetto with a broad English accent—"I am *so*
busy with my *Introductory* Ketchup as Metaphor, my *Intermediate*
Mauling, Murdering and Disemboweling the Competition and my
Advanced WASPs Make Me Puke, which is a required course you
know, every term, double credit, with a lab... So I'm afraid I simply
don't have the time...' " In his normal voice: "*Physics is beyond me* is
merely the polite, socially-approved way of saying *I'm too goddamned
lazy. And you're too mush-brained to make me.* And this is precisely
the *greatest thing* about Mirror Worlds..."

They pause as a beat-up Volvo station wagon shoots past, then
cross the street—

"They will *energize* people, once they're real. By placing a considerable explosive charge right in front of their noses. Hey, wanna be
a second class citizen? No? Then turn on your brain and *learn.* It's
like putting someone in a spacesuit, and loading him into a space
ship on top of a rocket, and then telling him *here we go.* We're
about to blast off. Now: *Would you like to know how this space ship
works?* The answer is going to be—*hmmmm,* actually—*yes.*" He

grabs a gray-green pine-needle from a tree by the sidewalk and rolls its ridginess between his fingers.

"Let's forget about relative likelihoods," says Ed. "I can't predict them accurately and neither can you. But *do you agree with me that...* If people *don't*, as you say, wise up, and *maybe* they won't, right?" "Yes. *Maybe* they won't." "Maybe they won't. Could be. Do you agree with me that, *if they don't*—they drown? Or they get blown to bits? Or, they become intellectual serfs, in *some limited sense at least,* to the Lords of the Mirror World Manor? Do you agree?—doesn't it *concern* you, *at least a little?*"

John stops walking, sticks his hands in his jacket pockets, stiffens his arms and looks at the sky. He stands that way for half a minute or more. In an oak-tree full of dry leaves the breeze makes a tinkling-crisp rustling.

He nods his head and looks down.

"Okay. Yes. It concerns me. At least a little."

And they walk on silently.

The waterfall comes over a stone dam capped with concrete. A clear arc over the rounded lip spills into white parallel lines, then feathers downward in broken silver-brown sheets. The sound is high-pitched from a distance and deepens as they approach. They walk through the covered bridge. The sound is muffled inside. Across from the waterfall, the stream slips under some fallen trees and disappears into the woods; as New England streams do.

"Here is my last problem," says Ed. They emerge on the other side and stand side-by-side, watching the waterfall. "Two guys struggling on top of a train. In an old Western. Picture it. One is going to make it. The other is going to get thrown off. And between us, chances are, he's going to die. The two guys struggling on top there are the science and technology worldview and the romantic worldview. And the romantic worldview has lost it. It's exhausted. Mirror Worlds are going to throw it off the train. And it's going to die."

"Huh?" says John. "Now you've lost me." They watch the waterfall.

"There's been a retreat going on at least since the early nineteenth century. From the country to the city, from outdoors to indoors, from natural to synthetic environments—old news. Our mental life runs through a riverbed that is getting paved, so to speak, piece by piece. But now the retreat will be pursued all the way out of mundane reality altogether. All the way into a little box on your desk, into your mind. You see: It's not just a sentimental attraction to birds and flowers..."

"What're you talking about?" says John. "*We're* outside." "But there's no connection between what we're seeing and what we're thinking—to a romantic, nature is *the driving engine* of thought. It's the engine under the hood—the electricity in the outlet—the vodka in the screwdriver, it's—just *one* grand poetic gesture? If you don't mind?" "Sure," says John— "the *blade* at the *bottom of the food processor.* Take that away, the constant chafing between natural-outer and human-inner, and the heat it generates, and thought stops. *To me, the meanest flower that blows*— That worldview still exists: instead of Wordsworth, *nature was all in all*, you've got Greenpeace; same thing, only it has a nasty, desperate edge today, because it's dying."

Near the other side of the bridge is a picnic table. A woman is sitting there and they can hear her calling something towards the parking lot repeatedly, indistinctly.

"I don't mean a sentimental attraction to birds and flowers," Ed begins again. "I'm not talking about air pollution or *recycling* or whatever. I'm talking about a worldview in which chaotic multi-sensual reality—*polyperceptiveness*, Goethe called it—is dying, because it's inefficient. It has been *shown* to be a losing way to think. It doesn't *produce* anything. Except maybe a vague sense of well-being; but so does a bottle of cheap wine. The sights, the sounds, the smells, the character of the people all buy you *nothing* intellectually. They waste your time. How do I know? Well, the Mirror World edits them out completely. And it gives you a vastly deeper look into the real nature of things. Romantics are *shallow*. They don't know much but they *feel* a lot. The future is clear. Know everything, feel nothing. Romanticism held its own against Technology for a couple of centuries, a couple dozen rounds or whatever, but now it's on its last legs, *staggering*. And Mirror Worlds have the stuff to kill it."

"Hey... *it's only software*, for God's sake!"

"Maybe I take Mirror Worlds more seriously than you do?" "No I take them *seriously*, it's just that—"

"They didn't *start* it, obviously," Ed puts in. "The fight has been going on for two centuries. I'm not saying Mirror Worlds created this state of affairs. They're just ambling casually onstage in the middle of it. What I *am* saying is that—if I had to envision the *capstone of the pyramid*—that *final concrete panel* in our *boffo* paving-the-riverbed project—it would look *exactly* like a Mirror World. Like a telescope, or a microscope, but focussed not on an isolated specimen but on the whole human world, reality, and like a microscope it shows you *deeply, seriously, completely, analytically*—it's *captivating*—and in an untaste-able, unsmellable way, in perfect clean neat analytic *silence*, what's going on. And it's done. The riverbed is paved."

"No, look, a biologist..." John shakes his head and sighs. "A biologist who uses a microscope doesn't *stop* seeing and feeling in a normal human way; he's merely *adding* something; he's *adding* to his sensory equipment, not diminishing it."

"But if his microscope shows him the *whole world...* Leonardo or Goethe or Ruskin were scientists after a fashion, or at least *in sympathy with* the science of their day. But the sensual isolation of powerful instruments drove this type *out* of science—*good riddance*, I mean, between Goethe and the electron microscope, *you must choose* the electron microscope, I'm not disputing it; and now they'll be driven back again. And the gain in clarity of vision will be just as great, but no longer confined only to science, and potentially even more important—but where does that leave Goethe? My only question—" and he repeats, not as a question but as a flat statement: "where does that leave Goethe. It all reminds me in the end of Ruskin talking about the railroad. 'There was always more in the world than men could see, walked they ever so slowly. They will see it no better for going fast.' "

"No. Ruskin is wrong. He's wrong in a bunch of ways. And so are you. You guys—you're attacking the idea of *going fast*: by which, implicitly, you mean *technological progress*—okay, not you," (Ed was protesting), "but Ruskin. Progress *means* forward motion. Going fast."

He pauses; then starts again.

"Did you ever ride at the front of a New York City subway when you were a kid, looking out the front window as the car roars down the track—rocking, screeching like hell, careening round the corners? With the blue tunnel lights batting past? Remember the first time

you rode in a plane and it started barreling down the runway? Remember running, when you were a kid, just for the hell of it? Just for
fun? *That's progress.* That's *forward motion.* That's *moving fast.*
Progress *means* the thrill of motion. That is: transformed childhood
joy. That's why we *do* technology...You've got it inside out. We
aren't isolating ourselves from the emotional side of anything...*Feel
nothing?* It's *all* emotion. When you think of technology, *that's* what
you ought to think of. The kid riding his bike, or sledding downhill,
or charging over a grass field trying to get his kite to fly, just because
it feels great, it's the human thing to do."

"But," says Ed, "you're saying...I don't care what the consequences are, we're having so much fun we're going to charge on
anyway? I accept that. I *accept* that these things are inevitable."
"No, *more* than that—forgetting about romanticism proper, more
broadly—the real live warm joyful *emotional* cutting edge of human
experience today *is* science and *is* technology. *That's* what I'm saying."

He crouches down, by the tangle of spiky dead wildflowers next to
the stream. The air out here is chilly, with the faint smell of burning
leaves.

They watch the waterfall.

"Ruskin is wrong in another way too," John continues. "He says,
you'll see it no better for going fast. Wrong. In one sense, at least,
you see *much* better. Because, you see a bigger piece. So much *more*
gets crammed into your field of view, and as a result, instead of a
handful of fragments and loose ends, the *big picture* gradually starts
to add up. And in this sense, Mirror Worlds are a natural culmination
of all these technologies of motion and communication; because they
show you so much more, a huge sweep instead of a narrow puny
medieval sliver, and for precisely that reason, they show you *better.*"
He picks up a pebble and tosses it into the water. "All right, they
move you farther from some of the concrete physical details, the
smells and chirps and oinks and rustlings and all that, and that's
regrettable. But at the same time, and for the very same reason,
they move you closer to *the whole.* You can't see the chickens clucking
from on top of the Eiffel Tower either, but people come from all over
the world to go to the top; they don't just stare at the thing, they
want to go to the top, because they know and feel that it's *good to*

see what the top of that tower has to show them. I think you see much better for building towers, and going fast. And after all, no Act of Parliament ever told Ruskin he couldn't take a walk in the woods if he felt like it, for all his whining, railroads or no; and you have the same privilege."

"But *I could be bounded in a nut-shell, and count myself a king of infinite space...*" He breaks off.

A full minute passes. They watch the waterfall and listen to its steady rush.

Ed begins again: "I've never said that the possibilities aren't tantalizing. All I'm saying is that the dangers are also frightening. I'm saying *I'm worried* and you're saying *sorry, I can't help it.* We're talking at right angles, aren't we? Do you *see*, at least, why I'm worried?"

The choppy stream has sky-blue facets angled at the waterfall, and burnt orange ones facing the bridge, and picks up a wintery yellow-brown from the faded plants near the far bank.

Eventually John asks "Do you see why I'm *not*, why I'm exhilarated?"

They watch some gulls circling the bare gray tangle of the distant lakeshore. "Look, anyway." He picks up another pebble and examines it carefully. "It's only a piece of software."

Ed shakes his head, and smiles wryly.

And the author snaps his two alter-egos back into place like the blades of a penknife, and pockets them. And there he is, smiling wryly, watching the waterfall.

New Haven, Connecticut
April, 1991

Notes

1. John Ruskin, *Modern Painters* Vol. 3; cited in Wolfgang Kemp, *The Desire of My Eyes. The Life and Work of John Ruskin,* Translated by J.V. Heurck (New York: Farrar, Straus and Giroux, 1990), 155.
2. From a letter of Fanny Kemble, a young actress at the time, describing her trip beside George Stephenson during a pre-inaugural trial of the Liverpool and Manchester Railway. Cited in L.T.C. Rolt, *George and Robert Stephenson. The Railway Revolution* (Westport, Conn.: Greenwood Press, 1960), 191.

Chapter 1

1. James Walvin, *English Urban Life 1776-1851* (London: Hutchinson, 1984), 7.
2. Adam Smith, *The Wealth of Nations* (London: Penguin Classics, 1986), 115.
3. Cited in Phyllis Deane, *The First Industrial Revolution* (Cambridge: Cambridge University Press, 1965), 19.
4. See Sigvard Strandh, *The History of the Machine* (New York: Dorset Press, 1989), 26.

Chapter 2

1. *New York Times,* Nov. 23, 1990:A1.
2. *Wall Street Journal,* Nov. 29, 1990:B1.
3. See for example Tekla S. Perry, *Slashing Development Time,* in *IEEE* [Institute of Electrical and Electronics Engineers] *Spectrum,* **27**,10 (Oct. 1990):64.

4. Hans Moravec, *Mind Children. The Future of Robot and Human Intelligence* (Cambridge, Mass.: Harvard University Press, 1988).

5. Edward R. Tufte, *The Visual Display of Quantitative Information* (Cheshire, Conn.: Graphics Press, 1983); Edward R. Tufte, *Envisioning Information* (Cheshire, Conn.: Graphics Press, 1990).

6. James Madison, *The Federalist Papers* Number 10, Edited by Clinton Rossiter (New York: New American Library, 1961), 78.

7. *Wall Street Journal,* January 11, 1991:A1. The quotation is attributed to John H. White Jr., retired transportation curator at the Smithsonian Institution.

8. Lynn B. Scarlett, "Make Your Environment Dirtier — Recyle." *Wall Street Journal,* January 14, 1991:A12. See Martin B. Hocking's "Paper Versus Polystyrene: A Complex Choice." *Science* **251**,4993 (Feb. 1991):504-505, for a detailed look at the underlying issue.

9. Edmund Burke, *Speech to Electors of Bristol* (1774), in Louis I. Bredvold and Ralph G. Ross, eds., *The Philosophy of Edmund Burke* (Ann Arbor: University of Michigan Press, 1960), 148.

10. Roger Starr, *The Rise and Fall of New York City* (New York: Basic Books, 1985), 199.

11. Cited in Martin Greif, *Depression Modern, The Thirties Style in America* (New York: Universe Books, 1975), 32.

12. Inaugural Address of President Reagan, January 20, 1981, cited in James A. Marone, *The Democratic Wish. Popular Participation and the Limits of American Government* (Basic Books, 1990), 324.

13. *Ibid.,* 330.

14. *Ibid.,* 336.

15. *Ibid.,* 333.

16. Georges Duby, *The Age of the Cathedrals. Art and Society, 980-1420,* Translated by Eleanor Levieux and Barbara Thomson (Chicago: The University of Chicago Press, 1981), 14.

Chapter 3

1. David Gelernter and Suresh Jagannathan, *Programming Linguistics* (Cambridge, Mass.: MIT Press, 1990).

2. David Pears, *Ludwig Wittgenstein* (Cambridge, Mass.: Harvard University Press, 1986), 13.

3. George Henderson, *Chartres* (Middlesex UK: Penguin Books, 1968), 15.
4. Benoit B. Mandelbrot, *The Fractal Geometry of Nature* (New York: W.H. Freeman, 1977).
5. Douglas R. Hofstadter, *Gödel, Escher, Bach: An Eternal Golden Braid* (New York: Basic Books, 1979).

Chapter 4

1. *Science* **248**,29 (June 1990):1608.
2. "Linda" is a registered trademark of Scientific Computing Associates.
3. Nicholas Carriero and David Gelernter, *How to Write Parallel Programs: A First Course* (Cambridge, Mass.: MIT Press, 1990).
4. George Lakoff and Mark Johnson, *Metaphors We Live By* (Chicago: The University of Chicago Press , 1980), 6.
5. See Isaiah Berlin, *Against the Current. Essays in the History of Ideas* (New York: The Viking Press 1978), 93.
6. Bernardo Huberman, *The Ecology of Computation* (Amsterdam: North-Holland, 1988).
7. Carriero and Gelernter, *How to Write Parallel Programs.*

Chapter 5

1. *New York Times,* May 12, 1990:A16.
2. *New York Times,* Aug. 11, 1990:A28.
3. *The Federal High Performance Computing Program,* (Sept. 1989) Appendix A: Summary of grand challenges:49-50.
4. *Science* **247**,26 (Jan. 1990):407.
5. *Science* **248**,11 (May 1990):675.
6. *Science* **248**,11 (May 1990):674.
7. David P. Billington, "Engineer as Artist—From Roebling to Khan," in David P. Billington and Myron Goldsmith, eds., *Technique and Aesthetics in the Design of Tall Buildings* (Bethlehem, Penn.: Institute for the Study of the High-Rise Habitat, Lehigh University, 1986), 73 and 71.
8. Cited in Ian Hamilton, *Robert Lowell, A Biography* (New York: Random House, 1982), 262.

9. Elwood Hennneman, "Organization of the motor systems—a preview," in Vernon B. Mountcastle, ed., *Medical Physiology Vol. 1, Thirteenth Edition* (Saint Louis: C.V. Mosby Company, 1974), 606.
10. See James P. Womack, Daniel T. Jones and Daniel Roos, *The Machine That Changed the World* (New York: Rawson Associates 1990), for a fascinating discussion of coordination in the Japanese auto industry.

Chapter 6

1. W.V. Quine, *Ontological Relativity and Other Essays* (New York: Columbia University Press, 1969), 31.
2. See R.V. Guha and Douglas B. Lenat, "Cyc: A Midterm Report," in *AI Magazine* Fall 1990:32-59.
3. By K.J. Gilhooly in *Thinking: Directed, Undirected, Creative* (Orlando: Academic Press 1988), 149.
4. See e.g. R.E. Snow and E. Yalow, "Education and intelligence," in R.J. Sternberg, ed., *Handbook of Human Intelligence* (Cambridge: Cambridge University Press, 1982), 493-585.
5. See Gilhooly, *Thinking*, 166.
6. Granted, under the guise of literary criticism having nothing to do with computers. See D. Gelernter, "Tsipporah's Bloodgroom," in *Orim* **3**,2 (Spring 1988): 46-57; D. Gelernter, "The Sea-Song Resounds," in *Tel Aviv Review* **4** (1991) (forthcoming). These pieces argue that some of the oddest and hardest passages in the Hebrew Bible become comprehensible if you approach them with your "concentration knob" dialed back to a far lower setting than we usually take for granted; the rules of textual coherence are transformed completely as you approach the far end of the dial.

Chapter 7

1. Christopher Thacker, *The History of Gardens* (Berkeley and Los Angeles: University of California Press, 1979), 72.
2. John Brookes, *Gardens of Paradise. The History and Design of Great Islamic Gardens* (New York: New Amsterdam Books, 1987), 23.

3. Stefan Koppelkamm, *Glasshouses and Wintergardens of the Nineteenth Century,* Translated by Kathrine Talbot (New York: Rizzoli, 1981), 40.

4. Otto von Simpson, *The Gothic Cathedral* (Princeton: Princeton University Press 1962), 35.

5. Cited in William Manchester, *Winston Spencer Churchill. The Last Lion. Visions of Glory 1874-1932* (New York: Laurel Trade Paperbacks, 1989), 667.

6. Cited in Morris Dickstein, "From the Thirties to the Sixties: The New York World's Fair in its Own Time," in The Queens Museum, ed., *Remembering the Future* (New York: Rizzoli, 1989), 22.

7. Albert Blankert, John Michael Montias and Gilles Aillaud, *Vermeer* (New York: Rizzoli 1988), 22.

8. *Ibid.*

9. Octavio Paz, "*Water always falls in* plural," in Anne D'Harnoncourt and Kynaston McShine, eds., *Marcel Duchamp* (New York and Philadelphia: The Museum of Modern Art and Philadephia Museum of Art, 1973), 145.

10. Kenneth T. Brown, "Physiology of the Retina," in Mountcastle, *Medical Physiology,* fig. 15-1, 459.

11. Tufte, *Envisioning Information,* 50.

12. John Hughes, "CAD Meets the Beaux Arts: Rennaissance of Grand Central Station." *Architectural Record,* March 1991:56.

13. Cited in William Boddy, *Fifties Television. The Industry and its Critics* (Urbana and Chicago: University of Illinois Press, 1990), 101.

14. *Ibid.,* 20.

Index